P9-DYZ-289

THE PENGUIN
ITALIAN
PHRASEBOOK

Fourth Edition

Jill Norman
Pietro Giorgetti
Daphne Tagg
Sonia Gallucci

PENGUIN BOOKS

PENGUIN BOOKS

Published by the Penguin Group
Penguin Books Ltd, 80 Strand, London WC2R ORL, England
Penguin Group (USA) Inc., 375 Hudson Street, New York, New York 10014, USA
Penguin Group (Canada), 90 Eglinton Avenue East, Suite 700, Toronto, Ontario, Canada M4P 2Y3
(a division of Pearson Penguin Canada Inc.)
Penguin Ireland, 25 St Stephen's Green, Dublin 2, Ireland (a division of Penguin Books Ltd)
Penguin Group (Australia), 707 Collins Street, Melbourne, Victoria 3008, Australia
(a division of Pearson Australia Group Pty Ltd)
Penguin Books India Pvt Ltd, 11 Community Centre, Panchsheel Park, New Delhi – 110 017, India
Penguin Group (NZ), 67 Apollo Drive, Rosedale, Auckland 0632, New Zealand
(a division of Pearson New Zealand Ltd)
Penguin Books (South Africa) (Pty) Ltd, Block D, Rosebank Office Park, 181 Jan Smuts Avenue,
Parktown North, Gauteng 2193, South Africa

Penguin Books Ltd, Registered Offices: 80 Strand, London WC2R ORL, England

www.penguin.com

First edition 1968
Second edition 1979
Third edition 1988
This revised and updated edition published 2013
002

Copyright © Jill Norman and Pietro Giorgetti, 1968, 1979
Third edition material © Jill Norman and Daphne Tagg, 1988
Revised and updated material copyright © Jill Norman and Sonia Gallucci, 2013

All rights reserved

Set in 9/12 pt TheSans and TheSerif
Typeset by Jouve (UK), Milton Keynes
Printed in England by Clays Ltd, St Ives plc

ISBN: 978-0-141-03905-3

www.greenpenguin.co.uk

MIX
Paper from
responsible sources
FSC
www.fsc.org   FSC™ C018179

Penguin Books is committed to a sustainable
future for our business, our readers and our planet.
This book is made from Forest Stewardship
Council™ certified paper.

ALWAYS LEARNING   **PEARSON**

CONTENTS

INTRODUCTION

This series of phrasebooks includes words and phrases essential to travellers of all kinds: the business traveller; the holiday-maker, whether travelling alone, with a group or the family; and the owner of a house, an apartment or a time-share. For easy use the phrases are arranged in sections that deal with specific situations and needs.

The book is intended to help travellers who never had the opportunity to learn Italian, as well as serving as an invaluable refresher course for those whose Italian has gone rusty.

Pronunciation is given *in italics* for each phrase and for all words in the extensive vocabulary. See pages xi–xvi for the pronunciation guide which should be read carefully before starting to use this book.

Some of the Italian phrases are marked with an **asterisk*** – these give an indication of the kind of reply you might get to your questions, and of questions you may be asked.

For those who would like to know a little more about the Italian language, a brief survey of the main points of its grammar is provided at the end of the book (pages 246–257).

PRONUNCIATION GUIDE

The pronunciation guide is intended for people with no knowledge of Italian. As far as possible the system is based on English pronunciation. This means that complete accuracy may sometimes be lost for the sake of simplicity, but you should be able to understand Italian pronunciation, and make yourself understood, if you read this section carefully. The pronunciation symbol(s) are highlighted in bold. When there are two possible pronunciation symbols available for the same syllable, these are indicated with a 'slash', e.g. [e/eh].

Vowels

All vowels are sounded distinctly; unstressed vowels keep their pure sound and are never slurred as in English. Final **e** is always pronounced.

A	as a in father	[a]	e.g. pane – bread (*pa-neh*)
	as a in apple	[a]	e.g. alto – high (*al-to*)
E	as e in wet	[e/eh]	e.g. ponte – bridge (*pon-teh*)
	as ai in fair	[ai]	e.g. aperto – open (*a-pair-to*)
I	as i in machine	[ee]	e.g. litro – litre (*lee-tro*)
O	as o in soft	[o]	e.g. opera – opera (*o-pair-a*)
U	as oo in moon	[oo]	e.g. punto – point (*poon-to*)

Compound Vowels

In the combinations **ia, ie, io, iu** the sound of the **i** tends to be shortened, and the syllables are usually pronounced as a combination of the English sound **y** with other vowel(s).

IA	as in yahoo	[ya]	e.g. piano – slow (*pya-no*)
IE	as in yet	[ye]	e.g. piede – foot (*pye-deh*)
IO	as in York	[yo]	e.g. fiore – flower (*fyo-reh*)
IU	as in you	[yoo]	e.g. aiuto – help (*a-yoo-to*)

In the combinations **ue, ui, uo** the sound of the **u** tends to be shortened, and the syllables are usually pronounced as a combination of the English sound **w** with other vowel(s).

UE	as in wet	[we]	e.g. guerra – war (*gwer-ra*)
UI	as in weed	[wee]	e.g. guida – guide (*gwee-da*)
UO	as in word	[wo]	e.g. buono – good (*bwo-no*)

In the combinations **au, ei** the sound of the syllable tends to be prolonged.

AU	as how	[ow]	e.g. auto – car (*ow-to*)
EI	as in day	[ay]	e.g. sei – six (*say*)

Consonants

In general consonants are pronounced much as in English, although the sound of the **r** is always pronounced very distinctly.

The consonants **c** and **g** followed by **e** or **i**, are pronounced as a combination of the English sounds **ch** and **j** with other vowel(s).

CE	as in chair	[che]	e.g. cena – dinner (*che-na*)
GE	as in jet	[je]	e.g. gente – people (*jen-te*)
CI	as in chin	[chee]	e.g. cibo – food (*chee-bo*)
GI	as in jeep	[jee]	e.g. giro – tour (*jee-ro*)

When the consonants **c** and **g** are followed by **a, o, u** they are pronounced with a sound like the English **k** and **g**.

CA	as in card	[ka]	e.g. casa – house (*ka-za*)
GA	as in gala	[ga]	e.g. gatto – cat (*gat-to*)
CO	as in core	[ko]	e.g. arco – arch (*ar-ko*)
GO	as in goal	[go]	e.g. gola – throat (*go-la*)
CU	as in cool	[koo]	e.g. cura – cure (*koo-ra*)
GU	as in guru	[goo]	e.g. gusto – taste (*goos-to*)

The consonants **s** and **z** have two sounds.

S	as in taste	[s]	e.g. sigaro – cigar (*see-ga-ro*)
S	as in nose	[z]	e.g. rosa – rose (*ro-za*)
Z	as in cuts	[ts]	e.g. prezzo – price (*pret-so*)
Z	as in birds	[dz]	e.g. mezzo – half (*med-zo*)

The consonant **q** is always in combination with the vowel **u**, and is pronounced [**koo**].

The consonant **h** is never pronounced, e.g. the word hotel is pronounced in Italian [*o-tel*].

Groups of consonants

Double consonants, like **cc** and **gg**, always represent a single heavily stressed sound. The following groups represent a single sound.

CHI	as in king	[**kee**]	e.g. chi – who (***kee***)
CHE	as in Kent	[**keh**]	e.g. che – what (***keh***)
GHI	as in gear	[**gee**]	e.g. ghisa – cast iron (***gee**-za*)
GHE	as in guest	[**ge**]	e.g. traghetto – ferry (*tra **get**-to*)

The combination of **g** and **l** followed by the vowel **i** is pronounced as double **ll** in English.

GLI	as in million	[**ly**]	e.g. figlio – son (*fee-**lyo***)

The combination of **g** and **n** followed by any vowel is pronounced as shown below.

GN	as in onion	[**ny**]	e.g. bagno – bath (*ba-**nyo***)

The combination of **s** and **c** followed by the vowels **i** and **e** is pronounced as shown below.

SCI	as in ship	[**shee**]	e.g. sci – ski (***shee***)
SCE	as in shed	[**she**]	e.g. scemo – stupid (***she**-mo*)

The combination of **s** and **c** followed by the vowels **a, o** and **u** is pronounced as shown below.

SCA	as in scarf	[**ska**]	e.g. scarso – scarse (*skar-so*)
SCO	as in scone	[**sko**]	e.g. scorso – last (*skor-so*)
SCU	as in scoop	[**sku**]	e.g. scuro – dark (*sku-ro*)

Stress
Most Italian words are stressed on the next to last syllable. If the last syllable is stressed it is written with an accent. Irregular stress is indicated in the pronunciation guide by printing the stressed syllable in **bold type**.

The Italian Alphabet

Italian letters

A	a [as in **a**pple]	I	i [as in l**i**tre]	Q	cu [as in ty**coo**n]
B	bi [as in **bee**]	L	elle [as in se**ller**]	R	erre [as in **Ferrero**]
C	ci [as in **chin**]	M	emme [as in **Emme**rdale]	S	esse [as in **Esse**x]
D	di [as in **dee**]	N	enne [as in **Kenne**dy]	T	ti [as in **tin**]
E	e [as in w**e**t]			U	u [as in m**oo**n]
F	effe [as in **effe**ct]	O	o [as in s**o**ft]	V	vu [as in **vu**lnerable]
G	gi [as in **j**oy]	P	pi [as in **pin**]		
H	acca [as in D**a**kar]			Z	zeta [as in **Zeta**]

Foreign letters

These letters are only used with foreign words, since there are no Italian words that contain them.

J	i lunga	X	ics
K	cappa	Y	ipsilon or 'ee' greca
W	vu doppia or doppia vu		

Spelling

For spelling out words in Italian, the names of Italian cities are often used (except for the Italian letters H, Q and Z, and for the foreign letters, for which there are no Italian cities starting with these letters). Note the following:

A	come (*as in*) Ancona	H	come Hotel	R	come Roma
		I	come Imola	S	come Savona
B	come Bari	L	come Lucca	T	come Torino
C	come Como	M	come Milano	U	come Udine
D	come Domodossola	N	come Napoli	V	come Venezia
E	come Empoli	O	come Otranto	Z	come Zorro
F	come Firenze	P	come Palermo		
G	come Genova	Q	come Quadro		

ESSENTIALS

First Things

Key Phrases		
Yes	**Sì**	*See*
No	**No**	*No*
That's all right (OK)	**Va bene (OK)**	*Va be-neh (OK)*
Please[1]	**Per favore**	*Pair fa-vor-eh*
Thank you	**Grazie**	*Grat-syeh*
You're welcome	**Prego**	*Pre-go*
Sorry	**Mi dispiace**	*Mee dees-pya-cheh*

Greetings

Key Phrases		
Good morning/ good day	**Buongiorno**	*Bwon-jor-no*
Good afternoon/ evening	**Buonasera**	*Bwo-na-se-ra*

1. In Italian the word please (per favore) is not used as much as it is in English.

Good night	**Buonanotte**	*Bwo-na-not-teh*
Hello/goodbye (informal)	**Ciao**	*Chow*
How are you?	**Come sta?**	*Ko-me sta*
Fine, thank you	**Bene, grazie**	*Be-neh, grat-syeh*
Goodbye (formal)	**Arrivederci**	*Ar-ree-ve-dair-chee*

See you soon	**A presto**	*A pre-sto*
See you tomorrow	**A domani**	*A do-ma-nee*
Have a good journey	**Buon viaggio**	*Bwon vyad-jo*
Good luck	**Buona fortuna**	*Bwo-na for-too-na*
All the best	**I migliori auguri**	*Ee mee-lyo-ree ow-goo-ree*
Have a good time	**Buon divertimento**	*Bwon dee-vair-tee-men-to*

Polite Phrases

Key Phrases

Excuse me	**Mi scusi**	*Mee skoo-zee*
Excuse me (*to pass, to enter*)	**Permesso**	*Pair-mes-so*
It's OK (*after thanks*)	**Prego**	*Pre-go*
Is everything all right?	**Tutto bene?**	*Toot-to be-neh*

| Good/that's fine | **Bene/va bene così** | *Be-neh/va be-neh ko-zee* |
| Thanks for your help | **Grazie per l'aiuto** | *Grat-syeh per la-yoo-to* |

Not at all	**Nient'affatto**	*Nyent-af-fat-to*
With pleasure	**Prego**	*Pre-go*
I beg your pardon?	**Prego?**	*Pre-go*
Don't worry	**Non si preoccupi**	*Non see pre-ok-koo-pee*
It doesn't matter	**Non fa niente**	*Non fa nyen-teh*
Am I disturbing you?	**La disturbo?**	*La dees-toor-bo*
Sorry to have troubled you	**Scusi il disturbo**	*Skoo-zee eel dees-toor-bo*

Language Problems

Key Phrases

Do you speak English?	**Parla inglese?**	*Par-la een-gle-zeh*
Does anyone speak English?	**Qualcuno parla inglese?**	*Kwal-koo-no par-la een-gle-zeh*
I don't speak Italian	**Non parlo italiano**	*Non par-lo ee-ta-lya-no*
I (don't) understand	**(Non) capisco**	*(Non) ka-pee-sko*

| Please write it down | **Per favore, lo scriva** | *Pair fa-vor-eh, lo **skree**-va* |
| Can you say that again? | **Può ripetere?** | *Pwo ree-pe-tair-eh* |

I'm English/American	**Sono inglese/ americano/ americana**	*So-no een-gle-zeh/ a-me-ree-ka-no/ a-me-ree-ka-na*
I speak a little Italian	**Parlo un po' d'italiano**	*Par-lo oon po dee-ta-lya-no*
Am I making myself clear?	***Sono chiaro/chiara?**	*So-no kya-ro/kya-ra*
What does it mean?	**Cosa significa?**	*Ko-za see-ny-fee-ka*
Can you translate it for me?	**Me lo può tradurre?**	*Meh lo pwo tra-door-reh*
How do you write it?	**Come si scrive?**	*Ko-meh see skree-veh*
Please speak slowly/ quietly	**Parli piano, per favore**	*Par-lee pya-no, pair fa-vor-eh*
How do you say it in Italian?	**Come si dice in italiano?**	*Ko-me see dee-che een ee-ta-lya-no*
I'll look it up in my book	**Lo cerco nel mio libretto**	*Lo cher-ko nel mee-o lee-bret-to*
Does anyone speak English?	**Qualcuno parla inglese?**	*Kwal-koo-no par-la een-gle-zeh*

Questions

Key Phrases

Who?	**Chi?**	*Kee*
Where is/are . . . ?	**Dov'è/dove sono . . . ?**	*Dov-**eh**/do-veh so-no*
When?	**Quando?**	*Kwan-do*
Why?	**Perché?**	*Pair-**keh***
What?	**(Che) cosa?**	*(Keh) ko-za*
How?	**Come?**	*Ko-meh*
How much is/are . . . ?	**Quanto costa/ costano?**	*Kwan-to kos-ta/**kos**-ta-no*
How far?	**Quanto dista?**	*Kwan-to **dee**-sta*
Is there . . ./are there . . . ?	**C'è . . ./ci sono . . . ?**	*Cheh . . ./chee so-no . . .*

Where?	**Dove?**	*Do-veh*
How much/many?	**Quanto/quanti?**	*Kwan-to/kwan-tee*
How long?	**Quanto tempo?**	*Kwan-to tem-po*
What's this?	**Cos'è questo?**	*Koz-**eh** kwes-to*
What would you like?	**Cosa desidera?**	*Ko-za de-**zee**-dair-a*
What do I have to do?	**Cosa devo fare?**	*Ko-za de-vo far-eh*
What is the matter?	**Cosa c'è/cosa succede?**	*Ko-za cheh/ko-za soo-che-deh*
Have you . . ./do you sell . . . ?	**Ha . . ./vende . . . ?**	*A . . ./ven-deh . . .*

Have you seen . . . ?	**Ha visto . . . ?**	*A vees-to . . .*
Where can I find . . . ?	**Dove posso trovare . . . ?**	*Do-veh pos-so tro-var-eh . . .*
May I have . . . ?	**Posso avere . . . ?**	*Pos-so a-vair-eh . . .*
Can you help me?	**Potrebbe aiutarmi?**	*Pot-reb-beh a-yu-tar-mee*
Can I help you?	***Posso aiutarla?**	*Pos-so a-yu-tar-la*
Could you tell me . . . ?	**Potrebbe dirmi . . . ?**	*Pot-reb-beh deer-mee . . .*
Can you show/give me . . . ?	**Può mostrarmi/ darmi . . . ?**	*Pwo mos-trar-mee/ dar-mee . . .*

Useful Statements

Key Phrases

Here (it) is/(they) are . . .	**Ecco (lo/li) . . .**	*Ek-ko (lo/lee) . . .*
I should like . . .	**Vorrei . . .**	*Vor-**ray** . . .*
I need . . .	**Ho bisogno di . . .**	*O bee-zo-nyo dee . . .*
I (don't) want . . .	**(Non) voglio . . .**	*(Non) vol-yo . . .*
I (don't) know	**(Non) lo so**	*(Non) lo so*
It's urgent	**È urgente**	*Eh oor-jen-teh*

It is . . .	**È . . .**	*Eh . . .*
It isn't . . .	**Non è . . .**	*Non eh . . .*
I (don't) have . . .	**(Non) ho . . .**	*(Non) o . . .*
I (don't) want . . .	**(Non) voglio . . .**	*(Non) vol-yo . . .*

I (don't) like it/them	**(Non) mi piace/ mi piacciono**	*(Non) mee pya-cheh/ mee pya-cho-no*
OK/that's fine	**OK/va bene**	*OK/va be-neh*
There is/are . . .	**C'è/ci sono . . .**	*Cheh/chee so-no . . .*
Here (it) is/(they)are . . .	**Ecco (lo/li) . . .**	*Ek-ko (lo/lee) . . .*
I (don't) know	**(Non) lo so**	*(Non) lo so*
I did (not) know	**(Non) lo sapevo**	*(Non) lo sa-pe-vo*
I think so	**Credo di sì**	*Kre-do dee see*
I'm hungry/thirsty	**Ho fame/sete**	*O fa-meh/se-teh*
I'm tired	**Sono stanco/stanca**	*So-no stan-ko/stan-ka*
I'm in a hurry	**Ho fretta**	*O fret-ta*
I'm ready	**Sono pronto/pronta**	*So-no pron-to/pron-ta*
Leave me alone!	**Mi lasci stare!**	*Mee la-shee star-eh*
Go away!	**Se ne vada!**	*Se ne va-da*
I'm lost	**Mi sono perso/ persa**	*Mee so-no pair-so/ pair-sa*
We're looking for . . .	**Cerchiamo . . .**	*Chair-kya-mo . . .*
Just a moment	***Un momento**	*Oon mo-men-to*
This way, please	***Da questa parte, per favore**	*Da kwes-ta par-teh, pair fa-vo-reh*
Take a seat	***Si accomodi**	*See ak-ko-mo-dee*
Come in!	***Entri/avanti!**	*En-tree/a-van-tee*
It's important	**È importante**	*Eh eem-por-tan-teh*

It's urgent	**È urgente**	*Eh oor-jen-teh*
That's all	**Questo è tutto**	*Kwe-sto eh toot-to*
You are wrong	**Si sbaglia**	*See zbal-ya*
You're right	**Ha ragione**	*A ra-jo-neh*

SIGNS AND PUBLIC NOTICES[1]

Acqua (non) potabile	(Not) drinking water
Affittasi	To let
Aperto	Open
Aperto dalle . . . alle . . .	Open from . . . to . . .
Ascensore	Lift/elevator
Attenzione	Caution
Bagno (WC/Servizi)	Lavatory/toilet
Bagno per donne	Ladies
Bagno per uomini	Gentlemen
Banca	Bank
Bussare	Knock
Carabinieri	(Military) police station
Chiuso	Closed
Divieto di entrata	No entry
Entrata/ingresso	Entrance
Guida	Guide
Ingresso libero	Admission free
Interprete	Interpreter

1. See also Signs at Airports and Stations (p. 15) and Road Signs (p. 50)

In vendita	For sale
I trasgressori verranno puniti ai termini di legge	Trespassers will be prosecuted
Libero	Vacant/free/unoccupied
Occupato	Engaged/occupied
Pedoni	Pedestrians
Pericolo	Danger
Posti in piedi	Standing room only
Posto di blocco	Check point
Privato	Private
Riservato	Reserved
Si prega di non ...	Do not ...
Spingere	Push
Stanza da affittare	Room to let
Stazione di polizia	Police station
Suonare	Ring
Svendita	Sale
Sconti	Discounts
Siete pregati di non .../ Si prega di non ...	You are requested not to ...
Tenere la destra/sinistra	Keep right/left
Tirare	Pull
Tutto esaurito	House full (*cinema, etc.*)
Tutto occupato	No vacancies

Ufficio informazioni	Information office
Ufficio postale	Post office
Uscita	Exit
Uscita di emergenza	Emergency exit
Vietato fumare	No smoking
Vietato l'ingresso	No admission

GETTING AROUND

Arrival

Key Phrases

I've lost my passport, I must have dropped it on the plane	**Ho perso il (mio) passaporto, mi dev'essere caduto in aereo**	*O pair-so eel (mee-o) pas-sa-por-to, mee de-ves-se-reh ka-du-to in a-air-e-o*
My luggage is lost	**I miei bagagli si sono persi**	*Ee myay ba-gal-yee see so-no pair-see*
My luggage is damaged	**I miei bagagli sono rovinati**	*Ee myay ba-gal-yee so-no ro-vee-na-tee*
Is there an ATM/a currency exchange office?	**C'è un bancomat/un ufficio di cambio?**	*Cheh oon ban-co-mat/ oon oof-fee-cho dee kam-byo*
Is there a train into the town?	**C'è un treno per il centro?**	*Cheh oon tre-no pair eel chen-tro*
How can I get to . . .?	**Come si arriva a . . .?**	*Ko-meh see ar-ree-va a . . .*

Passports

passport control	***il controllo passaporti**	*kon-trol-lo pas-sa-por-tee*
Your passport, please	***Passaporto, prego**	*Pas-sa-por-to, pre-go*
Are you together?	***Siete insieme?**	*Sye-teh een-sye-meh*

I'm travelling with a group	**Viaggio in gruppo**	*Vyad-jo een grup-po*
I'm travelling alone	**Viaggio da solo/sola**	*Vyad-jo da so-lo/so-la*
I'm travelling with . . .	**Viaggio con . . .**	*Vyad-jo kon . . .*
I'm here on business	**Sono qui per affari**	*So-no kwee pair af-fa-ree*
I'm here on holiday	**Sono qui in vacanza**	*So-no kwee een va-kan-tsa*
What is your address?	***Qual'è il suo indirizzo?**	*Kwal-eh eel soo-o een-dee-ree-tso*
How long are you staying?	***Quanto tempo rimane?**	*Kwanto tem-po ree-ma-neh*

Customs

customs	***la dogana**	*do-ga-na*
goods/nothing to declare	***merci/niente da dichiarare**	*Mair-chee/nyen-teh da dee-kya-rar-eh*
Which is your luggage?	***Quali sono i suoi bagagli?**	*Kwal-ee so-no ee swoy ba-gal-yee*
Anything to declare?	***Niente da dichiarare?**	*Nyen-teh da dee-kya-rar-eh*
You must pay duty (on this)	***Deve pagare il dazio**	*De-veh pa-gar-eh eel dat-syo*
This is my luggage	**Ecco i miei bagagli**	*Ek-ko ee myay ba-gal-yee*
Do you have any more luggage?	***Ha altri bagagli?**	*A alt-ree ba-gal-yee*

There are only personal things	**Ci sono solo effetti personali**	*Chee so-no so-lo ef-fet-tee pair-so-na-lee*
Open the bag, please	***Apra la valigia, per favore**	*Ap-ra la va-lee-ja, pair fa-vor-eh*
Can I shut my case?	**Posso chiudere la valigia?**	*Pos-so **kyoo**-dair-eh la va-lee-ja*
May I go?	**Posso andare?**	*Pos-so an-dar-eh*

Luggage

porter	**il facchino/portinaio**	*fak-kee-no/ por-tee-na-yo*
left luggage office	**deposito bagagli**	*de-**po**-zee-to ba-gal-yee*
luggage lockers	**armadietti per i bagagli**	*Ar-ma-dyet-tee per ee ba-gal-yee*
One suitcase is missing	**Manca una valigia**	*Man-ka oon-a va-lee-ja*
Are there any trolleys?	**Ci sono dei carrelli?**	*Chee so-no day ka-rel-lee*
Would you call a taxi?	**Può chiamare un taxi?**	*Pwo kya-mar-eh un taxi*
My luggage is lost	**I miei bagagli si sono persi**	*Ee myay ba-gal-yee see so-no pair-see*
My luggage is damaged	**I miei bagagli sono rovinati**	*Ee myay ba-gal-yee so-no ro-vee-na-tee*

Moving on

I'll take this myself	**Questa la porto io**	*Kwe-sta la por-to ee-o*
That's not mine	**Questa non è mia**	*Kwes-ta non eh mee-ya*
How much do I owe you?	**Quanto le devo?**	*Kwan-to leh de-vo*
Is there an ATM/ a currency exchange office?	**C'è un bancomat/un ufficio di cambio?**	*Cheh oon ban-co-mat/ oon oof-fee-cho dee kam-byo*
Is there a train into the town?	**C'è un treno per il centro?**	*Cheh oon tre-no pair eel chen-tro*
How can I get to . . .?	**Come si arriva a . . .?**	*Ko-meh see ar-ree-va a . . .*
How much is it per piece?	**Quanto costa a collo?**	*Kwan-to kos-ta a kol-lo?*
Where is the information bureau?	**Dov'è l'ufficio informazioni?**	*Dov-eh loof-fee-cho een-for-ma-tsyo-nee*
Could you take these bags to the taxi/bus/ car rental office?	**Può portare questi bagagli al taxi/ all'autobus/ all'ufficio noleggio auto?**	*Pwo por-tar-eh kwes-tee ba-gal-yee al taxi/al-low-to-boos/al-loof-fee-cho no-led-jo ow-to*

Signs at Airports and Stations

Arrivals	**Arrivi**
Booking office	**Prenotazioni**
Bus/coach	**Autobus/pullman**

Car rental	**Noleggio macchine/auto**
Connections	**Coincidenze**
Departures	**Partenze**
Exchange	**Cambio/cambiavalute**
Gentlemen	**WC/bagni per signori/uomini**
Hotel reservations	**Prenotazioni alberghi**
Information (desk)	**(Ufficio) informazioni**
Internet access	**Accesso Internet**
Ladies' room	**WC/bagni per signore/donne**
Left luggage	**Deposito bagagli**
Lost property	**Oggetti smarriti**
Main lines	**Linee principali**
News-stand	**Edicola**
No smoking	**Vietato fumare**
Platform	**Binario**
Refreshments	**Rinfreschi/ristorazione**
Reservations	**Prenotazioni**
Shuttle (for passengers)	**Navetta (passeggeri)**
Suburban lines	**Linee locali**
Tickets	**Biglietti**
Toilets	**Bagni/WC/servizi igienici**
Tourist office	**Ufficio turistico**
Transit desk	**Passeggeri in transito**
Underground	**Metropolitana**
Waiting room	**Sala d'aspetto**

By Air

Key Phrases

What's the (baggage) allowance?	**Quant'è il peso limite?**	*Quan-teh eel pe-zo lee-mee-teh*
I have only hand luggage	**Ho solo il bagaglio a mano**	*O so-lo eel ba-gal-yo a ma-no*
I'd like to change my reservation to . . .	**Vorrei cambiare la mia prenotazione per . . .**	*Vor-ray kam-byar-eh la mee-a pre-no-tat-syo-neh pair . . .*
Can I check in online?	**Posso fare il check-in online?**	*Pos-so fa-reh eel check-in online*
(The) flight to . . . has been delayed/ cancelled	***(Il) volo per . . . è in ritardo è stato/cancellato**	*(Eel) vo-lo pair . . . eh in ree-tar-do eh sta-to kan-chel-la-to*

Where's the airline office?	**Dov'è l'ufficio della compagnia aerea?**	*Dov-eh loof-fee-cho del-la kom-pan-yee-a a-air-e-a*
I'd like to book a flight to/for . . .	**Vorrei prenotare un volo per . . .**	*Vor-ray pre-no-tar-eh oon vo-lo pair . . .*
Is this the cheapest tariff?	**Questa è la tariffa meno cara?**	*Kwes-ta eh la ta-reef-fa me-no ka-ra*
I'd like an aisle/ window seat	**Vorrei un posto in corridoio/vicino al finestrino**	*Vor-ray oon pos-to een kor-ree-do-yo/vee-chee-no al fee-ne-stree-no*
When does the next plane leave?	**Quando parte il prossimo aereo?**	*Kwan-do par-teh eel pros-see-mo a-air-e-o*

Please cancel my reservation to . . .	**Vorrei disdire la mia prenotazione per . . .**	*Vor-ray dees-deer-eh la mee-a pre-no-tat-syo-neh pair . . .*
first class	**prima classe**	*pree-ma klas-seh*
economy	**seconda classe**	*se-kon-da klas-seh*
What is the flight number?	**Qual'è il numero di volo?**	*Kwa-leh eel noo-mai-ro dee vo-lo*
When does it leave/ arrive?	**Quando parte/ arriva?**	*Kwan-do par-teh/ ar-ree-va*
I have an open ticket	**Ho un biglietto aperto**	*O oon beel-yet-to a-pair-to*
Can I change it?	**Posso cambiarlo?**	*Pos-so kam-byar-lo*
Will it cost more?	**Costerà di più?**	*Kos-te-ra dee pyoo*
Is there a bus to . . .?	**C'è un autobus per . . .?**	*Cheh oon ow-to-bus pair . . .*
When must I check in?	**Quando devo fare il check-in?**	*Kwan-do de-vo fa-reh eel check-in*
Can I check in online?	**Posso fare il check-in online?**	*Pos-so fa-reh eel check-in online*
The plane leaves from gate . . .	***L'aereo parte dol'uscita . . .**	*La-air-e-o par-teh doloo-shee-ta . . .*
How long is the flight?	**Quanto dura il volo?**	*Kwan-to doo-ra eel vo-lo*
Is there a flight to . . .?	**C'è un volo per . . .?**	*Cheh oon vo-lo pair . . .*
Where are the check-in desks for . . .?	**Dove sono i banchi del check-in per' . . .?**	*Do-veh so-no ee ban-kee del check-in pair . . .*

Which airport/ terminal does the flight leave from?	**Da quale aeroporto/ terminale parte l'aereo?**	*Da kwa-leh a-air-o-por-to/ter-mee-na-leh par-teh la-air-e-o*
I've booked a wheelchair to take me to the plane	**Ho prenotato una sedia a rotelle per portarmi all'aereo**	*O pre-no-ta-to oon-a sed-ya a ro-tel-leh pair por-tar-mee al-la-air-e-o*
You must pay for excess baggage	***Deve pagare per l'eccedenza bagaglio**	*Deve pa-ga-reh pair le-che-den-tsa ba-gal-yo*
I've lost my boarding card	**Ho perso la mia carta d'imbarco**	*O pair-so la mee-a car-ta deem-bar-ko*
(The) flight to . . . has been delayed/ cancelled	***(Il) volo per . . . è stato posticipato/ cancellato**	*(Eel) vo-lo pair . . . eh sta-to po stee-chee-pa-to/ kan-chel-la-to*

By Boat or Ferry

Key Phrases

Is there a boat from here to . . .?	**C'è un servizio marittimo per . . .?**	*Cheh oon sair-veet-syo mar-eet-tee-mo pair . . .*
When does the next boat leave?	**Quando parte il prossimo battello?**	*Kwan-do par-teh eel pros-see-mo bat-tel-lo*
I'd like a one way/ return ticket	**Vorrei un biglietto di sola andata/andata e ritorno**	*Vor-ray oon beel-yet-to dee so-la an-da-ta/ an-da-ta eh ree-tor-no*

Where is the port/ harbour?	**Dov'è il porto?**	*Do-veh eel por-to*
How long does it take to get to ...?	**Quanto tempo ci mette per arrivare a ...?**	*Kwan-to tem-po chee met-teh pair ar-ree-var-eh a ...*
How often do the boats leave?	**Ogni quanto partono i battelli?**	*On-yee kwan-to par-to-no ee bat-tel-lee*
Does it call at ...?	**Si ferma a ...?**	*See fair-ma a ...*
What does it cost for	**Quanto costa per**	*Kwan-to ko-sta pair*
a child?	**un bambino?**	*oon bam-bee-no*
a bicycle?	**una bicicletta**	*oon-a bee-chee-klet-ta*
a motor cycle?	**una motocicletta?**	*oon-a mo-to-chee-klet-ta*
a caravan/camper van?	**un camper/una roulotte?**	*oon kam-pair/oon-a roo-lot*
Can I book a single berth cabin?	**Posso riservare una cabina con un letto?**	*Pos-so ree-zair-var-eh oon-a ka-bee-na kon oon let-to*
How many berths are there in this cabin?	**Quante cuccette ci sono in questa cabina?**	*Kwan-teh koo-chet-teh chee so-no een kwes-ta ka-bee-na*
When must we go on board?	**A che ora dobbiamo essere a bordo?**	*A keh or-a dob-bya-mo es-se-reh a bor-do*
How do we get on to the deck?	**Come si arriva al ponte?**	*Ko-meh see ar-ree-va al pon-teh*
When do we dock?	**A che ora arriviamo in porto?**	*A keh or-a ar-ree-vya-mo een por-to*
How long do we stay in port?	**Quanto rimaniamo in porto?**	*Kwan-to ree-ma-nya-mo een por-to*

Where are the toilets?	**Dove sono i bagni?**	*Do-veh so-no ee ban-yee*
I feel seasick	**Ho mal di mare**	*O mal dee ma-reh*
(car) ferry	**il traghetto**	*tra-get-to*
lifevest	**il giubbotto di salvataggio**	*joo-bot-to dee sal-va-tad-jo*
lifeboat	**il battello di salvataggio**	*bat-tel-lo dee sal-va-tad-jo*

By Bus or Coach

Key Phrases

Where can I buy a bus ticket?	**Dove posso comprare un biglietto per l'autobus?**	*Do-veh pos-so com-pra-reh oon beel-yet-to pair l-low-to-boos*
Do I pay the driver?	**Devo pagare l'autista?**	*De-vo pa-ga-reh low-tee-sta*
What time is the next bus?	**A che ora c'è il prossimo autobus?**	*A keh or-a cheh eel pros-see-mo ow-to-boos*
Which bus goes to...?	**Quale autobus va a...?**	*Kwal-eh ow-to-boos va a...*
Where do I get off?	**Dove devo scendere?**	*Do-veh de-vo shen-dair-eh*

Where's the bus station?	**Dov'è la stazione degli autobus?**	*Dov-eh la stat-syo-neh del-yee ow-to-boos*
Where's the coach station?	**Dov'è la stazione dei pullman?**	*Dov-eh la stat-syo-neh day pool-man*

bus stop	*fermata dell'autobus	*fair-ma-ta del-**low**-to-boos
request stop	*fermata a richiesta	*fair-ma-ta a ree-kyes-ta
Is there a daily/ weekly ticket?	C'è un biglietto giornaliero/ settimanale?	Cheh oon beel-yet-to jor-nal-ye-ro/set-tee-ma-na-leh
What is the fare?	Quanto costa?	Kwan-to ko-sta
I'd like to reserve a seat in the coach	Vorrei prenotare un posto in pullman	Vor-**ray** pre-no-ta-reh oon pos-to een pool-man
When does the coach leave?	Quando parte il pullman?	Kwan-do par-teh eel pool-man
What time do we get to ...?	A che ora arriviamo a ...?	A keh or-a ar-ree-vya-mo a ...
What stops does it make?	In quali posti si ferma?	Een kwa-lee pos-tee see fair-ma
Is it a long journey?	È un viaggio molto lungo?	Eh oon vyad-jo mol-to loon-go
How often does the bus run?	Ogni quanto passa l'autobus?	On-yee kwan-to pas-sa **low**-to-boos
What time is the last bus?	A che ora è l'ultimo pullman?	A keh or-a eh lool-tee-mo pool-man
Does this bus go to the centre?	Passa dal centro quest' autobus?	Pas-sa dal chen-tro kwes-t **ow**-to-boos
Does it go to the beach?	Va alla spiaggia?	Va al-la spyad-ja
Does this bus go to the station?	Va alla stazione questo autobus?	Va al-la stat-syo-neh kwes-to **ow**-to-boos
Does it go near ...?	Passa vicino a ...?	Pas-sa vee-chee-no a ...

Where can I get a bus to...?	**Dove posso prendere un autobus per...?**	*Do-veh pos-so pren-dair-eh oon ow-to-boos pair...*
Is this the right stop for...?	**È questa la fermata giusta per...?**	*Eh kwes-ta la fair-ma-ta joos-ta pair...*
Which bus goes to...?	**Quale autobus va a...?**	*Kwal-eh ow-to-boos va a...*
I want to go to...	**Voglio andare a...**	*Vol-yo an-dar-eh a...*
Where do I get off?	**Dove devo scendere?**	*Do-veh de-vo shen-dair-eh*
I want to get off at...	**Voglio scendere a...**	*Vol-yo shen-dair-eh a...*
The bus to...stops over there	***L'autobus per... ferma là**	*Low-to-boos pair... fair-ma la*
The number...goes to...	***Il numero... va a...**	*Eel noo-mair-o... va a...*
You must take a number...	***Lei deve prendere il numero...**	*Lay de-ve pren-dair-eh eel noo-mair-o...*
You get off at the next stop	***Scenda alla prossima fermata**	*Shen-da al-la pros-see-ma fair-ma-ta*
The buses run every ten minutes/every hour	***C'è un autobus ogni dieci minuti/ ogni ora**	*Cheh oon ow-to-boos on-yee dye-chee mi-noo-tee/on-yee or-a*

By Taxi

Key Phrases

Please get me a taxi	**Vuol chiamarmi un taxi, per favore?**	*Vwol kya-mar-mee oon taxi, pair fa-vor-eh*
Where can I get a taxi?	**Dove posso prendere un taxi?**	*Do-veh pos-so **pren**-dair-eh oon taxi*
Please wait a minute	**Aspetti un momento, per favore**	*As-pet-tee oon mo-men-to, pair fa-vor-eh*
Stop here	**Fermi qui**	*Fair-mee kwee*

I'd like to book a taxi for tomorrow at . . .	**Vorrei prenotare un taxi per domani alle . . .**	*Vor-**ray** pre-no-tar-eh un taxi pair do-ma-nee al-leh. . .*
Are you free?	**È libero?**	*Eh **lee**-bair-o*
Please take me	**Mi porti**	*Mee por-tee*
to Hotel Central	**all' Hotel Centrale**	*al-lo-**tel** chen-tra-leh*
to the station	**alla stazione**	*al-la stat-syo-neh*
to the city centre	**al centro**	*al chen-tro*
to this address	**a questo indirizzo**	*a kwes-to een-dee-reet-so*
Can you hurry, I'm late?	**Può andare più in fretta, sono in ritardo?**	*Pwo an-dar-eh pyoo een fret-ta, so-no een ree-tar-do*
Is it far?	**È molto lontano?**	*Eh mol-to lon-ta-no*
How far is it to . . .?	**Quanto manca de qui a . . .?**	*Kwan-to man-ka de kwee a . . .*

Turn right/left at the next corner	**Si gira a destra/ sinistra al prossimo angolo**	*See jeer-a a des-tra/ see-nees-tra al pros-see-mo an-go-lo*
Straight on	**Va diritto**	*Va dee-reet-to*
How much do you charge by the hour/ for the day?	**Quanto prende all'ora/a giornata?**	*Kwan-to pren-deh al-lor-a/a jor-na-ta*
I'd like to go to ... How much would you charge?	**Vorrei andare a ... Quanto costa?**	*Vor-ray an-dar-eh a ... Kwan-to kos-ta*
How much is it?	**Quant' è?**	*Kwan-teh*
That's too much	**È troppo**	*Eh trop-po*
I am not prepared to spend that much	**No, grazie, è più di quanto posso spendere**	*No, grat-syeh, eh pyoo dee kwan-to pos-so spen-dair-eh*
It's a lot, but all right	**È un po' caro, ma va bene**	*Eh oon po kar-o, ma va be-neh*

By Train[1]

Key Phrases

Where's the railway station?	**Dov'è la stazione?**	*Dov-eh la stat-syo-neh*
What's the cheapest fare to ...?	**Quanto costa la tariffa più economica per ...?**	*Kwan-to kos-ta la ta-reef-fa pyoo e-kon-om-ee-ka pair ...*

1. For help in understanding the answers to these and similar questions see Time and Dates (p. 228), Numbers (p. 237) and Directions (p. 53).

Is there a day return?	C'è un biglietto gionaliero (di) andata e ritorno?	*Cheh oon beel-yet-to jor-nal-ye-ro (dee) an-da-ta eh ree-tor-no*
Where do I change?	Dove devo cambiare?	*Do-veh de-vo kam-byar-eh*
Excuse me, what station is this?	Scusi, che stazione è questa?	*Skoo-zee, keh stat-syo-neh eh kwe-sta*

Reservations and enquiries

Where is the ticket office?	Dov'è la biglietteria?	*Dov-eh la beel-yet-tair-ee-a*
Do you have a timetable, please?	Ha un orario, per favore?	*A oon or-ar-yo, pair fa-vor-eh*
How much is it first class to . . .?	Quanto costa un biglietto di prima classe per . . .?	*Kwan-to kos-ta oon beel-yet-to dee pree-ma klas-seh pair . . .*
A second class single to . . .	Un biglietto di seconda classe, solo andata, per . . .	*Oon beel-yet-to dee se-kon-da klas-seh, so-lo an-da-ta, pair . . .*
A single ticket to . . .	Un biglietto di solo andata per . . .	*Oon beel-yet-to dee so-lo an-da-ta pair . . .*
A return ticket to . . .	Un biglietto di andata e ritorno per . . .	*Oon beel-yet-to dee an-da-ta eh ree-tor-no pair . . .*

When are you coming back?	*Quando ritorna?	Kwan-do ree-tor-na
Is there a supplementary charge?	C'è da pagare un supplemento?	Cheh da pa-gar-eh oon soop-ple-men-to
Is there a cheaper midweek/weekend fare?	C'è un biglietto feriale/festivo?	Cheh oon beel-yet-to fer-ya-leh/fes-tee-vo
How much is the child fare?	Quanto costa la tariffa per bambini?	Kwan-to ko-sta la ta-ree-fa pair bam-bee-nee
How old is he (she)/ are they?	*Quanti anni ha/ hanno?	Kwan-tee an-nee a/ an-no
How long is this ticket valid?	Per quanti giorni è valido questo biglietto?	Pair kwan-tee jor-nee eh va-lee-do kwes-to beel-yet-to
Do I need to reserve a seat?	È necessario prenotare un posto?	Eh ne-ches-sa-ryo pre-no-ta-reh oon pos-to?
I would like	Vorrei	Vor-ray
a window seat	un posto vicino al finestrino	oon pos-to vee-chee-no al fee-nes-tree-no
an aisle seat	un posto in corridoio	oon pos-to een kor-ree-do-yo
I want to reserve a sleeper	Vorrei riservare un posto in vagone letto	Vor-ray ree-zair-var-eh oon pos-to een va-go-neh let-to

When is the next train to ...?	Quando parte il prossimo treno per ...?	*Kwan-do par-teh eel pros-see-mo tre-no pair ...*
Is it an express or a local train?[1]	È un treno diretto o locale?	*Eh oon tre-no dee-ret-to o lo-ka-leh*
Is there an earlier/later train?	Ci sono altri treni prima di questo/dopo questo?	*Chee so-no alt-ree tre-nee pree-ma dee kwes-to/do-po kwes-to*
Is there a restaurant car on the train?	C'è un vagone ristorante su questo treno?	*Cheh oon va-go-neh rees-tor-an-teh soo kwes-to tre-no*
Does the train stop at ...?	Il treno si ferma a ...?	*Eel tre-no see fer-ma a ...*
I'd like to make a motorail reservation	Vorrei fare una prenotazione per i servizi treni con auto accompagnate	*Vor-ray far-eh oon-a pre-no-tat-syo-neh pair ee sair-veet-see tre-nee kon ow-to ak-kom-pan-ya-teh*
Where is the motorail loading platform?	Dov'è il binario motorail?	*Dov-eh eel bee-nar-yo motorail*

Changing

| Is there a through train to ...? | C'è un treno diretto per ...? | *Cheh oon tre-no dee-ret-to pair ...* |
| Do I have to change? | Devo cambiare? | *De-vo kam-byar-eh* |

1. Trains are classified as follows: **Rapido** – fast trains running between main towns, sometimes only first class. A supplement is charged (about 25 per cent of normal single fare). **Espresso** – long-distance express trains, first and second class. **Diretto** – express trains, first and second class. **Locale** – local trains. Luggage can often be transported for the whole journey in the luggage car, and this service is called *bagaglio a seguito passeggero*. Certain Trans-European Express trains go through Italy. They are only first class and a supplement must be paid.

Where do I change?	**Dove devo cambiare?**	*Do-veh de-vo kam-byar-eh*
Excuse me, what station is this?	**Scusi, che stazione è questa?**	*Skoo-zee, keh stat-syo-neh eh kwe-sta*
Is this where I change for...?	**È qui che devo cambiare per...?**	*Eh kwee keh de-vo kam-byar-eh pair...*
What time is there a connection to...?	**A che ora c'è la coincidenza per...?**	*A keh or-a cheh la ko-een-chee-dent-sa pair...*
When does it get to...?	**A che ora arriva a...?**	*A keh or-a ar-ree-va a...*
When does the train from...get in?	**A che ora arriva il treno da...?**	*A keh or-a ar-ree-va eel tre-no da...*
At which platform?	**Su quale binario?**	*Soo kwa-leh bee-nar-yo*
Is the train late?	**È in ritardo questo treno?**	*Eh een ree-tar-do kwes-to tre-no*
Change at...and take the local train	***Cambiare a...e prendere il treno locale**	*Kam-byar-eh a...eh **pren**-dair-eh eel tre-no lo-ka-leh*

Departure

When does the train leave?	**A che ora parte il treno?**	*A keh or-a par-teh eel tre-no*
Which platform does the train to...leave from?	**Da quale binario parte il treno per...?**	*Da kwal-eh bee-nar-yo par-teh eel tre-no pair...*
Is this the train for...?	**È questo il treno per...?**	*Eh kwes-to eel tre-no pair...*
There will be a delay of...	***Ci sarà un ritardo di...**	*Chee sa-**ra** oon ree-tar-do dee...*

On the train

ticket inspector	**il controllore**	*kon-trol-lo-reh*
We have reserved seats	**Abbiamo posti riservati**	*Ab-bya-mo pos-tee ree-zair-va-tee*
Is this seat free?	**È libero questo posto?**	*Eh lee-bair-o kwes-to pos-to*
This seat is taken	**Questo posto è occupato**	*Kwes-to pos-to eh ok-koo-pa-to*
dining car	**la carrozza ristorante**	*kar-rot-sa rees-tor-an-teh*
When is the buffet car open?	**Quand' apre la carrozza ristorante?**	*Kwan-d a-preh la kar-rot-sa rees-tor-an-teh*
Where is the sleeping car?	**Dov'è il vagone letto?**	*Dov-eh eel va-go-neh let-to*
Which is my sleeper?	**Qual'è la mia cuccetta?**	*Kwal-eh la mee-a koo-chet-ta*
Could you wake me at . . . please?	**Mi potrebbe svegliare alle . . . per favore?**	*Mee pot-reb-beh svel-ya-reh al-leh . . . pair fa-vor-eh*
The heating is too high/too low	**Bisogna abbassare/alzare il riscaldamento**	*Bee-zon-ya ab-bas-sar-eh/ alt-sar-eh eel rees-kal-da-men-to*
I can't open/close the window	**Non riesco ad aprire/a chiudere il finestrino**	*Non ree-es-ko ad ap-reer-eh/a kyoo-dair-eh eel fee-nes-tree-no*
What station is this?	**Che stazione è?**	*Keh stat-syo-neh eh*
How long do we stop here?	**Quanto tempo si ferma qui?**	*Kwan-to tem-po see fair-ma kwee*

By Underground

Key Phrases

Where is the nearest underground station?	**Dov'è la stazione della metropolitana la più vicina?**	*Dov-eh la stat-syo-neh del-la met-ro-po-lee-ta-na la pyoo vee-chee-na*
Do you have a map of the underground?	**Ha una carta della metropolitana?**	*A oon-a kar-ta del-la met-ro-po-lee-ta-na*
Does this train go to...?	**Questo treno va a...?**	*Kwes-to tre-no va a ...*

A book of tickets, please	**Un mazzetto di biglietti, per favore**	*Oon mad-zet-to dee beel-yet-tee, pair fa-vor-eh*
Can I use it on the bus/underground too?	**È valido pure per l'autobus/la metropolitana?**	*Eh va-lee-do poo-reh pair low-to-boos/la met-ro-po-lee-ta-na*
Is there a day/weekly ticket?	**C'è un biglietto giornaliero/ settimanale?**	*Cheh un beel-yet-to jor-nal-ye-ro/ set-tee-ma-na-leh*
Which line goes to...?	**Quale linea va a...?**	*Kwa-leh lee-ne-a va a ...*
Does this train go to...?	**Questo treno va a...?**	*Kwes-to tre-no va a ...*
Where do I change for...	**Dove si cambia per...?**	*Do-veh see kam-bya pair ...*
Is the next station...?	**La prossima stazione è...?**	*La pros-see-ma stat-syo-neh eh ...*
What station is this?	**Qual'è questa stazione?**	*Kwal-eh kwes-ta stat-syo-neh*

By Car[1]

Key Phrases

Do you have a road map, please?	**Ha una carta stradale, per favore?**	*A oon-a kar-ta stra-da-leh, pair fa-vor-eh*
Where is the nearest car park?	**Dov'è il parcheggio più vicino**	*Dov-eh eel par-ked-jo pyoo vee-chee-no?*
May I see your licence, please?	***Posso vedere la sua patente, per favore?**	*Pos-so ve-dair-eh la soo-a pa-ten-teh, pair fa-vor-eh*
I've run out of petrol	**Ho finito la benzina**	*O fee-nee-to la bend-zee-na*
I've lost my car key	**Ho perso le (mie) chiavi della macchina**	*O pair-so leh mee-eh kya-vee del-la mak-kee-na*
Can you repair it?	**Può ripararla?**	*Pwo ree-pa-rar-la*

(How long) can I park here?	**(Per quanto tempo) si può parcheggiare qui?**	*(Pair kwan-to tem-po) see pwo par-keh-ja-re kwee*
Can I park here?	**Si può tenere la macchina qui?**	*See pwo te-nair-eh la mak-kee-na kwee*
Do you have any change for the meter, please?	**Ha mica degli spiccioli per il parchimetro?**	*A mee-ka del-yee spee-cho-lee pair eel par-kee-met-ro*

1. See also Road Signs (p. 50) and Directions (p. 53).

How far is the next petrol station?	**A che distanza è il distributore (di benzina) più vicino?**	*A keh dees-tant-sa eh eel dees-tree-boo-tor-eh (dee bend-zee-na) pyoo vee-chee-no*
No parking	***Divieto di parcheggio/ parcheggio vietato**	*Dee-vye-to dee par-ked-jo/par-ked-jo vye-ta-to*
Is this your car?	***È sua questa macchina?**	*Eh soo-a kwes-ta mak-kee-na*
You were speeding	***Stava andando troppo veloce**	*Sta-va an-dan-do tro-po ve-lo-cheh*
Speed limit	***Limite di velocità**	*Lee-mee-teh dee ve-lo-chee-ta*
Pedestrian precinct	***Zona pedonale**	*Dzo-na pe-do-na-leh*

Car Rental

Where can I hire a car?	**Dove posso noleggiare una macchina?**	*Do-veh pos-so no-led-jar-eh oon-a mak-kee-na*
I want to hire a car	**Vorrei noleggiare una macchina**	*Vor-ray no-led-ja-reh oon-a mak-kee-na*
I want to hire a car and a driver	**Vorrei noleggiare una macchina con autista**	*Vor-ray no-led-jar-eh oon-a mak-kee-na kon ow-tees-ta*
I would like to hire an automatic/a manual	**Vorrei noleggiare una macchina automatica/ manuale**	*Vor-ray no-led-jar-eh oon-a mak-kee-na ow-to-ma-tee-ka/man-wa-leh*
I'd like a car with a sun roof/air conditioning	**Vorrei una macchina col tettuccio pieghevole/con l'aria condizionata**	*Vor-ray oon-a mak-kee-na kol tet-too-cho pye-ge-vo-leh kon lar-ya kon-deet-syo-na-ta*

Does it have a GPS system/CD player?	Ha il sistema GPS/ il lettore CD?	*A eel see-ste-ma jee-pee-esse/eel let-tor-eh chee dee*
We've reserved a camper van	Abbiamo prenotato un camper	*Ab-bya-mo pre-no-ta-to oon kam-per*
Can we rent a baby/ child seat?	Possiamo noleggiare un seggiolino?	*Pos-sya-mo no-led-ja-reh oon sed-jo-lee-no*
What kind of fuel does it take?	Che tipo di benzina devo mettere?	*Keh tee-po dee bend-zee-na de-vo **met**-te-re*
Is there a special weekend rate?	C'è una tariffa speciale per il fine settimana?	*Cheh oon-a ta-reef-fa spe-cha-leh pair eel fee-neh set-tee-ma-na*
Is there a midweek rate?	C'è una tariffa infrasettimanale?	*Cheh oon-a ta-reef-fa een-fra-set-tee-ma-na-le*
How much is it	Quanto costa	*Kwan-to kos-ta*
by the day?	a giornata?	*a jor-na-ta*
by the week?	per settimana?	*pair set-tee-ma-na*
I need a car for two days/a week	Ho bisogno di una macchina per due giorni/una settimana	*O bee-zon-yo dee oon-a **mak**-kee-na pair doo-eh jor-nee/oon-a set-tee-ma-na*
Does that include unlimited mileage?	Il chilometraggio illimitato è compreso?	*Eel kee-lo-met-rad-jo eel-lee-mee-ta-to eh kom-pre-zo*
The charge per kilometre is . . .	*La tariffa è di . . . euro a chilometro	*La ta-reef-fa eh dee . . . e-oor-o a kee-**lo**-met-ro*

Do you want comprehensive insurance?	*Vuole un'assicurazione inclusa?	*Vwo-leh oon-us-see-koo-rat-syo-neh een-kloo-za*
You have to pay the first . . . euros	*Deve pagare i primi . . . euro	*De-ve pa-gar-eh ee pree-mee . . . e-oor-o*
May I see your driving licence?	*Posso vedere la sua patente?	*Pos-so ve-dair-eh la soo-a pa-ten-teh*
Driving licence and car registration papers, please	*Patente e libretto (di circolazione), prego	*Pa-ten-teh e lee-bret-to (dee cheer-ko-lat-syo-neh), pre-go*
Do you want a deposit?	Vuole una cauzione?	*Vwo-leh oon-a kowt-syo-neh*
I will pay by credit card	Pagherò con la carta di credito	*Pa-ge-ro kon la kar-ta dee kre-dee-to*
Can I return the car in . . .?	Posso restituire la macchina in . . .?	*Pos-so res-tee-twee-reh la mak-kee-na in . . .*
Could you show me how the controls/lights work?	Può mostrarmi come funzionano i comandi/le luci?	*Pwo mo-strar-mee ko-me foont-syo-na-no ee ko-man-dee/leh loo-chee*
The car is scratched/dented here	La macchina è graffiata/ammaccata qui	*La mak-kee-na eh graf-fya-ta/am-mak-ka-ta kwee*

At a garage or petrol station

How much is petrol a litre?	Quanto costa un litro di benzina?	*Kwan-to kos-ta oon leet-ro dee bend-zee-na*
. . . litres of petrol	. . . litri di benzina	*. . . leet-ree dee bend-zee-na*

... litres of diesel	... litri di nafta	... leet-ree dee naf-ta
... euros worth of petrol, please	... euro di benzina, per favore	... e-oor-o dee bend-zee-na, pair fa-vor-eh
Can you fill it up, please?	Mi può fare il pieno, per favore?	Mee pwo fa-reh eel pye-no pair fa-vor-eh
The oil needs changing	Bisognerebbe cambiare l'olio	Bee-zon-yair-eb-beh kam-byar-eh lol-yo
Please change the tyre	Vuol cambiare la gomma, per favore	Vwol kam-byar-eh la gom-ma, pair fa-vor-eh
Please check	Per favore, controlli	Pair fa-vor-eh, kon-trol-lee
the battery	la batteria	la bat-tair-ee-a
the brakes	i freni	ee fre-nee
the oil and water	l'olio e l'acqua	lol-yo eh lak-wa
the transmission fluid	il giunto idraulico	eel joon-to ee-**drow**-lee-ko
the tyre pressure, including the spare	le gomme, inclusa la ruota di scorta	leh gom-meh, een-kloo-za la rwo-ta dee skor-ta
Would you clean the windscreen, please?	Può pulirmi il parabrezza, per favore?	Pwo poo-leer-mee eel pa-ra-bred-za, pair fa-vor-eh
I want the car serviced	Vorrei far revisionare l'automobile	Vor-**ray** far re-vee-zyo-nar-eh low-to-**mo**-bee-leh
Please wash the car	Vuol lavare la macchina, per favore	Vwol la-var-eh la **mak**-kee-na, pair fa-vor-eh
Can I garage the car here?	Posso lasciare la macchina in questo garage?	Pos-so la-shar-eh la **mak**-kee-na een kwes-to ga-**raj**

What time does the garage close?	**A che ora chiude il garage?**	*A keh or-a kyoo-deh eel ga-raj*
Where are the toilets?	**Dove sono le toilette?**	*Do-veh so-no leh twa-let-teh*
Please pay at the cash desk	***Per favore paghi alla cassa/allo sportello**	*Pair fa-vor-eh pa-gee al-la cas-sa/al-lo spor-tel-lo*

Problems and repairs

I've run out of petrol	**Ho finito la benzina**	*O fee-nee-to la bend-zee-na*
I've locked/left the keys in the car	**Ho lasciato le chiavi dentro la macchina**	*O la-sha-to leh kya-vee den-tro la mak-kee-na*
I've lost my car key	**Ho perso le (mie) chiavi della macchina**	*O pair-so leh mee-eh kya-vee del-la mak-kee-na*
The lock is broken/jammed	**La serratura è rotta/bloccata**	*La ser-ra-too-ra eh rot-ta/blok-ka-ta*
My car won't start	**La mia macchina non parte**	*La mee-a mak-kee-na non par-teh*
My car's broken down	**Ho un guasto alla macchina**	*O oon gwas-to al-la mak-kee-na*
Can you give me a lift	**Può darmi un passaggio**	*Pwo dar-mee oon pas-sad-jo*
to a telephone?	**al telefono più vicino?**	*al te-le-fo-no pyoo vee-chee-no*
to the garage?	**all'autofficina**	*al-low-tof-fee-chee-na*

May I use your phone?	Posso usare il telefono?	*Pos-so oo-zar-eh eel te-le-fo-no*
Where is there a ... agency?	Dov'è l'agenzia della ...?	*Dov-eh la-jent-see-a del-la ...*
Do you have a breakdown service?	Ha un servizio riparazioni?	*A oon sair-veet-syo ree-pa-rat-syo-nee*
Is there a mechanic?	C'è un meccanico?	*Cheh oon mek-ka-nee-ko*
Can you send someone to repair it/ tow it?	Può mandare qualcuno a ripararla/ rimorchiarla?	*Pwo man-dar-eh kwal-koo-no a ree-pa-rar-la/ ree-mor-kyar-la*
It is an automatic	È automatica	*Eh ow-to-ma-tee-ka*
Where is your car?	*Dov'è la macchina?	*Dov-eh la mak-kee-na*
Where are you now?	*Dove si trova lei adesso?	*Do-veh see tro-va lay a-des-so*
I am on the road from ... to ... near kilometre post ...	Sono sulla strada da ... a ... vicino al chilometro ...	*So-no sool-la stra-da da ... a ... vee-chee-no al kee-lo-met-ro ...*
How long will you be?	Fra quanto tempo sarà qui?	*Fra kwan-to tem-po sa-ra kwee*
The battery is flat, it needs charging	La batteria è scarica, ha bisogno di essere caricata	*La bat-tair-ee-a eh ska-ree-ka, a bee-zon-yo dee es-se-reh ka-ree-ka-ta*
This tyre is flat/ punctured	Questa gomma è sgonfia/forata	*Kwes-ta gom-ma eh zgon-fya/fo-ra-ta*
The exhaust is broken	Lo scappamento è guasto	*Lo skap-pa-men-to eh gwas-to*
The windscreen wipers do not work	Non funzionano i tergicristalli	*Non foont-syo-na-no ee tair-jee-krees-tal-lee*

This valve Is leaking	**Questa valvola perde**	*Kwes-ta **val**-vo-la pair-deh*
The radiator is leaking	**Il radiatore perde acqua**	*Eel ra-dya-tor-eh pair-deh ak-wa*
It's not running properly	**Procede a scosse**	*Pro-che-deh a skos-seh*
The engine is overheating	**Il motore riscalda troppo**	*Eel mo-tor-eh rees-kal-da trop-po*
I've got electrical trouble	**Dev'esserci un guasto nel sistema elettrico**	*Dev-**es**-sair-chee oon gwas-to nel sees-te-ma el-et-tree-ko*
There's a rattle/squeak	**C'è un cigolio**	*Cheh oon chee-go-lee-o*
The engine is firing badly	**L'accensione è difettosa**	*La-chen-syo-neh eh dee-fet-to-za*
Can you change this plug?	**Può cambiare questa candela?**	*Pwo kam-byar-eh kwes-ta kan-de-la*
There's a petrol/oil leak	**C'è una perdita di benzina/d'olio**	*Cheh oon-a **pair**-dee-ta dee bend-zee-na/dol-yo*
There's a smell of petrol/rubber	**Si sente odore di benzina/di gomma**	*See sen-teh o-dor-eh dee bend-zee-na/dee gom-ma*
The carburettor needs adjusting	**Il carburatore dev'essere regolato**	*Eel kar-boo-ra-tor-eh dev-**es**-se-reh re-go-la-to*
Something is wrong with	**Ho un guasto**	*O oon gwas-to*
my car	**alla macchina**	*al-la **mak**-kee-na*
the engine	**nel motore**	*nel mo-tor-eh*
the lights	**ai fanali**	*a-ee fa-na-lee*

the clutch	nella frizione	nel-la freet-syo-neh
the gearbox	nella scatola del cambio	nel-la **ska**-to-la del kam-byo
the brakes	ai freni	a-ee fre-nee
the steering	allo sterzo	al-lo stairt-so
Can you repair it?	Può ripararla?	Pwo ree-pa-rar-la
How long will it take to repair?	Quanto tempo ci vuole per ripararla?	Kwan-to tem-po chee vwo-leh pair ree-pa-rar-la
What will it cost?	Quanto costerà?	Kwan-to kos-tair-**a**
When can I pick the car up?	Quando posso venire a prendere la macchina?	Kwan-do pos-so ve-neer-eh a **pren**-dair-eh la **mak**-kee-na
I need it	Ne ho bisogno ...	Neh o bee-zon-yo
as soon as possible	il più presto possibile	eel pyoo pres-to pos-**see**-bee-leh
in three hours	fra tre ore	fra treh or-eh
tomorrow morning	domani mattina	do-ma-nee mat-tee-na
It will take two days	*Ci vorranno due giorni	Chee vor-**ran**-no doo-eh jor-nee
We can repair it temporarily	*La possiamo riparare provvisoriamente	La pos-sya-mo ree-pa-rar-eh prov-vee-zor-ya-men-teh
We don't have the right spares	*Non abbiamo i pezzi di ricambio	Non ab-bya-mo ee pet-see dee ree-kam-byo
We have to send for the spares	*Dobbiamo far venire i pezzi di ricambio	Dob-bya-mo far ve-neer-eh ee pet-see dee ree-kam-byo

You will need a new ...	*Ci vuole un nuovo ...	*Chee vwo-leh oon nwo-vo ...*
Could I have an itemized bill, please?	Può farmi il conto articolo per articolo, per favore?	*Pwo far-mee eel kon-to ar-tee-ko-lo pair ar-tee-ko-lo, pair fa-vor-eh*

Parts of a car and other useful words

accelerate (to)	accelerare	*a-che-le-rar-eh*
accelerator	l'acceleratore *m*	*a-che-le-ra-tor-eh*
aerial	l'antenna *f*	*an-ten-na*
air pump	la pompa d'aria	*pom-pa dar-ya*
alarm	l'allarme *m*	*al-lar-meh*
alternator	l'alternatore *m*	*al-ter-na-tor-eh*
anti-freeze	l'anticongelante *m*	*an-tee-kon-je-lan-teh*
automatic transmission	la transmissione automatica	*traz-mees-syo-neh ow-to-ma-tee-ka*
axle	l'asse *m*	*as-seh*
battery	la batteria	*bat-tair-ee-a*
bonnet	il cofano	*ko-fa-no*
boot/trunk	il portabagagli	*por-ta-ba-gal-yee*
brake	il freno	*fre-no*
brake lights	le luci dei freni	*loo-chee day fre-nee*
brake lining	la guarnizione del freno	*gwar-neet-syo-neh del fre-no*
brake pads	la ganascia del freno	*ga-na-sha del fre-no*

breakdown	il guasto	gwas-to
bulb	la lampadina	lam-pa-dee-na
bumper	il paraurti	pa-ra-oor-tee
carburettor	il carburatore	kar-boo-ra-tor-eh
CD player	il lettore CD	let-to-reh chee dee
clutch	la frizione	freet-syo-neh
cooling system	il sistema di raffreddamento	sees-te-ma dee raf-fred-da-men-to
crank-shaft	la manovella	ma-no-vel-la
cylinder	il cilindro	chee-leen-dro
differential gear	il differenziale	deef-fer-ent-sya-leh
dip stick	la coppa dell'olio	kop-pa del-lol-yo
distilled water	l'acqua distillata f	ak-wa dees-teel-la-ta
distributor	il distributore	dees-tree-boo-tor-eh
door	lo sportello/la portiera	spor-tel-lo/por-tyair-a
door handle	la maniglia dello sportello	ma-neel-ya del-lo spor-tel-lo
drive (to)	guidare	gwee-dar-eh
drive shaft	l'albero di trasmissione m	al-be-ro dee tras-mees-syo-neh
driver	l'autista m	ow-tees-ta
dynamo	la dinamo	dee-na-mo
engine	il motore	mo-tor-eh
exhaust	lo scappamento	skap-pa-men-to

fan	il ventilatore	*ven-tee-la-tor-eh*
fanbelt	la cinghia del ventilatore	*cheen-gya del ven-tee-la-tor-eh*
(oil) filter	il filtro (dell'olio)	*feel-tro (del-lol-yo)*
flat tyre	la gomma sgonfia	*gom-ma zgon-fya*
foglamp	il fanale antinebbia	*fan-al-eh an-tee-neb-bya*
fuse box	la valvola	*val-vo-la*
gasket	la guarnizione	*gwar-neet-syo-neh*
gear	la marcia/la velocità	*mar-cha/ve-lo-chee-ta*
gear-box	la scatola del cambio	*ska-to-la del kam-byo*
gear lever	la leva del cambio	*le-va del kam-byo*
grease (to)	ingrassare	*een-gras-sar-eh*
handbrake	il freno a mano	*fre-no a ma-no*
headlights	i fari/fanali	*fa-ree/fa-na-lee*
heater	il riscaldamento	*rees-kal-da-men-to*
horn	il clacson	*klak-son*
hose	il tubo	*too-bo*
ignition	l'accensione *f*	*a-chen-syo-neh*
ignition key	la chiavetta dell'accensione	*kya-vet-ta del-la-chen-syo-neh*
indicator	l'indicatore *m*/la freccia	*een-dee-ka-tor-eh/fre-cha*
jack	il martinetto/il cricco	*mar-tee-net-to/kreek-ko*

lights – head/rear/side	i fanali anteriori/posteriori/di posizione	*fa-na-lee an-ter-yor-ee/pos-ter-yor-ee/dee po-zeet-syo-neh*
lock/catch	la serratura	*ser-ra-too-ra*
mirror	lo specchietto	*spek-kyet-to*
number plate	la targa	*tar-ga*
nut	il dado	*da-do*
oil	l'olio *m*	*ol-yo*
parking lights	le luci di posizione	*loo-chee dee po-zeet-syo-neh*
pedal	il pedale	*pe-da-leh*
petrol	la benzina	*bend-zee-na*
petrol can	il bidone di benzina	*bee-do-neh dee bend-zee-na*
piston	il pistone	*pees-to-neh*
plug	la candela	*kan-de-la*
pump	la pompa	*pom-pa*
puncture	la foratura	*fo-ra-tu-ra*
radiator	il radiatore	*ra-dya-tor-eh*
rear axle	il ponte posteriore	*pon-teh pos-ter-yor-eh*
rear lights	le luci posteriori	*loo-chee pos-ter-yor-ee*
rear-view mirror	lo specchietto retrovisore	*spek-kyet-to re-tro-vee-zo-reh*
reverse (to)	fare marcia indietro	*fa-reh mar-cha een-dye-tro*
reverse	la retromarcia	*ret-ro-mar-cha*

reversing lights	le luci della retromarcia	*loo-chee del-la ret-ro-mar-cha*
screwdriver	il cacciavite	*ka-cha-vee-teh*
seat	il sedile	*se-dee-leh*
seatbelt	la cintura di sicurezza	*cheen-too-ra dee see-koo-ret-sa*
shock absorber	l'ammortizzatore *m*	*am-mor-teed-za-tor-eh*
silencer	il silenziatore	*see-lent-sya-tor-eh*
spanner	la chiave inglese	*kya-veh een-gle-zeh*
spare tyre	la gomma di scorta	*gom-ma dee skor-ta*
spares	i pezzi di ricambio	*pet-see dee ree-kam-byo*
spark plug	la candela	*kan-de-la*
speed	la velocità	*ve-lo-chee-ta*
speedometer	il tachimetro	*ta-kee-me-tro*
spring	la molla	*mol-la*
stall (to)	fermarsi a scosse	*fair-mar-see a skos-seh*
starter motor	il motorino d'avviamento	*mo-to-ree-no dav-vya-men-to*
steering	lo sterzo	*stert-so*
steering wheel	il volante	*vo-lan-teh*
sunroof	la cappotta	*kap-pot-ta*
suspension	la sospensione	*sos-pen-syo-neh*
tank	il serbatoio	*sair-ba-to-yo*
tappets	le punterie	*poon-ter-ee-eh*
transmission	la trasmissione	*tras-mees-syo-neh*

tyre pressure	la pressione delle gomme	*pres-syo-neh del-leh gom-meh*
tyres	le gomme	*gom-meh*
valve	la valvola	***val**-vo-la*
warning lights	le spie luminose	*spee-eh loo-mee-no-zeh*
wheel – back/front/ spare	la ruota posteriore/ anteriore/di scorta	*rwo-ta pos-ter-yor-eh/ an-ter-yor-eh/dee skor-ta*
window	il vetro	*ve-tro*
windscreen	il parabrezza	*pa-ra-bred-za*
windscreen washers	gli spruzzatori	*sproot-sa-tor-ee*
windscreen wipers	i tergicristalli	*tair-jee-krees-tal-lee*

By Bike or Moped

Key Phrases

Where can I hire	Dove posso affittare	*Do-veh pos-so af-feet-tar-eh*
a bicycle?	una bicicletta?	*oon-a bee-chee-klet-ta*
a moped?	un ciclomotore	*oon chee-klo-mo-to-reh*
a motorbike?	una moto(cicletta)	*oon-a mo-to (chee-klet-ta)*
Is it obligatory to wear a helmet?	È obbligatorio indossare un casco?	*Eh ob-blee-ga-tor-yo een-dos-sar-eh oon ka-sko*
Do you repair bicycles?	Riparate le biciclette?	*Ree-pa-ra-teh leh bee-chee-klet-teh*

What does it cost	**Quanto costa**	*Kwan-to ko-sta*
per day?	**al giorno?**	*al jor-no*
per week?	**a settimana?**	*a set-tee-ma-na*
I'd like a lock, please	**Vorrei un lucchetto per favore**	*Vor-**ray** oon look-ket-to pair fa-vor-eh*
The saddle is too high/too low	**Il sellino è troppo alto/basso**	*Eel sel-lee-no eh trop-po al-to/bas-so*
Where is the cycle shop?	**Dov'è il negozio di bici?**	*Dov-**eh** eel ne-got-syo dee bee-chee*
The brake isn't working	**Il freno non funziona**	*Eel fre-no non foont-syo-na*
Could you tighten/ loosen the brake cable?	**Può aggiustare il cavo del freno?**	*Pwo ad-joos-tar-eh eel ka-vo del fre-no*
A spoke is broken	**Si è rotto un raggio**	*See eh rot-to oon rad-jo*
The tyre is punctured	**Il pneumatico è forato**	*Eel pne-oo-**ma**-tee-ko eh fo-ra-to*
The gears need adjusting	**Bisogna aggiustare i cambi**	*Bee-zon-ya ad-joos-tar-eh ee kam-bee*
Could you straighten the wheel?	**Potrebbe raddrizzare la ruota?**	*Pot-reb-beh rad-dreet-sar-eh la rwo-ta*
The handlebars are loose	**Il manubrio si è allentato**	*Eel ma-noob-ryo see eh al-len-ta-to*
Could you please lend me	**Mi potrebbe prestare**	*Mee pot-reb-beh pres-tar-eh*
a spanner?	**una chiave fissa?**	*oon-a kya-veh fees-sa*
a tyre lever?	**un livello?**	*oon lee-vel-lo*

Can I take my bike on the boat/train?	Posso portare la (mia) bici in nave/ treno?	*Pos-so por-ta-reh la (mee-a) bee-chee een na-veh/tre-no*

Parts of a bicycle and other useful words

axle	l'asse *m*	*as-seh*
basket	il cestino	*che-stee-no*
bell	il campanello di bicicletta	*kam-pa-nel-lo dee bee-chee-klet-ta*
brake (front/rear)	il freno (anteriore/ posteriore)	*fre-no (an-ter-yor-eh/ pos-ter-yor-eh)*
brake cable	il cavo del freno	*ka-vo del fre-no*
brake lever	la leva del freno	*le-va del fre-no*
bulb	la lampadina	*lam-pa-dee-na*
chain	la catena	*ka-te-na*
chain guard	la catena di sicurezza	*ka-te-na dee see-koo-ret-sa*
child's seat	il seggiolino	*sed-jo-lee-no*
dynamo	la dinamo	***dee**-na-mo*
fork	la forcella	*for-chel-la*
frame	il telaio	*te-la-yo*
gear lever	la leva del cambio	*le-va del kam-byo*
gears	i cambi	*kam-bee*
handlebars	il manubrio	*ma-noob-ryo*

helmet	**il casco**	*kas-ko*
high visibility jacket	**il giubbotto ad alta visibilità**	*joo-bot-to ad al-ta vee-zee-bee-lee-ta*
inner tube	**la camera d'aria**	*ka-mair-a dar-ya*
light – front/rear	**il fanale/il fanalino posteriore**	*fa-na-leh/fa-na-lee-no pos-ter-yor-eh*
mudguard	**il parafango**	*pa-ra-fan-go*
panniers	**i cestini**	*ches-tee-nee*
pedal	**il pedale**	*pe-da-leh*
pump	**la pompa**	*pom-pa*
puncture	**la foratura**	*fo-ra-too-ra*
puncture repair kit	**il kit per la foratura**	*keet pair la fo-ra-too-ra*
reflector	**il catarifrangente**	*ka-ta-reef-ran-jen-teh*
rim	**il cerchione**	*chair-kyo-neh*
saddle	**la sella/il sellino**	*sel-la/sel-lee-no*
saddlebag	**la borsa porta-attrezzi**	*bor-sa por-ta-at-tret-see*
spoke	**il raggio**	*rad-jo*
suspension	**la sospensione**	*so-spen-syo-neh*
tyre	**il pneumatico**	*pne-oo-**ma**-tee-ko*
valve	**la valvola**	*val-vo-la*
wheel	**la ruota**	*rwo-ta*

Road Signs

Attraverso il traffico	Through traffic
Caduta massi	Falling stones
Camion	Lorries
Casello/pedaggio (autostradale)	(Motorway) toll
Cautela	Caution
Corsia degli autobus/dei pullman	Bus lane
Curve	Winding road
Diluvio	Flooding
Disco blu	Parking disc required
Diversione	Diversion
Dogana	Customs
Fermata	Stop
Fine del divieto di parcheggio	End of no-parking zone
Lavori in corso	Road works ahead
Limite di velocità	Speed limit
Limite massimo di velocità	Maximum speed
Materiale instabile sulla strada	Loose chippings
Parcheggio limitato	Restricted parking
Parcheggio per disabili	Parking for disabled
Parcheggio vietato	No parking

Passaggio a livello	Level crossing
Pericolo	Danger
Prudenza	Attention/caution
Rallentamento traffico	Slow traffic
Rallentare	Slow
Salita ripida	Steep hill
Semaforo	Traffic lights
Senso unico	One way (street)
Senso vietato	No entry
Sosta autorizzata	Parking allowed
Strada bloccata	No through road
Strada interrotta	Road blocked
(Strada) senza uscita	Dead end (street)
Strada stretta	Narrow road
Superficie ghiacciata	Icy surface
Superficie irregolare/ sdrucciolevole	Uneven/slippery surface
Svolte/curve	Bends/curves
Tenere la destra/la sinistra	Keep right/left
Tenere la destra/stare nella corsia a destra	Keep in the right-hand lane
Tenersi in corsia	Keep in lane
Usare i fanali	Lights on/use headlights

Uscita autoveicoli	Exit for lorries
Vicolo cieco	Cul de sac
Vietato (il sorpasso/sorpassare)	(Overtaking) prohibited
Zona pedonale	Pedestrians only

DIRECTIONS

Key Phrases

Where is …?	**Dov'è …?**	*Dov-eh …*
Is this the way to …?	**È questa la strada per …?**	*Eh kwes-ta la stra-da pair …*
How many kilometres?	**Quanti chilometri?**	*Kwan-tee kee-lo-met-ree*
Please show me on the map	**Può farmi vedere sulla mappa, per favore**	*Pwo far-mee ve-dair-eh sool-la map-pa, pair fa-vor-eh*
You are going the wrong way	***Ha sbagliato strada**	*A zbal-ya-to stra-da*

Excuse me, could you tell me the way to	**Mi scusi, può indicarmi la strada per**	*Mee skoo-zee, pwo een-dee-kar-mee la stra-da pair*
the station	**la stazione**	*la stat-syo-neh*
the post office	**l'ufficio postale**	*loof-fee-cho pos-ta-leh*
the town centre	**il centro (città)**	*eel chen-tro (cheet-ta)*
I'm looking for	**Sto cercando**	*Sto chair-kan-do*
a pharmacy	**una farmacia**	*oon-a far-ma-chee-a*
an ATM/cashpoint	**un bancomat**	*oon ban-ko-mat*
an Internet café	**un Internet caffè**	*oon internet kaf-feh*

It isn't far	*Non è lontano da qui	Non eh lon-ta-no da kwee
It's on the square	*È nella piazza	Eh nel-la pyat-sa
It's opposite the ... hotel	*È di fronte all'... hotel	Eh dee fron-teh al ... o-tel
It's at the end of this street	*È alla fine di questa strada	Eh al-la fee-neh dee kwe-sta stra-da
It's in the pedestrian area	*È nella zona pedonale	Eh nel-la dzo-na pe-do-na-leh
Where is ...?	Dov'è ...?	Dov-eh ...
Which is the road for ...?	Qual'è la strada per ...?	Kwal-eh la stra-da pair ...
How far is it to ...?	Quanto c'è di qui a ...?	Kwan-to cheh dee kwee a ...
We want to get on to the motorway to ...	Vorremmo prendere l'autostrada per ...	Vor-rem-mo pren-dair-eh low-to-stra-da pair ...
Which is the best road to ...?	Qual'è la migliore strada per ...?	Kwal-eh la meel-yor-eh stra-da pair ...
Is this the right road for ...?	È questa la strada giusta per ...?	Eh kwes-ta la stra-da joos-ta pair ...
Is there a scenic route to ...?	C'è una strada panoramica per ...?	Cheh oon-a stra-da pa-no-ra-mee-ka pair ...
Where does this road lead to?	Dove porta questa strada?	Do-veh por-ta kwes-ta stra-da
Is it a good road?	È una strada in buone condizioni?	Eh oon-a stra-da een bwo-neh kon-deet-syo-nee
Is it a motorway?	È un'autostrada?	Eh oon ow-to-stra-da

Is there a toll?	C'è un pedaggio?	*Cheh oon pe-dad-jo*
Is the tunnel/pass open?	È aperta la galleria/aperto il passo?	*Eh a-pair-ta la gal-lair-ee-a/a-pair-to eel pas-so*
Is the road to . . . clear?	È aperta la strada per . . .?	*Eh a-pair-ta la stra-da pair . . .*
How far is	A che distanza è	*A keh dees-tand-za eh*
the next village?	il prossimo paese?	*eel **pros**-see-mo pa-e-zeh*
the petrol station?	la prossima stazione di rifornimento?	*la **pros**-see-ma stat-syo-neh dee ree-for-nee-men-to*
Is there any danger of	C'è pericolo di	*Cheh pair-**ee**-ko-lo dee*
avalanches?	valanghe?	*va-lan-geh*
snowdrifts?	ammassi di neve?	*a-mas-see dee ne-veh*
Will we get to . . . by evening?	Arriveremo a . . . prima di sera?	*Ar-ree-vair-em-o a . . . pree-ma dee se-ra*
How long will it take	Quanto tempo ci si mette	*Kwan-to tem-po chee see met-teh*
by car?	in macchina?	*een **mak**-kee-na*
by bicycle?	in bicicletta?	*een bee-chee-klet-ta*
on foot?	a piedi?	*a pye-dee*
Where are we now?	Dove siamo adesso?	*Do-veh sya-mo a-des-so*
What is the name of this place?	Come si chiama questo posto?	*Ko-meh see kya-ma kwes-to pos-to*
I'm lost	Mi sono perso/persa	*Mee so-no pair-so/pair-sa*
We're lost	Ci siamo persi	*Chee sya-mo pair-see*

Please show me on the map	Può farmi vedere sulla mappa, per favore	Pwo far-mee ve-dair-eh sool-la map-pa, pair fa-vor-eh
It's that way	*È in questa direzione/di qui	Eh een kwes-ta dee-ret-syo-neh/dee kwee
Follow signs for . . .	*Segua le indicazioni per . . .	Seg-wa teh een-dee-ka-syo-nee pair . . .
Follow this road for . . . kilometres	*Segua questa strada per . . . chilometri	Seg-wa kwes-ta stra-da pair . . . kee-lo-met-ree
Keep straight on	*Continui diritto	Kon-teen-wee dee-reet-to
Turn right at the crossroads/ roundabout	*Al crocevia/alla rotatoria, volti a destra	Al kro-che-vee-a/al-la ro-ta-tor-ya, vol-tee a des-tra
Take the second road on the left	*Prenda la seconda strada a sinistra	Pren-da la se-kon-da stra-da a see-nees-tra
Turn right at the traffic lights	*Al semaforo, volti a destra	Al se-ma-fo-ro, vol-tee a des-tra
Turn left after the bridge	*Dopo il ponte, giri a sinistra	Do-po eel pon-teh, jee-ree a see-nees-tra
Take the next left/ right	*Prenda la prima a sinistra/destra	Pren-da la pree-ma a see-nee-stra/de-stra
The best road is . . .	*La strada migliore è . . .	La stra-da meel-yor-eh eh . . .
Take this road as far as . . . and ask again	*Segua questa strada fino a . . . e chieda di nuovo	Seg-wa kwes-ta stra-da fee-no a . . . eh kye-da dee nwo-vo

Take junction 12/the exit for . . .	*Prenda il bivio 12/l'uscita per . . .	*Pren-da eel bee-vyo do-dee-chee/loo-shee-ta pair . . .*
You are going the wrong way	*Ha sbagliato strada	*A zbal-ya-to stra-da*
one-way system	la circolazione a senso unico	*cheer-ko-lat-syo-neh a sen-so **oo**-nee-ko*
north	nord	*nord*
south	sud	*sood*
east	est	*est*
west	ovest	*o-vest*

ACCOMMODATION

campsite	il campeggio	kam-ped-jo
cottage	la villetta	veel-let-ta
country inn	l'agriturismo *m*	ag-ree-too-ree-smo
hotel	l'albergo *m*	al-ber-go
youth hostel	l'ostello della gioventù *m*	os-tel-lo del-la jo-ven-**too**
Rooms to let / vacancies	*Affittasi/camere da affittare	Af-**fee**-ta-see/**ka**-mair-eh da af-fee-tar-eh
No vacancies	*Tutto occupato	Toot-to ok-koo-pa-to
No camping	*Vietato campeggiare	Vye-ta-to kam-ped-jar-eh
Can you show me on the map where the hotel is?	Potrebbe mostrarmi sulla cartina dove si trova l'albergo?	Pot-reb-beh mo-strar-mee sool-la kar-tee-na do-veh see tro-va lal-ber-go
Is it in the centre?	È in centro?	Eh een chen-tro
Is it near a bus stop?	È vicino alla fermata del pullman?	Eh vee-chee-no al-la fer-ma-ta del pool-man
Is it on a train/metro route?	È nel tragitto del treno/della metro ?	Eh nel **tra**-geet-to del tre-no/del-la me-**tro**

Check In

Key Phrases

Do you have a room for the night?	**Ha una camera per stanotte?**	*A oon-a ka-mair-a pair sta-not-teh*
Does the hotel have wi-fi?	**L'albergo ha il sistema wi-fi?**	*Lal-bair-go a eel see-ste-ma wi-fi*
I've reserved a room. My name is . . .	**Ho riservato una camera. Mi chiamo . . .**	*O ree-zair-va-to oon-a ka-mair-a. Mee kya-mo . . .*
Is there a lift/ elevator?	**C'è l'ascensore?**	*Cheh la-shen-sor-eh*
How much is the room per night?	**Quanto costa questa camera per notte?**	*Kwan-to kos-ta kwes-ta ka-mair-a pair not-teh*

double room	**camera matrimoniale**	*ka-mair-a mat-ree-mon-ya-leh*
twin room	**doppia**	*dop-pya*
single room	**singola**	*seen-go-la*
triple room	**tripla**	*tree-pla*
Do you know	**Può indicarmi**	*Pwo een-dee-kar-mee*
another hotel?	**un altro albergo?**	*oon al-tro al-bair-go*
an inexpensive hotel?	**un albergo economico?**	*oon al-bair-go e-ko-no-mee-ko*
a moderately priced hotel?	**un albergo a prezzi modici?**	*oon al-bair-go a pret-see mo-dee-chee*

Is there an Internet connection in the room?	C'è la connessione Internet in camera?	*Cheh la kon-ne-syo-ne internet een ka-mair-a*
Yes, it's free/it costs ... euros per day/hour	*Sì, è libera/costa ... euro al giorno/a ora	*See, eh lee-bair-a/ko-sta ... e-oo-ro al jor-no/a o-ra*
Is there a business centre in the hotel?	C'è un centro business nell'albergo?	*Cheh oon chen-tro beez-ness nel-lal-bair-go*
Is there a spa/fitness centre?	C'è un centro benessere/fitness?	*Cheh un chen-tro ben-es-se-reh/feet-ness*
Does the hotel have a swimming pool/private beach?	L'albergo ha una piscina/spiaggia privata?	*Lal-bair-go a oon-a pee-shee-na/spyad-ja pree-va-ta*
I'd like a single room with a shower	Vorrei una camera ad un letto con doccia	*Vor-ray oon-a ka-mair-a ad oon let-to kon do-cha*
We'd like	Vorremmo	*Vor-rem-mo*
a room with a double bed and a bathroom/a private toilet	una camera matrimoniale con bagno/un gabinetto privato	*oon-a ka-mair-a mat-ree-mon-ya-leh kon ban-yo/oon ga-bee-net-to pree-va-to*
a family room	una camera familiare	*oon-a ka-mair-a fa-mee-lyar-eh*
adjoining rooms	camere adiacenti	*ka-mair-eh ad-ya-chen-tee*
Do you have a room with	Ha una camera con	*A oon-a ka-mair-a kon*
twin beds?	due letti?	*doo-eh let-tee*
a king-size bed?	un letto matrimoniale (molto spazioso)?	*oon let-to mat-ree-mo-nya-leh (mol-to spat-syo-zo)*

Is there air conditioning in the room?	C'è l'aria condizionata in camera?	*Cheh lar-ya kon-deet-syo-na-ta een ka-mair-a*
How long will you be staying?	*Quanto tempo rimane (rimangono pl)?	*Kwan-to tem-po ree-man-eh (ree-**man**-go-no)*
Is it for one night only?	*Rimane (rimangono pl) solo una notte?	*Ree-man-eh (ree-**man**-go-no) so-lo oon-a not-teh*
I want a room	Vorrei una camera	*Vor-**ray** oon-a ka-mair-a*
for two or three days	per due o tre giorni	*pair doo-eh o treh jor-nee*
for a week	per una settimana	*pair oon-a set-tee-ma-na*
until Friday	fino a venerdì	*fee-no a ven-air-**dee***
What floor is the room on?	A che piano è questa camera?	*A keh pya-no eh kwes-ta ka-mair-a*
Is there a lift/elevator?	C'è l'ascensore?	*Cheh la-shen-sor-eh*
Are there facilities for the disabled?	Può accomodare le persone disabili?	*Pwo ak-ko-mo-dar-eh leh pair-so-neh dee-za-bee-lee*
Do you have a room on the first floor?	Ha una camera al primo piano?	*A oon-a ka-mair-a al pree-mo pya-no*
May I see the room?	Posso vedere la camera?	*Pos-so ve-dair-eh la ka-mair-a*
I like this room, I'll take it	Questa camera mi piace, la prendo	*Kwes-ta ka-mair-a mee pya-cheh, la pren-do*

I don't like this room	**Questa camera non mi piace molto**	*Kwes-ta ka-mair-a non mee pya-cheh mol-to*
Do you have another one?	**Ne ha un'altra?**	*Neh a oon-al-tra*
I want a quiet room/a bigger room	**Vorrei una camera molto tranquilla/ una camera più grande**	*Vor-ray oon-a ka-mair-a mol-to tran-kweel-la/ oon-a ka-mair-a pyoo gran-deh*
There's too much noise	**C'è troppo rumore**	*Cheh trop-po roo-mor-eh*
I'd like a room with a balcony	**Vorrei una camera con balcone**	*Vor-ray oon-a ka-mair-a kon bal-ko-neh*
Do you have a room	**Ha una camera**	*A oon-a ka-mair-a*
looking on to the street/sea?	**che dà sulla strada/ sul lungomare?**	*keh da sool-la stra-da/ sool loon-go-mar-eh*
near the swimming pool?	**vicino alla piscina?**	*vee-chee-no al-la pee-shee-na*
We've only a double room	***Abbiamo solo una camera matrimoniale**	*Ab-bya-mo so-lo oon-a ka-mair-a mat-ree-mon-ya-leh*
This is the only room vacant	***Questa è l'unica camera libera**	*Kwes-ta eh loo-nee-ka ka-mair-a lee-bair-a*
We shall have another room tomorrow	***Avremo un'altra camera libera domani**	*Av-re-mo oon al-tra ka-mair-a lee-bair-a do-ma-nee*
The room is only available tonight	***Possiamo darle questa camera solo per stanotte**	*Pos-sya-mo dar-leh kwes-ta ka-mair-a so-lo pair sta-not-teh*
How much is the room per night?	**Quanto costa questa camera per notte?**	*Kwan-to kos-ta kwes-ta ka-mair-a pair not-teh*

Have you nothing cheaper?	**Non ha niente di meno costoso?**	*Non a nyen-teh dee me-no kos-to-zo*
What do we pay for the children?	**Quanto pagano i bambini/i ragazzi?**	*Kwan-to pa-ga-no ee bam-bee-nee/ee ra-gat-see*
Could you put a cot/ an extra bed in the room, please?	**Può mettere una culla/un letto in più, per piacere?**	*Pwo met-tair-eh oon-a kool-la/oon let-to een pyoo pair pya-chair-eh*
Are service and tax Included?	**Il servizio e le tasse sono compresi nel prezzo?**	*Eel sair-veet-syo eh leh tas-seh so-no kom-pre-zee nel pret-so*
Is breakfast included in the price?	**La prima colazione è compresa nel prezzo?**	*La pree-ma ko-lat-syo-neh eh kom-pre-za nel pret-so*
How much is the room without meals?	**Quant'è la camera senza i pasti?**	*Kwan-teh la ka-mair-a send-za ee pas-tee*
How much is full board/half board?	**Quant'è la pensione completa/la mezza pensione?**	*Kwan-teh la pen-syo-neh kom-ple-ta/la med-za pen-syo-neh*
Do you have a weekly rate?	**Fa dei prezzi settimanali?**	*Fa day pret-see set-tee-ma-nal-ee*
What is the weekly rate?	**Qual'è il prezzo settimanale?**	*Kwal-eh eel pre-tso set-tee-ma-na-leh*
It's too expensive	**È troppo caro**	*Eh trop-po ka-ro*
Please fill in the registration form	***Compili la scheda di registrazione, per cortesia?**	*Kom-pee-lee la ske-da dee re-jees-trat-syo-neh, pair kor-te-zee-a*

Could I have a passport please?	*Potrei avere un documento d'identità, per favore?	Pot-ray a-vair-eh oon do-ku-men-to dee-den-tee-ta, pair fa-vor-eh
surname/first name	*cognome/nome	con-yo-meh/no-meh
address	*indirizzo	een-dee-ree-tso
date and place of birth	*data e luogo di nascita	da-ta eh lwo-go dee na-shee-ta
identity document/ passport number	*numero della carta d'identità/del passaporto	noo-mair-o del-la kar-ta dee-den-tee-ta/del pas-sa-por-to
What is your car registration number?	*Qual'è il numero di targa della sua macchina?	Kwal-eh eel noo-mair-o dee tar-ga del-la soo-a mak-kee-na

Check Out

Key Phrases

My bill please	Il conto per favore	Eel kon-to pair fa-vo-reh
There's a mistake on the bill	C'è un errore nel conto	Cheh oon er-ror-eh nel kon-to
Please store the luggage, we will be back at . . .	Tenga i bagagli in deposito, per favore. Torneremo alle . . .	Ten-ga ee ba-gal-yee een de-po-zee-to, pair fa-vor-eh. Tor-ne-re-mo al-le . . .

I have to leave tomorrow	**Devo partire domani**	*De-vo par-teer-eh do-ma-nee*
Can you make up my bill?	**Può prepararmi il conto?**	*Pwo pre-pa-rar-mee eel kon-to*
How would you like to pay?	***Come vuole pagare?**	*Ko-meh vwo-leh pa-ga-reh*
I'll pay by credit card/ in cash	**Pago con la carta di credito/in contanti**	*Pa-go kon la kar-ta dee **cre**-dee-to/een kon-tan-tee*
I shall be coming back on . . .; can I book a room for that date?	**Ritornerò il . . .; può riservarmi una camera per questa data?**	*Ree-tor-nair-o eel . . .; pwo ree-zair-var-mee oon-a **ka**-mair-a pair kwes-ta data*
Could you have my luggage brought down?	**Può far portare giù i bagagli?**	*Pwo far por-tar-eh joo ee ba-gal-yee*
Please call a taxi for me	**Per favore, vuol chiamare un taxi**	*Pair fa-vor-eh, vwol kya-mar-eh oon taxi*
Thank you for a pleasant stay	**Grazie di tutto. È stato un soggiorno molto piacevole**	*Grat-syeh dee toot-to. Eh sta-to oon sod-jor-no mol-to pya-**che**-vo-leh*

Problems and Complaints

The air conditioning doesn't work	**L'aria condizionata non funziona**	*la-rye kon-dee-tsyo-na-ta to ar-ya non foont-syo-na*
The television doesn't work	**La televisione non funziona**	*La te-le-vee-zyo-neh non foont-syo-na*
There are no towels in my room	**Nella mia camera non ci sono asciugamani**	*Een **ka**-mair-a mee-a non cee so-no a-shoo-ga-ma-nee*

There's no soap	**Non c'è sapone**	*Non cheh sa-po-neh*
There's no (hot) water	**Non c'è acqua (calda)**	*Non cheh ak-wa (kal-da)*
There's no plug in my washbasin	**Nel mio lavandino non c'è il tappo**	*Nel mee-o la-van-dee-no non cheh eel tap-po*
There's no toilet paper in the lavatory	**Nel bagno non c'è la carta igienica**	*Nel ban-yo non cheh la kar-ta ee-jen-ee-ka*
The lavatory won't flush	**Lo sciacquone non funziona**	*Lo sha-kwo-neh non foont-syo-na*
The bidet leaks	**Il bidè perde**	*Eel bee-**deh** pair-deh*
The light doesn't work	**La luce non funziona**	*La loo-cheh non foont-syo-na*
The lamp is broken	**La lampada è rotta**	*La **lam**-pa-da eh rot-ta*
The blind is stuck	**La persiana è bloccata**	*La pair-sya-na eh blok-ka-ta*
The curtains won't close	**Le tende non si possono chiudere**	*Le ten-deh non see pos-son-o **kyoo**-dair-eh*
The toilet is blocked	**Il WC è otturato**	*Eel vee-chee eh ot-too-ra-to*
The shower doesn't work/is flooded	**La doccia non funziona/è allagata**	*La do-cha non foont-syo-na/eh al-lag-at-a*

Camping

Key Phrases

Is there a camp site nearby?	**C'è un campeggio qui vicino?**	*Cheh oon kam-ped-jo kwee vee-chee-no*
May we camp	**Si può campeggiare**	*See pwo kam-ped-jar-eh*
here?	**qui?**	*kwee*
in your field?	**nel suo campo?**	*nel soo-o kam-po*
on the beach?	**sulla spiaggia?**	*sool-la spyad-ja*
Is there drinking water/electricity	**C'è l'acqua potabile/ l'elettricità?**	*Cheh lak-wa po-**ta**-bee-leh/le-let-tree-che-**ta***

Where should we put our tent/caravan?	**Dove dovremmo mettere la nostra tenda/roulotte?**	*Do-veh dov-rem-mo **met**-tair-eh la nos-tra ten-da/roo-**lot***
Can I park the car next to the tent?	**Posso parcheggiare la macchina accanto alla tenda?**	*Pos-so par-ked-jar-eh la **mak**-kee-na ak-kan-to al-la ten-da*
Can we hire a tent?	**Possiamo affittare una tenda?**	*Pos-sya-mo af-feet-tar-eh oon-a ten-da*
Are there showers/ toilets?	**Ci sono le docce/i bagni/servizi (WC)?**	*Chee so-no le do-cheh/ ee ban-yee/sair-veet-see (vee-chee)*
What does it cost	**Quanto costa**	*Kwan-to kos-ta*
per night?	**a notte?**	*a not-teh*
per week?	**a settimana?**	*a set-tee-ma-na*
per person?	**a persona?**	*a pair-so-na*

Is there	C'è	Cheh
a shop?	un negozio?	oon ne-got-syo
a swimming pool?	una piscina?	oon-a pee-shee-na
a playground?	un campo di ricreazione?	oon kam-po dee ree-kre-at-syo-neh
a restaurant?	un ristorante?	oon rees-tor-an-teh
a launderette?	una lavanderia?	oon-a la-van-dair-ee-a
Can I buy ice?	Si può comprare del ghiaccio?	See pwo kom-prar-eh del gya-cho
Where can I buy butane gas?	Dove posso comprare del gas butano?	Do-veh pos-so kom-prar-eh del gaz boo-ta-no
Where do I put rubbish?	Dove si buttano i rifiuti ?	Do-veh see **boot**-ta-no ee ree-fyoo-tee
Should we sort the rubbish for recycling?	Dobbiamo fare la raccolta differenziata (dei rifiuti)?	Dob-bya-mo fa-re la rak-kol-ta dee-fair-ent-sya-ta day ree-fyoo-tee
Where can I wash up?	Dove si lavano i piatti?	Do-veh see **la**-va-no ee pyat-tee
Where can I wash clothes?	Dove si fa il bucato?	Do-veh see fa eel boo-ka-to
Is there somewhere to dry clothes/ equipment?	Dove si possono asciugare i panni/ le cose?	Do-veh see **pos**-so-no a-shoo-gar-eh ee pan-nee/leh ko-zeh
My camping gas has run out	Il mio gas campeggio è finito	Eel mee-o gas cam-ped-jo eh fee-nee-to

May we light a fire?	**Possiamo accendere un fuoco?**	*Pos-sya-mo a-chen-dair-eh oon fwo-ko*
How long do you want to stay?	***Quanto tempo rimane?**	*Kwan-to tem-po ree-man-eh*
Please prepare the bill, we are leaving today	**Prepari il conto, per favore. Partiamo oggi**	*Pre-pa-ree eel kon-to, pair fa-vor-eh. Par-tya-mo od-jee*
I'm afraid the camp site is full	***Purtroppo il campeggio è pieno**	*Poor-trop-po eel kam-ped-jo eh pye-no*

Hostels

How long is the walk to the youth hostel?	**Quanto dista a piedi l'ostello della gioventù?**	*Kwan-to dees-ta a pye-dee los-tel-lo del-la jo-ven-**too***
Is there a youth hostel here?	**C'è un ostello della gioventù qui?**	*Cheh oon os-tel-lo del-la jo-ven-**too** kwee*
Do you have a room/ bed for the night?	**Si può avere una camera/un letto stanotte?**	*See pwo a-vair-eh oon-a ka-mair-a/oon let-to sta-not-teh*
How many days can we stay?	**Si può rimanere per quanti giorni?**	*See pwo ree-ma-nair-eh pair kwan-tee jor-nee*
Here is my membership card	**Ecco la mia tessera di socio**	*Ek-ko la mee-a tes-sair-a dee so-cho*
Do you serve meals?	**Si servono pasti?**	*See **sair**-vo-no pas-tee*
Can I use the kitchen?	**Posso servirmi della cucina?**	*Pos-so sair-veer-mee del-la koo-chee-na*
Is there somewhere cheap to eat nearby?	**C'è una trattoria non costosa qui vicino?**	*Cheh oon-a trat-tor-ee-a non kos-to-za kwee vee-chee-no*

| I want to rent sheets/ a sleeping bag | Vorrei noleggiare le lenzuola/un sacco a pelo | Vor-**ray** no-led-jar-eh leh lend-zwo-la/oon sak-ko a pe-lo |
| Is there an Internet connection? | C'è la connessione Internet? | Cheh la kon-nes-syo-neh internet |

Hotels

In your room

chambermaid	la cameriera d'albergo	ka-mair-yair-a dal-ber-go
room service	il servizio di camera	sair-veet-syo dee ka-mair-a
Could we have breakfast in our room?	Potremmo avere la prima colazione in camera?	Pot-rem-mo a-vair-eh la pree-ma ko-lat-syo-neh een **ka**-mair-a
I'd like some ice cubes	Vorrei dei cubetti di ghiaccio	Vor-**ray** day koo-bet-tee dee gya-cho
May I have more hangers, please?	Posso avere qualche altra gruccia?	Pos-so a-vair-eh kwal-keh al-tra groo-cha
Is there a socket for an electric razor?	C'è una presa per rasoio elettrico?	Cheh oon-a pre-za pair ra-zo-yo el-**et**-tree-ko
Where is the bathroom/the lavatory?	Dov'è il bagno/il WC?	Dov-**eh** eel ban-yo/ eel vee chee
Is there a shower?	C'è la doccia?	Cheh la do-cha
May I have another blanket/another pillow?	Posso avere un'altra coperta/un altro cuscino?	Pos-so a-vair-eh oon-al-tra ko-pair-ta/oon al-tro koo-shee-no

These sheets are dirty	**Queste lenzuola sono sporche**	*Kwes-teh lend-zwo-la so-no spor-keh*
I can't open my window, can you please open it?	**Non posso aprire la finestra. Può aprirla lei, per favore?**	*Non pos-so ap-reer-eh la fee-nes-tra. Pwo ap-reer-la lay, pair fa-vor-eh*
It's too hot/cold	**Fa troppo caldo/ freddo**	*Fa trop-po kal-do/ fred-do*
Can the heating be turned up/turned down/turned off?	**Può aprire/ abbassare/chiudere il riscaldamento?**	*Pwo ap-reer-eh/ab-bas-sar-eh/**kyoo**-dair-eh eel ree-skal-da-men-to*
Is the room air conditioned?	**In questa camera c'è l'aria condizionata?**	*Een kwes-ta **ka**-mair-a cheh lar-ya kon-deet-syo-na-ta*
Come in!	**Entri/avanti!**	*En-tree/a-van-tee*
Put it on the table, please	**Lo metta sulla tavola, per favore**	*Lo met-ta sool-la **ta**-vo-la, pair fa-vor-eh*
How long will the laundry take?	**Quanto ci metterà la lavanderia?**	*Kwan-to chee met-tair-**a** la la-van-dair-ee-a*
Do you have	**Ha mica**	*A mee-ka*
a needle and thread?	**ago e filo?**	*a-go eh fee-lo*
an iron and ironing board?	**un ferro e una tavola da stiro?**	*oon fer-ro eh oon-a **ta**-vo-la da stee-ro*
Would you clean these shoes, please?	**Mi può lucidare le scarpe, per favore?**	*Mee pwo loo-chee-dar-eh leh skar-peh, pair fa-vor-eh*
Would you clean this dress, please?	**Mi può pulire questo abito, per favore?**	*Mee pwo poo-leer-eh kwes-to **a**-bee-to, pair fa-vor-eh*

Would you press this suit, please?	Mi può stirare questo abito, per favore?	*Mee pwo stee-rar-eh kwes-to a-bee-to, pair fa-vor-eh*
When will it be ready?	Quando sarà pronto?	*Kwan-do sa-ra pron-to*
It will be ready tomorrow	*Sarà pronto domani	*Sa-ra pron-to do-ma-nee*

Other services

porter	il facchino/portinaio	*fak-kee-no/por-tee-na-yo*
hall porter	il portiere	*port-yair-eh*
page	il fattorino	*fat-tor-ee-no*
manager	il manager/direttore	*ma-na-ger/dee-ret-tor-eh*
telephonist	il/la centralinista	*chen-tra-lee-nees-ta*
My key, please	La chiave, per favore	*La kya-veh, pair fa-vor-eh*
A second key, please	Una seconda chiave, per favore	*Oon-a se-kon-da kya-veh, pair fa-vo-reh*
I've lost my key	Ho perso la mia chiave	*O pair-so la mee-a kya-veh*
Do you have a map of the town/ an entertainment guide?	Avete una cartina della città/ una guida per i divertimenti?	*A-veh-teh oon-a kar-tee-na del-la cheet-ta/oon-a gwee-da pair ee dee-vair-tee-men-tee*
Can you keep this in your safe?	Può tenere questo nella cassaforte?	*Pwo te-nair-eh kwes-to nel-la kas-sa-for-teh*
Are there any letters for me?	C'è posta per me?	*Cheh pos-ta pair meh*
Are there any messages for me?	Ci sono messaggi per me?	*Chee so-no mes-sad-jee pair meh*

What is the international dialling code?	Qual'è il prefisso internazionale?	Kwal-**eh** eel pre-fees-so een-tair-nat-syo-na-leh
Could you send a fax for me, please?	Potrebbe spedirmi un fax, per favore?	Po-treb-beh spe-deer-mee un fax, pair fa-vor-eh
Is there a computer for guests to use?	C'è un computer che possano usare gli ospiti?	Cheh oon computer ke pos-san-o oo-zar-eh lyee os-pee-tee
Is there a charge for this (service)?	C'è un sovraprezzo per questo (servizio)?	Cheh oon sov-ra-pret-so pair kwe-sto (sair-veet-syo)
Do I need a password/ID?	Ho bisogno di una password/un login	O bee-zon-yo dee oona password/oon login
Please post this	Mi potrebbe imbucare questo?	Mee pot-reh-beh eem-boo-kar-eh kwes-to
There's a lady/ gentleman to see you	*C'è una signora/un signore che desidera vederla	Cheh oon-a seen-yor-a/ oon seen-yor-eh keh de-**zee**-dair-a ve-dair-la
Please ask her/him to come up	Le/gli dica di salire, per favore	Leh/lyee dee-ka dee sa-leer-eh, pair fa-vor-eh
I'm coming down	Scendo subito	Shen-do **soo**-bee-to
Do you have	Ha	A
any writing paper?	della carta da lettere?	del-la kar-ta da **let**-tair-eh
any envelopes?	delle buste?	del-le boos-teh
any stamps?	dei francobolli?	day fran-ko-bol-lee
Please send the chambermaid/the waiter	Può mandare la cameriera/il cameriere, per favore	Pwo man-dar-eh la ka-mair-yair-a/eel ka-mair-yair-eh, pair fa-vor-eh

I need a guide/an interpreter	Vorrei una guida/un interprete	Vor-**ray** oon-a gwee-da/ oon een-**tair**-pre-teh
Does the hotel have a baby-sitting service?	C'è un servizio baby-sitting nell'albergo	Cheh oon sair-veet-syo baby-sitting nel-lal-bair-go
Where is the cloakroom?	Dov'è il guardaroba?	Dov-**eh** eel gwar-da-ro-ba
Where is the dining room?	Dov'è il ristorante?	Dov-**eh** eel rees-tor-an-teh
What time is	A che ora è	A keh or-a eh
breakfast?	la (prima) colazione?	la (pree-ma) ko-lat-syo-neh
lunch?	il pranzo?	eel prand-zo
dinner?	la cena?	la che-na
Is there a garage?	C'è un garage?	Cheh oon ga-**raj**
Where can I park the car?	Dove posso parcheggiare la macchina?	Do-veh pos-so par-ked-jar-eh la **mak**-kee-na
Is the hotel open all night?	Rimane aperto tutta la notte questo albergo?	Ree-ma-neh a-pair-to toot-ta la not-teh kwes-to al-bair-go
What time does it close?	A che ora chiude?	A keh or-a kyoo-deh
Please wake me at . . .	Mi può svegliare alle . . ., per favore	Mee pwo zvel-yar-eh al-leh . . ., pair fa-vor-eh

APARTMENTS AND VILLAS

Key Phrases

Please show us round	**Ci faccia vedere la casa, per favore**	*Chee fa-cha ve-dair-eh la ka-za, pair fa-vor-eh*
Please show me how this works	**Può mostrarmi come funziona questo?**	*Pwo mos-trar-mee ko-meh foont-syo-na kwes-to*
Which days does the maid come?	**Quali giorni viene la cameriera d'albergo?**	*Kwal-ee jor-nee vye-neh la ka-mair-yair-a del-ber-go*
When is the rubbish collected?	**Quando vengono raccolti i rifiuti?**	*Kwan-do ven-go-no rak-kol-tee ee ree-fyoo-tee*
Please give me another set of keys	**Mi dia un'altro mazzo di chiavi, per favore**	*Mee dee-a oon-al-tro mat-so dee kya-vee, pair fa-vor-eh*
How does the heating/hot water work?	**Come funziona il riscaldamento/l'acqua calda?**	*Ko-meh foon-tsyo-na eel rees-kal-da-men-to/lak-wa kal-da*

We have rented an apartment/villa	**Abbiamo affittato un appartamento/una villa**	*Ab-bya-mo af-feet-ta-to oon ap-par-ta-men-to/oon-a veel-la*
Here is our reservation	**Ecco la nostra prenotazione**	*Ek-ko la nos-tra pre-no-ta-syo-neh*

Does the cost include electricity/the gas cylinder?	È compresa l'elettricità/la bombola?	*Eh kom-pre-za le-let-tree-cee-ta/la **bom**-bo-la*
Is there a spare gas cylinder?	C'è un'altra bombola di gas?	*Cheh oon-al-tra **bom**-bo-la dee gaz*
Do gas cylinders get delivered?	Si consegnano le bombole di gas?	*See kon-**sen**-ya-no leh **bom**-bo-leh dee gaz*
Is the cost of the maid included?	È compreso il servizio della cameriera d'albergo?	*Eh kom-pre-zo eel sair-veet-syo del-la ka-mair-yair-a del-bair-go*
Which days does the maid come?	Quali giorni viene la cameriera d'albergo?	*Kwal-ee jor-nee vye-neh la ka-mair-yair-a del-bair-go*
For how long?	Per quanto tempo?	*Pair **kwan**-to tem-po*
Where is	Dov'è	*Dov-**eh***
the electricity mains switch?	il contattore?	*eel con-ta-tore-eh*
the water mains stopcock?	il rubinetto di arresto?	*eel roo-bee-net-to dee ar-res-to*
the light switch?	l'interruttore?	*leen-tair-root-tor-eh*
the power point?	la presa?	*la pre-za*
the fuse box?	la scatola delle valvole?	*la **ska**-to-la del-leh **val**-vo-leh*
Can you please show me how this works?	Potrebbe mostrarmi come funziona questo?	*Pot-reb-beh mos-trar-mee ko-meh foont-syo-na qwe-sto*
Is there a fly-screen?	C'è una zanzeriera?	*Cheh oona zan-ze-rye-reh*

When is the rubbish collected?	Quando vengono raccolti i rifiuti?	Kwan-do **ven**-go-no rak-kol-tee ee ree-fyoo-tee
The rubbish hasn't been collected	I rifiuti non sono stati raccolti	Ee ree-fyoo-tee non so-no sta-tee rak-kol-tee
Where can we buy logs for the fire?	Dove si può comprare leg na per il fuoco?	Do-veh see **pwo** komp-rar-eh le-nya pair eel fwo-ko
Is there a barbecue?	C'è una griglia?	Cheh oon-a greel-ya
Could someone come to service the swimming pool?	È possible avere il servizio in piscina?	Eh pos-**see**-bee-leh a-vair-eh eel sair-veet-syo een pee-shee-na
Is there an inventory?	C'è un inventario?	Cheh oon een-ven-ta-ryo
This was already broken when we arrived	Questo cra già rotto quando siamo arrivati	Kwes-to air-a ja rot-to kwan-do sya-mo ar-ree-va-tee
We have replaced the broken ...	Abbiamo sostituito il ... che abbiamo rotto	Ab-bya-mo sos-tee-twee-to eel ... che ab-bya-mo rot-to
Here is the bill	Ecco il conto	Ek-ko il kon-to
Please return my deposit against breakages	Mi restituisca la cauzione contro i danni, per favore	Mee res-tee-twees-ka la cowt-syo-neh kon-tro ee dan-nee, pair fa-vor-eh

Cleaning and Maintenance[1]

| Where is a DIY centre/ hardware shop? | Dov'è un negozio di ferramenta? | Dov-**eh** oon ne-got-syo dee fer-ra-men-ta |

1. See also Shops and Services (p. 194).

Where can I get butane gas?	Dove posso rifornire del gas butano?	*Do-veh pos-so ree-for-nee-reh del gas boo-ta-no*
bleach	la candeggina/varechina	*kan-de-jee-na/va-re-kee-na*
bracket	la mensola	*men-so-la*
broom	la scopa	*sko-pa*
brush	la spazzola	*spat-so-la*
bucket	il secchio	*sek-kyo*
charcoal	il carbone	*kar-bo-ne*
clothes line	il filo da stendere	*fee-lo da sten-deh-reh*
clothes peg	la molletta per il bucato	*mol-let-ta pair eel boo-ka-to*
detergent	il detergente	*de-tair-jen-teh*
dustbin	la pattumiera	*pat-toom-yair-a*
dustpan	la paletta per la spazzatura	*pa-let-ta pair la spat-sa-too-ra*
fire extinguisher	l'estintore del fuoco *m*	*es-teen-tor-eh del fwo-co*
hammer	il martello	*mar-tel-lo*
nails	i chiodi	*kyo-dee*
paint	la vernice	*vair-nee-cheh*
paint brush	il pennello	*pe-nel-lo*
plastic	la plastica	*plas-tee-ka*
pliers	le pinze	*peent-seh*

rubbish sacks	i sacchetti della spazzatura	sak-ket-tee del-la spat-sa-too-ra
saw	la sega	se-ga
screwdriver	il cacciavite	ka-cha-vee-teh
screws	le viti	vee-tee
spanner	la chiave fissa	kya-veh fees-sa
stainless steel	l'acciaio inossidabile m	a-cha-yo een-os-see-da-bee-leh
steel	l'acciaio m	a-cha-yo
tile	la mattonella	mat-to-nel-la
vacuum cleaner	l'aspirapolvere m	as-peer-a-**pol**-vair-eh
washing powder	il detersivo in polvere	de-tair-see-vo een **pol**-vair-eh
washing-up liquid	il detersivo	de-tair-see-vo
wire	il filo metallico	fee-lo me-**tal**-lee-ko
wood	il legno	len-yo

Furniture and Fittings

armchair	la poltrona	pol-tro-na
barbecue	la griglia	greel-ya
bath	il bagno	ban-yo
bed	il letto	let-to
blanket	la coperta	ko-pair-ta
bolt (*for door*)	il chiavistello	kya-vee-stel-lo

chair	la sedia	se-dya
clock	l'orologio m	o-ro-lo-jo
cooker	il fornello	for-nel-lo
cupboard	l'armadio m	ar-ma-dyo
curtains	le tende	ten-deh
cushions	i cuscini	koo-shee-nee
deckchair	la sedia a sdraio	se-dya a zdra-yo
dishwasher	la lavastoviglie	la-va-sto-veel-yeh
door	la porta	por-ta
doorbell	il campanello	kam-pa-nel-lo
doorknob	la maniglia della porta	ma-neel-ya del-la por-ta
hinge	il cardine	**kar**-dee-neh
immersion heater	il riscaldamento/ termosifone a immersione	ree-skal-da-men-to/ ter-mos-ee-fo-ne a eem-mair-syo-neh
iron	il ferro	fer-ro
lamp	la lampada	**lam**-pa-da
lampshade	il paralume	pa-ra-loo-meh
light bulb	la lampadina	lam-pa-dee-na
lock	la serratura	ser-ra-too-ra
mattress	il materasso	ma-tair-as-so
mirror	lo specchio	spek-kyo
padlock	il lucchetto	look-ket-to

pillow	il guanciale	gwan-cha-leh
pipe	il tubo	too-bo
plug (*electric*)	la presa	pre-za
plug (*bath*)	il tappo	tap-po
radio	la radio	ra-dyo
refrigerator	il frigorifero	free-go-**ree**-fair-o
sheet	il lenzuolo	lend-zwo-lo
shelf	lo scaffale	skaf-fa-leh
shower	la doccia	do-cha
sink	l'acquaio *m*	ak-wa-yo
sofa	il sofà/divano	so-**fa**/dee-va-no
stool	lo sgabello	zga-bel-lo
sun lounger	il lettino	let-tee-no
table	la tavola/il tavolo	**ta**-vo-la/**ta**-vo-lo
tap	il rubinetto	roo-bee-net-to
television	la televisione/TV	te-le-vee-zyo-neh/tee-voo
toilet	il WC	vee-chee
towel	l'asciugamano *m*	a-shoo-ga-ma-no
washbasin	il lavandino	la-van-dee-no
washing machine	la lavatrice	la-va-tree-cheh
window latch	la fermafinestre	fair-ma-fee-nes-treh
window sill	il davanzale	da-vand-za-leh

Kitchen Equipment

bottle opener	l'apribottiglie *m*	ap-ree-bot-teel-yeh
bowl	la ciotola	**cho**-to-la
can opener	l'apriscatole *m*	a-pree-**ska**-to-leh
candles	le candele	kan-de-leh
chopping board	il tagliere	tal-yair-eh
coffee pot	la macchinetta del caffè	ma-kee-net-ta del kaf-**feh**
colander	il colino	ko-lee-no
coolbag	la borsa frigo	bor-sa free-go
corkscrew	il cavatappi	ka-va-tap-pee
cup	la tazza	tat-sa
fork	la forchetta	for-ket-ta
frying pan	la padella	pa-del-la
glass	il bicchiere	beek-kyair-eh
ice pack	la borsa per ghiaccio	bor-sa pair gya-cho
ice tray	il vassoio da ghiaccio	vas-so-yo da gya-cho
kettle	il bollitore	bol-lee-tor-eh
knife	il coltello	kol-tel-lo
matches	i fiammiferi	fyam-**mee**-fair-ee
microwave (oven)	(forno a) microonde	(for-no) a mee-kro-on-deh
pan with lid	la pentola con coperchio	**pen**-to-la kon ko-pair-kyo
plate	il piatto	pyat-to

scissors	**le forbici**	*for-bee-chee*
sieve	**il setaccio**	*se-ta-cho*
spoon	**il cucchiaio**	*kook-kya-yo*
tea towel	**il canovaccio**	*ka-no-va-cho*
toaster	**il tostapane**	*to-sta-pa-neh*
torch (electric)	**la torcia elettrica**	*tor-cha e-let-tree-ka*

Parts of a House and Grounds

balcony	**il balcone**	*bal-ko-neh*
bathroom	**il bagno**	*ban-yo*
bedroom	**la camera da letto**	*ka-mair-a da let-to*
ceiling	**il soffitto**	*sof-feet-to*
chimney	**il camino**	*ka-mee-no*
corridor	**il corridoio**	*kor-ree-do-yo*
door	**la porta**	*por-ta*
fence	**il recinto**	*re-cheen-to*
fireplace	**il caminetto**	*ka-mee-net-to*
floor	**il pavimento**	*pa-vee-men-to*
garage	**il garage**	*ga-raj*
garden	**il giardino**	*jyar-dee-no*
gate	**il cancello**	*kan-chel-lo*
hall	**l'entrata** *f*	*en-tra-ta*
kitchen	**la cucina**	*koo-chee-na*

living room	**il salotto**	*sa-lot-to*
patio/courtyard	**il cortile**	*kor-tee-leh*
roof	**il tetto**	*tet-to*
shutters	**le imposte/persiane**	*eem-pos-teh/pair-sya-neh*
stairs	**le scale**	*ska-leh*
swimming pool	**la piscina**	*pee-shee-na*
terrace	**la terrazza**	*ter-rat-sa*
wall	**il muro**	*moo-ro*
window	**la finestra**	*fee-nes-tra*

Problems

The drain . . .	**Il tubo di scarico . . .**	*Eel too-bo dee ska-ree-ko . . .*
The pipe . . .	**Il tubo . . .**	*Eel too-bo . . .*
The sink . . . is blocked	**Il lavandino . . . è otturato**	*Eel la-van-dee-no eh ot-too-ra-to*
The toilet doesn't flush	**Il WC non funziona**	*Eel vee-chee non foont-syo-na*
There is no water	**Non c'è acqua**	*Non cheh ak-wa*
We can't turn the water off/shower on	**Non riusciamo a chiudere l'acqua/ad aprire la doccia**	*Non ryoo-sha-mo a kyoo-dair-eh lak-wa/ad ap-reer-eh la do-cha*
There is a gas/water leak	**C'è una fuga di gas/ una perdita d'acqua**	*Cheh oon-a foo-ga dee gas/oon-a per-dee-ta dak-wa*

There is a broken window	C'è una finestra rotta	Cheh oon-a fee-nes-tra rot-ta
The shutters won't close	Non si chiudono le persiane	Non see **kyoo**-do-no le pair-sya-neh
The window won't open	Non si apre la finestra	Non see ap-re la fee-nes-tra
The electricity has gone off	Manca l'elettricità	Man-ka le-let-tree-chee-**ta**
The heating ...	Il riscaldamento ...	Eel rees-kal-da-men-to ...
The cooker ...	Il fornello ...	Eel for-nel-lo ...
The refrigerator ...	Il frigorifero ...	Eel free-go-**ree**-fair-o ...
The water heater ... doesn't work	Il riscaldamento acqua ... non funziona	Eel rees-kal-da-men-to ak-wa ... non foonl-syo-na
The lock is stuck	La serratura è bloccata	La ser-ra-too-ra eh blok-ka-ta
This is broken	Questo è guasto	Kwes-to eh gwas-to
This needs repairing	Bisogna riparare questo	Bee-zon-ya ree-pa-rar-eh kwes-to
The apartment/villa has been burgled	Il domicilio è stato violato	Eel do-mee-cheel-yo eh sta-to vee-o-la-to

COMMUNICATIONS

Key Phrases

Is there an Internet café near here?	C'è un caffé Internet qui vicino?	*Cheh oon kaf-feh internet kwee vee-chee-no*
Do I need a password?	Ho bisogno di una password?	*O bee-zon-yo dee oon-a password*
Can I print this?	Posso stampare questo?	*Pos-so stam-pa-reh kwe-sto*
What is your email address?	Qual'è il suo indirizzo email?	*Kwal-eh eel soo-o en-dee-reet-so email*
I want to get an Italian SIM card for this mobile phone	Voglio prendermi una sim card italiana per questo telefonino	*Vol-yo pren-dair-mee oon-a sim card ee-tal-ya-na pair kwes-to te-le-fo-nee-no*
Where's the nearest post office?	Dov'è l'ufficio postale più vicino?	*Dov-eh loof-fee-cho pos-ta-leh pyoo vee-chee-no*

Email and Internet

Does this café have wi-fi?	Questo caffé ha un sistema wi-fi?	*Kwe-sto kaf-feh a oon see-steh-ma wi-fi*
Is there a connection fee?	Bisogna pagare per la connessione?	*Bee-zon-ya pa-ga-reh pair la kon-nes-syo-neh*

Can I access the Internet?	**Posso accedere a Internet?**	*Pos-so ach-**ed**-air-eh a internet*
Can I check my email?	**Posso controllare le email?**	*Pos-so con-trol-lar-eh le email*
Can I use any computer?	**Posso usare qualsiasi computer?**	*Pos-so oo-zar-eh kwal-sya-zee computer*
How much does it cost for half an hour/ an hour?	**Quanto costa per mezz'ora/un'ora?**	*Kwan-to kos-ta pair med-zor-a/oon-or-a*
How do I turn on the computer?	**Come si accende il computer?**	*Ko-meh see a-chen-deh eel computer*
How do I log on/log off?	**Come mi connetto/ disconnetto?**	*Ko-meh mee kon-net-to/ dees-kon-net-to*
The computer doesn't respond	**Il computer non risponde ai comandi**	*Eel computer non ree-spon-deh a-ee ko-man-dee*
The computer has frozen	**Il computer si è bloccato**	*Eel computer see eh blok-ka-to*
Can you change this to an English keyboard?	**Può cambiarlo con una tastiera inglese?**	*Pwo cam-byar-lo kon oon-a tas-tye-ra een-gle-ze*
Where is the @ (at) sign on the keyboard?	**Dov'è il segno della chiocciola sulla tastiera?**	*Dov-**eh** eel sen-yo del-la **kyo**-cho-la sool-la tas-tye-ra*
I would need an adapter	**Avrei bisogno di un adattatore**	*Av-**ray** bee-zon-yo dee oon ad-at-ta-tor-eh*
My email address is ...	**Il mio indirizzo email è ...**	*Eel mee-o een-dee-reet-so email eh ...*

Did you get my email?	**Hai ricevuto la mia email?**	*A-ee ree-che-voo-to la mee-a email*
Email me, please	**Mi mandi un email, per favore**	*Mee man-dee-oon email, pair fa-vor-eh*
Do you have a website?	**Ha un sito Internet?**	*A oon see-to internet*

Faxing, Copying and Telegrams

I would like to send a fax	**Vorrei spedire un fax**	*Vor-ray spe-dee-reh oon fax*
Can I send/receive a fax here?	**Posso spedire/ ricevere un fax qui?**	*Pos-so spe-dee-reh/ree-che-vair-eh oon fax kwee*
How much does it cost per page?	**Quanto costa a pagina?**	*Kwan-to kos-ta a pa-jee-na*
Do you have a fax?	**Ha un fax?**	*A oon fax*
What is your fax number?	**Qual'è il suo numero di fax?**	*Kwal-eh eel soo-o noo-mair-o dee fax*
Please resend your fax	**Per favore rimandi il fax**	*Pair fa-vor-eh ree-man-dee eel fax*
Can I make photocopies here?	**Posso fare fotocopie qui?**	*Pos-so fa-reh fo-to-ko-pyeh kwee*
Could you scan this for me?	**Potrebbe scannerizzarmi questo?**	*Po-tre-be skan-ner-eet-sar-mee kwes-to*
I want to send a (reply-paid) telegram	**Voglio mandare un telegramma (con risposta pagata)**	*Vol-yo man-dar-eh oon te-le-gram-ma (kon rees-pos-ta pa-ga-ta)*

How much does it cost per word?	Quanto costa a parola?	Kwan-to kos-ta a pa-ro la
Write the message here and your own name and address	*Scriva qui il testo con il suo nome e indirizzo	Skree-va kwee eel tes-to kon eel soo-o no-meh eh een-dee-reet-so

Post

Where's the main post office?	Dov'è l'ufficio postale centrale?	Dov-**eh** loof-fee-cho pos-ta-leh chen-tra-leh
Where's the nearest post office?	Dov'è l'ufficio postale più vicino?	Dov-**eh** loof-fee-cho pos-ta-leh pyoo vee-chee-no
What time does the post office open/ close?	A che ora apre/ chiude l'ufficio postale?	A keh or-a a-preh/ kyoo-deh loof-fee-cho pos-ta-leh
Where's the post box?	Dov'è una buca per le lettere?	Dov-**eh** oon-a boo-ka pair le **let**-tair-eh
Is there a stamp machine?	C'è una macchinetta per francobolli?	Cheh oon-a mak-kee-net-ta pair fran-ko-bol-lee
Which counter do I go to for	Qual'è lo sportello per	Kwal-**eh** lo spor-tel-lo pair
telegrams?	i telegrammi?	ee te-le-gram-mee
stamps?	i francobolli?	ee fran-ko-bol-lee
poste restante?	fermo posta?	fer-mo po-sta
money orders?	vaglia postali?	val-ya pos-ta-lee

How much is a letter to Great Britain?	Che francobolli ci vogliono per la Gran Bretagna?	Keh fran-ko-bol-lee chee vol-yo-no pair la gran bre-tan-ya
How much is an airmail letter to the USA?	Quanto costa una lettera per via aerea per gli Stati Uniti?	Kwan-to kos-ta oon-a let-tair-a pair vee-a a-air-e-a pair lyee sta-tee oo-nee-tee
I want to send a parcel	Vorrei spedire un pacco	Vor-ray spe-deer-eh oon pak-ko
It's for Italy	È per l'Italia	Eh pair lee-ta-lya
Give me three . . . euro stamps, please	Vorrei tre francobolli da . . . euro	Vor-ray treh fran-ko-bol-lee da . . . e-oo-ro
I want to send this letter special delivery	Voglio spedire questa lettera in consegna espressa	Vol-yo spe-dee-reh kwe-sta let-tair-a een con-sen-ya es-pres-sa
I want to send this letter express	Voglio mandare questa lettera con posta espressa	Vol-yo man-dar-eh kwes-ta let-tair-a kon pos-ta es-pres-sa
I want to register this letter	Voglio mandare questa lettera raccomandata	Vol-yo man-dar-eh kwes-ta let-tair-a rak-ko-man-da-ta
Where is the poste restante section?	Dov'è lo sportello del fermo posta?	Dov-eh lo spor-tel-lo del fair-mo pos-ta
Are there any letters for me?	Ci sono lettere per me?	Chee so-no let-tair-eh pair me
What is your name?	*Il suo nome, per favore	Eel soo-o no-meh, pair fa-vor-eh
Do you have any identification?	*Ha qualche documento d'identità?	A kwal-keh do-koo-men-to dee-den-tee-ta

Telephones, Mobiles and SMS

Do you have a mobile (cell phone)?	**Ha un telefonino?**	*A oon te-le-fo-nee-no*
What is your mobile (cell) number?	**Qual'è il suo numero di telefonino?**	*Kwal-**eh** eel soo-o **noo**-mair-o dee te-le-fo-nee-no*
My mobile (cell phone) isn't working here	**Il mio telefonino non funziona qui**	*Eel mee-o te-le-fo-nee-no non foont-syo-na kwee*
I want to get an Italian SIM card for this mobile phone	**Voglio prendermi una sim card italiana per questo telefonino**	*Vol-yo **pren**-dair-mee oon-a sim card ee-tal-ya-na pair kwes-to te-le-fo-nee-no*
Can you give me your mobile number?	**Puoi darmi il suo numero di telefonino?**	*Pwo dar-mee eel soo-o **noo**-mair-o dee te-le-fo-nee-no*
I'll send you a text	**Ti mando un messaggino**	*Tee man-do oon mes-sad-jee-no*
Where's the nearest phone box?	**Dov'è la cabina telefonica la più vicina?**	*Dov-**eh** la ka-bee-na te-le-fo-nee-ka la pyoo vee-chee-na*
I would like a phonecard	**Vorrei una carta telefonica**	*Vor-**ray** oon-a kar-ta te-le-**fo**-nee-ka*
I want to make a phone call	**Voglio fare una telefonata**	*Vol-yo far-eh oon-a te-le-fo-na-ta*
May I use your phone?	**Posso usare il suo telefono?**	*Pos-so oo-zar-eh eel soo-o te-**le**-fo-no*
Do you have a telephone directory for . . .?	**Ha l'elenco telefonico di . . .?**	*A le-len-ko te-le-**fo**-nee-ko dee . . .*

Could you give me the number for international directory enquiries?	**Potrebbe darmi il numero per le richieste internazionali?**	*Pot-reb-beh dar-me eel noo-mair-o pair leh ree-kyes-teh een-tair-nat-syo-na-leh*
Call 112 (*number for international emergencies*)	***Chiami il 112!**	*Kya-mee eel chen-to do-dee-chee*
What is the international/ country/area code?	**Qual'è il prefisso internazionale/ nazionale/urbano?**	*Kwal-eh eel pre-fees-so een-tair-nat-syo-na-leh/ nat-syo-na-leh/oor-ba-no*
What do I dial to get the international operator?	**Qual'è il numero del centralino internazionale?**	*Kwal-eh eel noo-mair-o del chen-tra-lee-no een-tair-nat-syo-na-leh*
Please give me . . . tokens (for the video game)	**Potrebbe darmi . . . gettoni (per il video game), per favore**	*Pot-reb-beh dar-mee . . . jet-to-nee (pair eel video game), pair fa-vor-eh*
Please get me . . .	**Desidero chiamare . . .**	*De-zee-dair-o kya-mar-eh . . .*
I want to telephone England	**Voglio telefonare l'Inghilterra**	*Vol-yo te-le-fo-nar-eh leen-geel-ter-ra*
We were cut off. Can you reconnect me?	**Ci hanno interrotto. Può rimettermi in linea?**	*Chee han-no een-tair-rot-to. Pwo ree-met-tair-mee een lee-ne-a*
The number is out of order	***Il numero è guasto**	*Eel noo-mair-o eh gwas-to*
The line is engaged	***La linea è occupata**	*La lee-ne-a eh ok-koo-pa-ta*
There's no reply	***Non c'è risposta**	*Non cheh rees-pos-ta*
You have the wrong number	***Il suo numero è sbagliato**	*Eel soo-o noo-mair-o eh zbal-ya-to*

On the phone

Hello	**Pronto**	*Pron-to*
I want extension . . .	**Voglio parlare con l'interno . . .**	*Vol-yo par-lar-eh kon leen-tair-no . . .*
May I speak to . . .	**Posso parlare con . . .**	*Pos-so par-lar-eh kon . . .*
Speaking	**Sono io**	*So-no ee-o*
Who's speaking?	**Chi parla?**	*Kee par-la*
Hold the line, please	***Rimanga in linea, prego**	*Ree-man-ga een **lee**-ne-a, pre-go*
He's not here	***Non è qui**	*Non eh kwee*
He's at . . .	***È a . . .**	*Eh a . . .*
When will he be back?	**Quando sarà di ritorno?**	*Kwan-do sa-**ra** dee ree-tor-no*
Can I leave a message?	**Posso lasciare un messaggio?**	*Pos-so la-shar-eh oon mes-sad-jo*
Tell him that . . . phoned	**Gli dica che gli ha telefonato . . .**	*Lyee dee-ka keh lyee a te-le-fo-na-to . . .*
I'll ring again later	**Chiamo più tardi**	*Kya-mo pyoo tar-dee*
Please ask him to phone me	**Per favore, gli dica di telefonarmi**	*Pair fa-vor-eh, lyee dee-ka dee te-le-fo-nar-mee*
Can you repeat that, please?	**Può ripetere, per favore?**	*Pwo ree-pe-tair-eh, pair fa-vor-eh*
Please speak slowly	**Per favore, parli lentamente**	*Pair fa-vo-reh, par-lee len-ta-men-teh*

I can't hear you	**Non la sento**	*Non la sen-to*
What's your number?	***Qual'è il suo numero?**	*Kwal-**eh** eel soo-o **noo**-mair-o*
My number is . . .	**Il mio numero è . . .**	*Eel mee-o **noo**-mair-o eh . . .*

DISABLED TRAVELLERS

Key Phrases

Is there a disabled parking area?	**C'è un parcheggio per persone disabili?**	*Cheh oon par-ked-jo pair pair-so-neh dee-za-bee-lee*
Are there facilities for the disabled?	**Ci sono attrezzature per persone disabili?**	*Chee so-no at-tret-sa-too-reh pair pair-so-neh dee-za-bee-lee*
I want to book a wheelchair from the check-in desk to the plane	**Voglio prenotare una sedia a rotelle dal check-in all'aereo**	*Vol-yo pre-no-ta-reh oon-a se-dya a ro-tel-leh dal check-in al-la-air-e-o*
I need a bedroom on the ground floor/near the lift	**Ho bisogno di una camera al piano terra/vicino all'ascensore**	*O bee-zon-yo dee oon-a ka-mair-a al pya-no ter-ra/vee-chee-no al-la-shen-sor-eh*
Does the bus/train/plane take wheelchairs/mobility scooters?	**Posso salire sul pullman/sul treno/sull'aereo con la sedia a rotelle/lo scooter di mobilità?**	*Pos-so sa-lee-reh sul pool-man/sul tre-no/sul-la-air-e-o kon la se-dya a ro-tel-leh/lo scooter dee mo-bee-lee-ta*

Access

Is there a disabled parking area?	C'è un parcheggio per persone disabili?	*Cheh oon par-ked-jo pair pair-so-neh dee-**za**-bee-lee*
Are there facilities for the disabled?	Ci sono attrezzature per persone disabili?	*Chee so-no at-tret-sa-too-reh pair pair-so-neh dee-**za**-bee-lee*
Can we borrow/ hire a wheelchair/a mobility scooter?	Possiamo prendere in prestito/affittare una sedia a rotelle/ uno scooter di mobilità?	*Pos-sya-mo **pren**-dair-eh een **pre**-stee-to/af-feet-tar-eh oon-a se-dya a ro-tel-leh/oon-o scooter dee mo-bee-lee-**ta***
I want to book a wheelchair from the check-in desk to the plane	Voglio prenotare una sedia a rotelle dal check-in all'aereo	*Vol-yo pre-no-ta-reh oon-a se-dya a ro-tel-leh dal check-in al-la-**air**-e-o*
Is it possible to visit the old town/the site in a wheelchair?	È possibile visitare il centro storico/il sito in sedia a rotelle?	*Eh pos-**see**-bee-leh vee-zee-tar-eh eel chen-tro sto-ree-co/eel see-to een se-dya a ro-tel-leh*
Is there wheelchair access to the gallery/ concert hall/theatre?	C'è l'accesso per la sedia a rotelle nella galleria/nella sala concerti/nel teatro?	*Cheh la-ches-so pair la se-dya a ro-tel-leh nel-la gal-le-ree-a/nel-la sa-la kon-chair-tee/nel te-at-ro*
Are the paths in the garden/park suitable for wheelchairs?	I viali del giardino/ del parco sono adatti per il passaggio delle sedie a rotelle?	*Ee vee-a-lee del jar-dee-no/del par-ko so-no a-dat-tee pair eel pas-sad-jo del-le se-dye a ro-tel-leh*
Is there a wheelchair ramp?	C'è una rampa d'accesso per la sedia a rotelle?	*Cheh oon-a ram-pa da-ches-so pair la se-dya a ro-tel-leh*

Are there seats reserved for the disabled?	**Ci sono posti riservati per le persone disabili?**	*Chee so-no pos-tee ree-sair-va-tee pair le pair-so-neh dee-za-bee-lee*
Is there a table with space for a wheelchair?	**C'è un tavolo con spazio per la sedia a rotelle?**	*Cheh un ta-vo-lo kon spat-syo pair la se-dya a ro-tel-leh*
Are mobility scooters allowed inside?	**È permesso entrare con gli scooter di mobilità?**	*Eh pair-mes-so en-tra-reh kon lyee scooter dee mo-bee-lee-ta*
Where is the lift?	**Dov'è l'ascensore?**	*Dov-eh la-shen-so-reh*
Are there/where are the disabled toilets?	**Ci sono/dove sono i bagni per i disabili?**	*Chee so-no/do-veh so-no ee ban-yee pair ee dee-za-bee-lee*
Is there a discount for the disabled?	**C'è uno sconto per portatori di handicap?**	*Cheh oo-no skun-to pair por-ta-to-ree dee han-dee-kap*
Are guide dogs allowed?	**È permesso entrare con i cani guida?**	*Eh pair-mes-so en-tra-reh con ee ka-nee gwee-da*
I can't walk far	**Non posso camminare per lunghi tragitti**	*Non pos-so kam-mee-na-reh pair lun-gee tra-jet-tee*
I can't climb stairs	**Non posso fare le scale**	*Non pos-so fa-re le ska-leh*
Is the bathroom equipped for the disabled?	**Il bagno è attrezzato per le persone disabili?**	*Eel ban-yo eh at-tret-sa-to pair le pair-so-neh dee-za-bee-lee*

Assistance

Please hold the door open, thank you	**Lasciare la porta aperta, grazie**	*La-shar-eh la por-ta a-pair-ta, grat-sye*
Can you help me?	**Potete aiutarmi?**	*Po-te-teh a-yoo-tar-mee*
I am (nearly) deaf, please speak louder	**Sono (quasi) sordo, per favore parlate più forte**	*So-no (qwa-see) sor-do, pair fa-vor-eh par-la-teh pyu for-teh*
I am deaf, please look at me when you speak, so I can read your lips	**Sono sordo, per favore mi guardi quando parla, così posso leggerle le labbra**	*So-no sor-do, pair fa-vo-re mee gwar-dee kwan-do par-la, ko-zee pos-so led-jair-eh leh lab-bra*
Could you help me cross the road, please?	**Potreste aiutarmi ad attraversare la strada, per favore?**	*Po-tres-teh ayu-tar-mee ad-at-tra-vair-sa-reh la stra-da, pair fa-vo-reh?*

Travel

Does the bus/ train/plane take wheelchairs/mobility scooters?	**Posso salire sul pullman/sul treno/ sull'aereo con la sedia a rotelle/lo scooter di mobilità?**	*Pos-so sa-lee-reh sul pool-man/sul tre-no/sul-la-air-e-o kon la se-dya a ro-tel-leh/lo scooter dee mo-bee-lee-ta*
Could you order a taxi that will take a wheelchair?	**Può prenotarmi un taxi che abbia spazio per la sedia a rotelle?**	*Pwo pre-no-tar-mee oon taxi keh ab-bya spat-syo pair la se-dya a ro-tel-leh*

EATING OUT

Key Phrases

Can you suggest	**Mi può indicare**	*Mee pwo een-dee-kar-eh*
a good restaurant?	**un buon ristorante?**	*oon bwon rees-tor-an-teh*
a cheap restaurant?	**un ristorante a buon mercato?**	*oon rees-tor-an-teh a bwon mair-ka-to*
a vegetarian restaurant?	**un ristorante vegetariano?**	*oon rees-tor-an-teh ve-je-tar-ya-no*
I've reserved a table. My name is . . .	**Ho riservato un tavolo. Sono . . .**	*O ree-zair-va-to oon ta-vo-lo. So-no . . .*
May I see the menu/ the wine list, please?	**Posso vedere il menù/la lista dei vini, per favore?**	*Pos-so ve-dair-eh eel me-noo/la lees-ta day vee-nee*
Is there a set menu for lunch?	**Ha un pranzo a prezzo fisso?**	*A oon prand-zo a pre-tso fees-so*
What is the dish of the day?	**Qual'è il piatto del giorno?**	*Kwal-eh eel pyat-to del jor-no*
It was very good	**Era molto buono**	*Er-a mol-to bwo-no*
The bill, please	**Il conto, prego**	*Eel kon-to, pre-go*
Does it include service?	**Il servizio è compreso?**	*Eel sair-veet-syo eh kom-pre-zo*

I'd like to book a table for four at 1 p.m.	**Vorrei riservare un tavolo per quattro persone per l'una**	*Vor-ray ree-zair-var-eh oon ta-vo-lo pair kwat-tro pair-so-neh pair loon-a*
We did not make a reservation	**Non abbiamo riservato un tavolo**	*Non ab-bya-mo ree-zair-va-to oon ta-vo-lo*
Do you have a table for three?	**Ha un tavolo per tre?**	*A oon ta-vo-lo pair treh*
Is there a table free	**Ha un tavolo**	*A oon ta-vo-lo*
on the terrace	**sulla veranda**	*sool-la ve-ran-da*
by the window	**vicino alla finestra**	*vee-chee-no al-la fee-nes-tra*
in a corner?	**in un angolo?**	*een oon an-go-lo*
This way, please	***Da questa parte, per favore**	*Da kwes-ta par-teh, pair fa-vor-eh*
We shall have a table free in half an hour	***Avremo un tavolo libero tra mezz'ora**	*Av-re-mo oon ta-vo-lo lee-bair-o tra med-zor-a*
You would have to wait about . . . minutes	***Dovrebbe aspettare circa . . . minuti**	*Dov-reb-beh as-pet-tar-eh cheer-ka . . . mee-noo-tee*
We don't serve lunch until 12.30	***Cominciamo a servire il pranzo alle dodici e mezzo**	*Ko-meen-chya-mo a sair-veer-eh eel prand-zo al-leh do-dee-chee eh med-zo*
We don't serve dinner until 8 p.m.	***Cominciamo a servire la cena alle otto**	*Ko-meen-chya-mo a sair-veer-eh la che-na al-leh ot-to*
We stop serving at 11 o'clock	***Smettiamo di servire alle undici**	*Smet-tya-mo dee sair-veer-eh al-leh oon-dee-chee*

Sorry, the kitchen is closed	**Mi dispiace, è chiusa la cucina**	*Mee dees-pya-cheh, eh kyoo-za la koo-chee-na*
Where are the toilets?	**Dove sono i bagni?**	*Do-veh so-no ee ban-yee*
It is downstairs/upstairs	***È al piano di sotto/al piano di sopra**	*Eh al pya-no dee sot-to/al pya-no dee sop-ra*
We are in a hurry	**Abbiamo fretta**	*Ab-bya-mo fret-ta*
Do you serve snacks?	**Si può fare uno spuntino?**	*See pwo far-eh oon-o spoon-tee-no*
I am a vegetarian	**Sono vegetariano/vegetariana**	*So-no ve-je-tar-ya-no/ve-je-tar-ya-na*
I am allergic to	**Sono allergico/allergica**	*So-no al-**lair**-jee-ko/al-**lair**-jee-ka*
wheat	**al grano/frumento**	*al gra-no/froo-men-to*
gluten	**al glutine**	*al **gloo**-tee-neh*
nuts	**alle noci**	*al-leh no-chee*
dairy products	**ai latticini**	*ay lat-tee-chee-nee*
I am coeliac	**Sono celiaco/celiaca**	*So-no che-lee-a-ko/che-lee-a-ka*

Ordering

cover charge	***il coperto**	*ko-pair-to*
service charge	***il servizio**	*sair-veet-syo*
service and VAT (not) included	***servizio e IVA (non) sono compresi**	*sair-veet-syo eh ee-va (non) so-no kom-pre-zee*

waiter/waitress (to address)	il cameriere/la cameriera	ka-mair-yair-eh/ ka-mair-yair-a
Excuse me (to call the waiter)	Scusi	Skoo-zee
May I see the menu/ the wine list, please?	Posso vedere il menù/la lista dei vini, per favore?	Pos-so ve-dair-eh eel me-noo/la lees-ta day vee-nee
Is there a set menu for lunch?	Ha un pranzo a prezzo fisso?	A oon prand-zo a pre-tso fees-so
I'll have the . . . euro menu	Prendo il menù da . . . euro	Pren-do eel me-noo da . . . e-oo-ro
today's special menu	la specialità di oggi	la spe-chya-lee-ta dee od-jee
As the first course	Come primo	Ko-meh pree-mo
second course	secondo	se-kon-do
side dish	contorno	kon-tor-no
dessert	dolce	dol-cheh
I would like something light	Vorrei qualcosa di leggero	Vor-ray kwal-ko-za dee led-je-ro
Do you have children's helpings?	Avete porzioni per bambini?	A-ve-te port-syo-nee pair bam-bee-nee
Could we have a small helping?	Potremmo avere una mezza porzione?	Pot-rem-mo a-vair-eh oon-a med-za port-syo-neh
What is the dish of the day?	Qualè il piatto del giorno?	Kwal-eh eel pyat-to del jor-no
What do you recommend?	Cosa raccomanda lei?	Ko-za rak-ko-man-da lay

Can you tell me what this is?	**Mi può dire che cos'è questo piatto?**	*Mee pwo deer-eh keh koz-eh kwes-to pyat-to*
Do you have any	**Ha delle**	*A del-leh*
local dishes?	**specialità regionali?**	*spe-cha-lee-ta re-jo-na-lee*
vegetarian dishes?	**dei piatti vegetariani?**	*day pyat-tee ve-je-tar-ya-nee*
What are the specialities of the restaurant/ of the region?	**Quali sono le specialità di questo ristorante/questa regione?**	*Kwal-ee so-no leh spe-cha-lee-ta dee kwes-to rees-tor-an-teh/kwes-ta re-jo-neh*
I'd like ...	**Vorrei ...**	*Vor-ray ...*
May I have peas instead of beans?	**Posso avere piselli invece di fagioli?**	*Pos-so a-vair-eh pee-zel-lee een-ve-cheh dee fa-jo-lee*
Is it hot or cold?	**E un piatto caldo o freddo?**	*Eh oon pyat-to kal-do o fred-do*
I don't want any oil/ sauce with it	**Lo voglio senza olio/ senza salsa**	*Lo vol-yo send-za ol-yo/ send-za sal-sa*
Some more bread, please	**Ancora del pane, per favore**	*An-kor-a del pa-neh, pair fa-vor-eh*
A little more, please	**Un po' di più, per favore**	*Oon po dee pyoo, pair fa-vor-eh*
Salt and pepper/ napkins, please	**Sale e pepe/ tovaglioli, per favore**	*Sa-leh eh peh-peh/to-va-lyo-lee pair fa-vo-reh*
Would you like to try ...?	***Vuol provare ...?**	*Vwol pro-var-eh ...*
There's no more ...	***Non abbiamo più ...**	*Non ab-bya-mo pyoo ...*
How would you like it (*the steak*) cooked?	***Come la vuole cotta?**	*Ko-meh la vwo-leh kot-ta*

Rare/medium/well done	**Al sangue/media/ben cotta**	*Al san-gwe/me-dya/ben kot-ta*
Would you like a dessert?	***Vuole un dolce?**	*Vwo-leh oon dol-cheh*
Something to drink?	***Qualcosa da bere?**	*Kwal-ko-za da be-reh*
The wine list, please	**La lista del vino, per favore**	*La lee-sta del vee-no, pair fa-vo-reh*
A quarter/half-litre of the house wine	**Un quartino/mezzo litro di vino della casa**	*Oon kwar-tee-no/med-zo lee-tro dee vee-no del-la ka-za*

Paying[1]

The bill, please	**Il conto, prego**	*Eel kon-to, pre-go*
Does it include service?	**Il servizio è compreso?**	*Eel sair-veet-syo eh kom-pre-zo*
Please check the bill. I don't think it's correct	**Vuol controllare il conto. Non mi sembra esatto**	*Vwol kon-trol-lar-eh eel kon-to. Non mee sem-bra e-zat-to*
What is this amount for?	**Quant'è per . . .?**	*Kwant-eh pair . . .*
I didn't have soup	**Non ho preso la minestra**	*Non o pre-zo la mee-nes-tra*
I had chicken, not steak	**Ho preso pollo, non bistecca**	*O pre-zo pol-lo, non bees-tek-ka*
May we have separate bills?	**Ci faccia il conto separato?**	*Chee fa-cha eel kon-to se-pa-ra-to*

1. Tipping is welcome, but not expected in restaurants, cafés or bars in Italy.

Can I pay with a credit card?	**Posso pagare con una carta di credito?**	*Pos-so pa-gar-eh kon oon-a kar-ta dee kre-dee-to*
Keep the change	**Tenga il resto**	*Ten-ga eel res-to*

Compliments

It was very good	**Era molto buono**	*Er-a mol-to bwo-no*
We enjoyed it, thank you	**Ci ha piaciuto, grazie**	*Chee a pya-choo-to, grat-syeh*
The food was delicious	**Il cibo era delizioso**	*Eel chee-bo air-a de-leet-syo-zo*
We particularly liked ...	**Ci è piaciuto soprattutto ...**	*Chee eh pya-choo-to so-prat-toot-to*

Complaints

Where are our drinks?	**Non ci ha ancora portato da bere**	*Non chee a an-kor-a por-ta-to da be-reh*
Why does it take so long?	**Perchè bisogna aspettare tanto?**	*Pair-**keh** bee-zon-ya as-pet-tar-eh tan-to*
This isn't what I ordered, I want ...	**Non ho ordinato questo, io voglio ...**	*Non o or-dee-na-to kwes-to, ee-o vol-yo ...*
This is	**Questo è**	*Kwes-to eh*
bad	**cattivo**	*kal-lee-vo*
uncooked	**poco cotto**	*po-ko kot-to*
stale	**andato a male**	*an-da-to a ma-leh*

cold	**freddo**	*fred-do*
too salty	**troppo salato**	*trop-po sa-la-to*
overcooked	**stracotto**	*stra-kot-to*
This isn't fresh	**Questo non è fresco**	*Kwes-to non eh fres-ko*
This plate/knife/spoon/glass is not clean	**Questo piatto/coltello/cucchiaio/bicchiere è sporco**	*Kwes-to pyat-to/kol-tel-lo/koo-kya-yo/bee-kyair-eh eh spor-ko*
I'd like to see the head waiter	**Mi fa vedere il capocameriere**	*Mee fa ve-dair-eh eel ka-po-ka-mair-yair-eh*
I'm sorry, I will bring you another	***Mi scusi, gliene porto un altro/un'altra**	*Mee skoo-zee, lye-ne por-to oon al-tro/oon-al-tra*

Breakfast and Tea

A coffee[1]	**Un caffè**	*Oon kaf-feh*
double (shot)	**lungo**	*loon-go*
single (shot)	**ristretto**	*ree-stret-to*
with a dash of milk	**macchiato**	*ma-kyat-to*
with a shot of alcohol	**corretto**	*kor-ret-to*
americano	**Nescaffé**	*Nescaffé*
coffee with milk	**caffelatte**	*kaf-fe-lat-teh*
cappuccino	**cappuccino**	*kap-poo-chee-no*
decaffeinated	**decaffeinato**	*de-kaf-fay-na-to*

1. A coffee in Italy is always an espresso, unless you specify a different kind.

breakfast	la colazione	ko-lat-syo-neh
What time is breakfast served?	A che ora servono la colazione?	A keh or-a *sair*-vo-no la ko-lat-syo-neh
A cup of tea/a herb tea, please	Un tè/una tisana, per favore	Oon teh/oon-a tee-za-na, pair fa-vor-eh
I'd like tea with milk/lemon	Vorrei tè con latte/al limone	Vor-**ray** teh kon lat-teh/al lee-mo-neh
A cup of chocolate	Una tazza di cioccolata	Oon-a tat-sa dee cho-ko-la-ta
Hot/cold milk	Latte caldo/freddo	Lat-teh kal-do/fred-do
May we have some sugar, please?	Lo zucchero, per favore	Lo **tsoo**-ke-ro, pair fa-vor-eh
Do you have sweeteners?	Ha dei dolcificanti?	A day dol-chee-fee-kan-tee
a roll and butter	un panino con burro	oon pa-nee-no kon boor-ro
bread	il pane	pa-neh
toast	il pane tostato	pa-neh tos-ta-to
We'd like more butter, please	Vorremmo ancora del burro, per favore	Vor-rem-mo an-kor-a del boor-ro, pair fa-vor-eh
Do you have some jam/marmalade?	Ha della marmellata/marmellata d'aranci?	A del-la mar-mel-la-ta/mar-mel-la-ta dar-an-chee
I'd like	Vorrei	Vor-**ray**
a hard-boiled egg	un uovo sodo	oon wo-vo so-do
soft-boiled egg	un uovo à la coque	oon wo-vo a la kok

fried eggs	**delle uova fritte**	*del-leh wo-va freet-teh*
scrambled eggs	**delle uove strapazzate**	*del-leh wo-va stra-pat-sa-teh*
What fruit juices do you have?	**Che succhi di frutta ha?**	*Keh sook-kee dee froot-ta a*
Orange/grapefruit/peach juice	**Un succo d'arancio/di pompelmo/di pesca**	*Oon sook-ko dar-an-cho/dee pom-pel-mo/dee pes-ka*
cereal	**i fiocchi d'avena**	*fyok-kee da-ve-na*
fresh fruit	**la frutta fresca**	*froot-ta fres-ka*
yogurt	**un yogurt**	*yo-**goort***
Help yourself at the buffet	***Servitevi al buffet**	*Sair-**vee**-te-vee al buffet*
We'd like a selection of pastries	**Vorremmo dei pasticcini**	*Vor-rem-mo day pas-tee-chee-nee*
Do you have ice creams or sorbets?	**Avete gelati o sorbetti?**	*A-ve-te je-la-tee o sor-bet-tee*
What flavours would you like?	***Che gusto desidera?**	*Keh gu-sto de-**zee**-dair-a*
We have chocolate/vanilla/strawberry/pistachio/lemon	***Abbiamo cioccolato/vaniglia/fragola/pistacchio/limone**	*Ab-bya-mo cho-ko-la-to/va-nee-lya/**fra**-go-la/pee-stak-kyo/lee-mo-neh*
a pastry	**pasticcino**	*pas-tee-chee-no*
a slice of cake	**una fetta di torta**	*fet-ta dee tor-ta*
a de-caf coffee	**un caffè decaffeinato**	*oon kaf-**feh** de-ka-fay-na-to*
an iced coffee	**un caffè freddo**	*oon kaf-**feh** fred-do*

ice cream (*flavours*, gusti *see above*)	**il gelato**	*je-la-to*
hot chocolate	**una cioccolata**	*chok-ko-la-ta*
iced tea	**un tè freddo**	*teh fred-do*
China tea	**un tè cinese**	*teh chee-ne-se*
tea with lemon	**un tè con limone**	*teh kon lee-mo-neh*
black tea	**un tè nero**	*teh ne-ro*
tea with milk	**un tè con latte**	*teh kon lat-teh*
camomile tea	**una camomilla**	*ka-mo-meel-la*
herbal tea	**una tisana**	*tee-za-na*
mint tea	**un tè alla menta**	*teh al-la men-ta*

Drinks[1]

What will you have to drink?	***Cosa desidera bere?**	*Ko-za de-**zee**-dair-a be-reh*
A bottle of the local wine, please	**Una bottiglia di vino locale, per favore**	*Oon-a bot-teel-ya dee vee-no lo-**ka**-leh, pair fa-vor-eh*
Do you serve wine by the glass?	**Vende vino a bicchieri?**	*Ven-deh vee-no a beek-kyair-ee*
Carafe/glass	**Una caraffa/un bicchiere**	*Oon-a ka-raf-fa/oon beek-kyair-eh*
Bottle/half bottle	**Una bottiglia/una mezza bottiglia**	*Oon-a bot-teel-ya/oon-a med-za bot-teel-ya*

1. For a list of drinks, see p. 130.

Do you serve cocktails?	**Si servono cocktail?**	*See sair-vo-no cocktail*
Two glasses of beer, please	**Due birre, per favore**	*Doo-eh beer-reh, pair fa-vor-eh*
Do you have draught beer?	**Ha birra alla spina?**	*A beer-ra al-la spee-na*
Two more beers	**Altre due birre**	*Al-treh doo-eh beer-reh*
A large/small beer	**Una birra grande/piccola**	*Oon-a beer-ra gran-deh/peek-ko-la*
I'd like	**Vorrei**	*Vor-ray*
a soft drink	**un analcolico**	*oon a-nal-ko-lee-ko*
an apple juice	**un succo di mela**	*oon sook-ko dee me-la*
an orange juice	**un succo d'arancia**	*oon sook-ko da-ran-cha*
a fruit juice	**un succo di frutta**	*oon sook-ko dee froot-ta*
a milk shake	**un frappé**	*oon frap-peh*
a smoothie	**un frullato**	*oon frool-la-to*
neat	**liscio**	*lee-sho*
on the rocks	**con ghiaccio**	*kon gya-cho*
with soda water	**. . . e soda**	*. . . eh so-da*
with water	**. . . e acqua**	*. . . eh ak-wa*
ice cubes	**i cubetti di ghiaccio**	*ku-bet-tee dee gya-cho*
mineral water (fizzy/still)	**l'acqua minerale (gassata/non gassata)**	*ak-wa meen-air-al-eh (gaz-za-ta/non gaz-za-ta)*
Cheers!	**Salute!/Cin cin!**	*Sa-luh-teh/Cheen-cheen*

I'd like another glass of water, please	**Vorrei un altro bicchiere d'acqua, per favore**	*Vor-__ray__ oon al-tro beek-kyair-eh dak-wa, pair fa-vor-eh*
The same again, please	**Lo stesso, per favore**	*Lo stes-so, pair fa-vor-eh*
Three coffees and one with cream	**Tre caffè uno con panna**	*Treh kaf-__feh__ oon-o kon pan-na*

Quick Meals and Snacks

snack bar	**la tavola calda**	*__ta__-vo-la kal-da*
What is there to eat?	**Cosa c'è da mangiare?**	*Ko-za cheh da man-ja re*
We are in a hurry, what can you suggest that won't take long?	**Abbiamo fretta, ci consiglia qualcosa di veloce?**	*Ab-bya-mo fret-ta, chee kon-see-lya kwal-ko-za dee ve-lo-cheh*
I only want a snack	**Voglio solo uno spuntino**	*Vol-yo so-lo oon-o spoon-tee-no*
To eat here or to take away?	***Da mangiar qui o da portar via?**	*Da man-jar kwee o da por-__tar__ vee-a*
It's to take away	**È da portar via**	*Eh da por-__tar__ vee-a*
What rolls/ sandwiches do you have?	**Che panini/ tramezzini avete?**	*Ke pa-nee-nee/ tra-med-zee-nee a-ve-te*
cheese	**il formaggio**	*for-mad-jo*
ham (cooked)	**il prosciutto cotto**	*pro-shoot-to kot-to*
Parma ham (cured)	**il prosciutto crudo**	*pro-shoot-to kroo-do*

salami	il salame	sa-la-meh
tuna and egg	tonno e uovo	ton-no eh wo-vo
toasted bread with ham and cheese	il toast con prosciutto e formaggio	toast kon pro-shoot-to eh for-mad-jo
with grilled vegetables	con verdure grigliate	kon ver-door-eh greel-ya-teh
vegetarian	vegetariano	ve-je-ta-rya-no
I'm sorry, we've run out	*Mi dispiace, l'abbiamo finito	Mee dee-spya-cheh, lab-bya-mo fee-nee-to
What is this?	Cos'è questo?	Koz-eh kwes-to
What are they made of?	Di cosa sono fatti?	Dee ko-za so-no fat-tee
What is in them?	Cosa c'è dentro?	Ko-za cheh den-tro
I'll have one of these, please	Me ne dia uno, per favore	Meh neh dee-a oon-o, pair fa-vor-eh
biscuits	i biscotti	bees-kot-tee
bread	il pane	pa-neh
cheese	il formaggio	for-mad-jo
chips	le patatine fritte	pa-ta-tee-neh freet-teh
chocolate bar	la tavoletta di cioccolata	ta-vo-let-ta dee cho-ko-la-ta
egg/eggs	l'uovo/uova m	wo-vo/wo-va
omelette	la frittata	freet-ta-ta
pancakes	le frittelle	freet-tel-leh
pastries	le paste/i pasticcini	pas-teh/pas-tee-chee-nee

pickles	**i sottaceti**	*sot-ta-che-tee*
pizza	**la pizza**	*peet-sa*
roll	**il panino**	*pa-nee-no*
salad	**l'insalata** *f*	*een-sa-la-ta*
sausage	**la salsiccia**	*sal-see-cha*
snack	**lo spuntino**	*spoon-tee-no*
soup	**la minestra**	*mee-nes-tra*
tomato	**il pomodoro**	*po-mo-do-ro*
waffles	**le cialde**	*chal-deh*

Restaurant Vocabulary

bill	**il conto**	*kon-to*
bowl	**la scodella**	*sko-del-la*
bread	**il pane**	*pa-neh*
butter	**il burro**	*boor-ro*
course (*dish*)	**la portata/il piatto**	*por-ta-ta/pyat-to*
cream	**la panna**	*pan-na*
cup	**la tazza**	*tat-sa*
coffee cup	**la tazzina**	*tat-see-na*
dessert	**il dolce**	*dol-cheh*
first course/starter	**il primo piatto/ antipasto**	*pree-mo pyat-to/ an-tee-pas-to*
fork	**la forchetta**	*for-ket-ta*

glass	il bicchiere	*beek-kyair-eh*
head waiter	il capocameriere	*ka-po-ka-mair-yair-eh*
hungry (*to be*)	aver fame	*avair fa-meh*
knife	il coltello	*kol-tel-lo*
main course	il piatto principale	*pyat-to preen-chee-pa-leh*
mayonnaise	la maionese	*ma-yo-neh-seh*
menu	il menù	*me-**noo***
mustard	la senape	*se-na-peh*
napkin	la salvietta/ il tovagliolo	*sal-vyet-ta/to-val-yo-lo*
oil	l'olio *m*	*ol-yo*
pepper	il pepe	*pe-peh*
plate	il piatto	*pyat-to*
salt	il sale	*sa-leh*
salt-cellar	la saliera	*sal-yair-a*
sauce	la salsa	*sal-sa*
saucer	il piattino	*pyat-tee-no*
service	il servizio	*sair-veet-syo*
set menu	il menù fisso	*me-**noo** fees-so*
spoon	il cucchiaio	*kook-kya-yo*
tea spoon	il cucchiaino	*kook-kya-ee-no*
straw	la cannuccia	*kan-noo-cha*
sweetener	il dolcificante	*dol-chee-fee-kan-teh*
table	la tavola/il tavolo	***ta**-vo-la/**ta**-vo-lo*

tablecloth	**la tovaglia**	*to-val-ya*
thirsty (*to be*)	**aver sete**	*a-**vair** se-teh*
tip	**la mancia**	*man-cha*
toilets	**i bagni**	*ban-yee*
toothpick	**lo stuzzicadenti**	*stoot-see-ka-den-tee*
vegetarian	**vegetariano**	*ve-je-tar-ya-no*
vinegar	**l'aceto** *m*	*a-che-to*
waiter	**il cameriere**	*ka-mair-yair-eh*
waitress	**la cameriera**	*ka-mair-yair-a*
water	**l'acqua** *f*	*ak-wa*
wine list	**la lista dei vini**	*lees ta day vee-nee*

THE MENU

Minestre / Soups

brodetto / fish soup

brodo di manzo / consommé

brodo di pollo / chicken broth

crema di piselli / cream of pea soup

crema di pollo / cream of chicken soup

fettuccine in brodo / noodle soup

minestra di cipolle / onion soup

minestra di fagioli / bean soup

minestra di lenticchie / lentil soup

minestra di pomodoro / tomato soup

minestra di riso / rice soup

minestrone / vegetable soup with noodles

pasta e fagioli / pasta and beans in broth

pasta in brodo / pasta in broth

stracciatella / broth with beaten egg and cheese

taglierini in brodo / thin noodles in broth

zuppa di cozze / mussel soup

zuppa pavese / consommé with fried bread, poached egg and grated cheese

zuppa di verdura / vegetable soup

Antipasti / Starters

acciughe/alici / anchovies

affettati / cold cuts

antipasto misto / mixed hors d'œuvres

bresaola / dried beef, thinly sliced

calamaretti / small squid

carciofini sott'olio / artichokes in olive oil

carpaccio / raw beef, thinly sliced

coppa / raw smoked ham

cozze / mussels

crostini di mare / shellfish on fried bread

datteri di mare / date-shell mussels

finocchiona / fennel-flavoured salami

frutti di mare / shellfish

funghi sott'olio / mushrooms in olive oil

granchio / crab

insalata di finocchi e cetrioli / fennel and cucumber salad

insalata di frutti di mare / seafood salad

insalata di funghi / salad of raw mushrooms

insalata di riso e scampi / salad of rice and scampi

insalata di tonno / tuna salad

lumache / snails

olive / olives

ostriche / oysters

peperoni con alici e capperi / peppers with anchovies and capers

peperoni sott'olio / peppers in oil

pomodori con tonno / tomatoes stuffed with tuna

prosciutto e melone / Parma ham and melon

prosciutto e fichi / Parma ham and figs

salame / salami

scampi / prawns

sardine / sardines

seppie / cuttlefish

tonno / tuna

totani / squid

uova sode agli spinaci / eggs florentine

uova tonnate / hard boiled eggs in tuna sauce

Pasta Asciutta / Pasta

cannelloni al forno / large tubes of pasta, stuffed and browned in the oven

cappelletti / rings of pasta filled with minced meat

fettuccine alla marinara / ribbon noodles with tomato sauce

gnocchi alla romana / gnocchi made with semolina and egg

gnocchi di patate / gnocchi made with potato, flour and egg

lasagne (verdi) al forno / lasagne (with spinach)

maccheroni / macaroni

pappardelle al sugo di lepre / wide pasta ribbons with hare sauce

penne/rigatoni / large macaroni

ravioli/tortellini / squares of pasta stuffed with meat or spinach and cream cheese

spaghetti alla bolognese / spaghetti with meat sauce

spaghetti al pomodoro / spaghetti with tomato sauce

spaghetti alle vongole / spaghetti with clam sauce

tagliatelle alla bolognese / ribbon noodles with meat sauce

tortellini al sugo di carne / small ravioli with meat sauce

Riso / Rice

risi e bisi / rice with green peas

riso ai gamberi / rice with shrimps

riso e ceci / a broth of rice and chickpeas with tomatoes and spices

riso alla genovese / rice with a sauce of minced beef or veal with vegetables

risotto alla milanese / risotto with butter, saffron, beef marrow and parmesan

risotto alla sbirraglia / risotto with chicken

risotto alla veronese / risotto with mushrooms and ham

risotto di frutti di mare / seafood risotto

risotto di peoci (di cozze) / mussel risotto

risotto alla romana / risotto with lamb and tomatoes

supplì di riso / rice croquettes filled with ham and cheese

Pesce / Fish

anguille / eel

aragosta / rock lobster

baccalà / salt cod

burrida / fish stew

calamari / squid

cappon magro / a pyramid of vegetables and fish

cefalo/muggine / grey mullet

cernia / grouper

coda di rospo / monkfish

cozze / mussels

fritto misto / mixed fried fish and seafood

gamberi / shrimps

granchio di mare / crab

merluzzo / hake

nasello / whiting

pagro / sea bream

pesce alla griglia / grilled fish

pesce arrosto / baked or roast fish

pesce fritto / fried fish

pesce San Pietro / John Dory

pesce spada / swordfish

polpi / octopus

ricci / sea urchins

salmone / salmon

sarde/sardine / sardines

scampi / prawns

seppie / cuttlefish

sgombro / mackerel

sogliola / sole

spigola / sea bass

storione / sturgeon

tonno / tuna

totani / squid

triglia / red mullet

trota / trout

ventresca / white meat tuna

vongole / small clams

Carne / Meat

agnello / lamb

animelle alla salvia / sweetbreads with sage

arista / roast loin of pork

bistecca alla pizzaiola / steak with tomato and garlic sauce

bollito / dish of slow cooked meats

braciola / rib steak

braciola di maiale / pork chop

capretto / kid

cervella / brain

cotechino / spicy pork sausage

cotoletta alla bolognese / fried veal cutlet with ham and tomato

cotoletta alla milanese / veal cutlet coated in egg and breadcrumbs and fried

fegato (alla veneziana) / liver (with onions)

filetto / fillet

girello / rump

lingua / tongue

maiale / pork

manzo / beef

manzo stufato al vino rosso / beef stewed in red wine

ossobuco alla milanese / stewed shin of veal with tomatoes, garlic and white wine

piccata di vitello / veal cooked with lemon and parsley

polpette / meat balls

polpettone / meat roll

porchetta / roast suckling pig

prosciutto affumicato / gammon

rognoncini al vino bianco / kidneys in white wine sauce

salsicce di maiale / pork sausages

saltimbocca alla romana / rolls of veal with ham

scaloppa milanese / escalope coated in egg and breadcrumbs and fried

scaloppa napoletana / escalope coated in breadcrumbs and fried, with tomato sauce

scaloppine al marsala / small escalopes in marsala sauce

scaloppine al vino bianco / small escalopes in white wine sauce

spezzatino di vitello / veal stew

stracotto / beef stew with pork sausage

trippa / tripe

vitello / veal

vitello tonnato / cold veal with tuna sauce

zampone di maiale / stuffed pig's trotter

Pollame e Cacciagone / Poultry and Game

anatra / duck

beccaccia / woodcock

cervo / venison

cinghiale / boar

coniglio / rabbit

fagiano / pheasant

faraona / guinea-fowl

lepre / hare

oca / goose

pernice / partridge

petto di pollo / chicken breast

piccione / pigeon

pollo / chicken

quaglie / quails

tacchino / turkey

tordi / thrush

uccelletti / small birds of all kinds

Contorni / Vegetables

acetosella / sorrel

aglio / garlic

arugula, rucola / rocket

asparagi / asparagus

barbabietola / beetroot

bietola / chard

caponata / cold dish of aubergines, courgettes and tomatoes

carciofi / artichokes

carote / carrots

castagne / chestnuts

cavolfiore / cauliflower

cavoli / cabbage

cavolini di bruxelles / brussels sprouts

ceci / chickpeas

cetriolo / cucumber

cipolla / onion

fagioli / dried white beans

fagiolini / green beans

fave / broad beans

finocchio / fennel

funghi / mushrooms

insalata verde / green salad

lattuga / lettuce

lenticchie / lentils

melanzane / aubergine, egg plant

patate / potatoes

peperonata / tomatoes, peppers and onions stewed together

peperoni / peppers

piselli / peas

polenta / cornmeal

pomodoro / tomato

porro / leek

radicchio / red chicory

ravanelli / radishes

rape / turnip

scarola / endive

sedano / celery

spinaci / spinach

zucchini / courgettes

Uova / Eggs

frittata / omelette

frittata al pomodoro / tomato omelette

frittata al prosciutto / ham omelette

frittata con spinaci / spinach omelette

uova al tegame con formaggio / fried eggs with cheese

uova alla coque / soft boiled eggs

uova sode / hard boiled eggs

uova strapazzate / scrambled eggs

Dolci / Desserts

amaretti / macaroons

budino alla toscana / cream cheese with raisins, almonds, sugar and egg yolks

cassata alla siciliana / ice cream with candied fruit

gelato al cioccolato / chocolate ice cream

gelato alle fragola / strawberry ice cream

gelato al limone / lemon ice cream

macedonia di frutta / fruit salad

Mont Blanc / puree of chestnuts with whipped cream

panettone / spiced cake with sultanas

panna montata / whipped cream

ricotta al maraschino / curd cheese with maraschino

tartufi al cioccolata / chocolate truffles

torrone / nougat

torta / gateau, cake

torta di cioccolata / chocolate cake

tortiglione / almond cakes

torta di mele / apple tart

zabaione / zabaglione

zuppa inglese / trifle

Frutta e Noci / Fruit and Nuts

albicocche / apricots

ananas / pineapple

arancia / orange

ciliege / cherries

cocomero/anguria / watermelon

datteri / dates

fichi / figs

fragole (di bosco) / (wild) strawberries

lamponi / raspberries

mandarini / tangerines

mandorle / almonds

mela / apple

melone / melon

mirtilli / blueberries

noci / walnuts

pera / pear

pesca / peach

pompelmo / grapefruit

prugna / plum

uva / grape

Some Cooking Methods and Sauces

al vapore / steamed

affumicato / smoked

ain agrodolce / with a dressing of vinegar or lemon juice and sugar

al burro / with butter

al forno / baked

al pesto / with basil, oil and garlic sauce

al ragù / stewed with vegetables

al sugo / with sauce

alla bolognese / with meat sauce

alla griglia / grilled

alla napoletana / with tomato sauce

alla panna / with cream

alla pizzaiola / with tomato and garlic sauce

arrosto / roast

bollito / boiled

carne / meat

  al sangue / rare

  media / medium

  ben cotta / well done

casareccio / home made

con aglio / with garlic

con bagna cauda / hot sauce of olive oil, garlic and anchovy for dipping raw vegetables

con pomodoro / with tomato

crudo / raw

fritto / fried

in camicia / poached

in padella / fried

in umido / stewed

marinato / marinated

passato / puréed

ripieno / stuffed

salsa verde / sauce made from oil, lemon juice, capers, parsley and garlic

stufato / braised

trifolato / with truffles

Bevande / Drinks

acqua minerale / mineral water

amaro / bitters

aranciata / orangeade

birra / beer

  alla spina / draught

  bionda / light

  in bottiglia / bottled

  in lattina / in a can

  scura / dark

brandy / brandy

caffè/caffè nero/espresso / black coffee

caffelatte/cappuccino / white coffee

caffè con panna / coffee with cream

cioccolata / hot chocolate

frullato/frappé / smoothie / milk shake

grappa / spirit made from grape pressings

limonata / lemonade

succo di frutta / fruit juice

succo di albicocca / apricot juice

succo d' arancia / orange juice

succo d' mela / apple juice

succo di mirtilli / blueberry juice

succo di uva / grape juice

tè cinese / China tea

tè indiano / Indian tea

tisana / herb tea

   al tiglio / lime

   alla menta / mint

   camomilla / camomile

vino / wine

   bianco / white

   rosso / red

   dolce / sweet

   secco / dry

   spumante / sparkling

EMERGENCIES[1]

Key Phrases		
Help!	**Aiuto!**	*A-yoo-to*
Danger!	**Pericolo!**	*Pair-**ee**-co-lo*
Call the police/ the emergency number (112)	**Chiami la polizia/ il numero d'emergenza (il cento dodici)**	*Kya-mee la po-leet-see-a/ eel **noo**-mair-o de-mair- jent-sa (eel chen-to **do**- dee-chee)*
Call a doctor	**Chiami un medico**	*Kya-mee oon **me**-dee-ko*
Call an ambulance	**Chiami un'ambulanza**	*Kya-mee oon-am-boo- lant-sa*
Where is the nearest A&E/ER/hospital?	**Dov'è il Pronto Soccorso/l'ospedale più vicino?**	*Dov-eh eel pron-to sok- kor-so/lo-spe-da-leh pyoo vee-chee-no*
Fire brigade	**i vigili del fuoco/ pompieri**	*vee-gee-lee del fwo-ko pomp-yair-ee*
My son/daughter is lost	**Mio figlio/mia figlia si è perso/persa**	*Mee-o feel-yo/mee-a feel-ya see eh pair-so/ pair-sa*

Where's the police station?	**Dov'è il posto/la stazione di polizia?**	*Dov-**eh** eel pos-to/ la stat-syo-neh dee po-leet-see-a*

1. For car breakdown see p37. For problems with a house rental see p84.

Call the police/ the emergency number (112)[1]	**Chiami la polizia/ il numero d'emergenza (il cento dodici)**	*Kya-mee la po-leet-see-a/ eel **noo**-mair-o de-mair-jent-sa (eel chen-to **do**-dee-chee)*
Where is the British consulate?	**Dov'è il consolato britannico?**	*Dov-**eh** eel kon-so-la-to bree-**tan**-nee-ko*
I want to speak to someone from the embassy	**Voglio parlare con qualcuno dell'ambasciata**	*Vol-yo par-lar-re kon kwal-koo-no del-lam-ba-sha-ta*
Please let the consulate know	**Informi il consolato, per favore**	*Een-for-mee eel kon-so-la-to, pair fa-vor-eh*
I want a lawyer who speaks English	**Voglio un avvocato che parla inglese**	*Vol-yo oon av-vo-ka-to keh par-la een-gle-zeh*
It's urgent	**È urgente**	*Eh oor-jen-teh*
Can you help me?	**Può aiutarmi?**	*Pwo ay-oo-tar-mee*

1. The control of traffic is performed by the **vigili urbani** as well as by **pubblica sicurezza** and the **carabinieri**, who are in fact a branch of the army. The **carabinieri** also perform other police duties, and on entering most towns and villages there is a notice which gives the telephone number of the local police under the words **pronto intervento**. Most other police work is done by officers of the **questura**, who combine some of the functions of a district attorney's department and the CID. Both the **vigili** and the **carabinieri** are empowered to give on-the-spot fines, for which they issue a receipt. These are best paid immediately – to dispute them is often time-consuming and comparatively expensive; but the police usually do no more than warn foreign visitors unless the offence is particularly blatant. In the event of an accident call the police. It is essential to get full details of the other driver's insurance, licence and registration.

Accidents[1]

Call a doctor	**Chiami un medico**	*Kya-mee oon **me**-dee-ko*
Call an ambulance	**Chiami un'ambulanza**	*Kya-mee oon-am-boo-lant-sa*
Where is the nearest A&E/ER/hospital?	**Dov'è il Pronto Soccorso/l'ospedale più vicino?**	*Dov-eh eel pron-to sok-kor-so/lo-spe-da-leh pyoo vee-chee-no*
paramedics	**i paramedici**	*pa-ra-**me**-dee-chee*
fire brigade	**i vigili del fuoco/pompieri**	*vee-gee-lee del fwo-ko pomp-yair-ee*
lifeguard	**il bagnino**	*ba-ny-no*
There has been an accident	**C'è stato un incidente**	*Cheh sta-to oon een-chee-den-teh*
Is anyone hurt?	**Qualcuno si è ferito?**	*Kwal-koo-no see eh fe-ree-to*
Do you need help?	**Ha bisogno di aiuto?**	*A bee-zon-yo dee ay-oo-to*
First aid, quickly	**Il pronto soccorso, subito**	*Eel pron-to sok-kor-so, **soo**-bee-to*
Emergency exit	**Uscita d'emergenza/di sicurezza**	*Oo-shee-ta de-mair-jent-sa/dee see-koo-ret-sa*
(Fire) extinguisher	**Estintore (del fuoco)**	*Es-teen-to-reh (del fwo-ko)*
He's badly hurt	**È ferito gravemente**	*Eh fe-ree-to gra-ve-men-teh*
He has fainted	**È svenuto**	*Eh zve-noo-to*
He's losing blood	**Perde sangue**	*Pair-deh san-gweh*

1. See Doctor (p. 146)

Her arm is broken	Si è rotta la braccia	*See eh rot-ta la bra-cha*
Please get some water/a blanket/some bandages	Porti un po' d'acqua/una coperta/delle fascie, per favore	*Por-tee oon po dak-wa/oon-a ko-pair-ta/del-le fa-sheh, pair fa-vor-eh*
I've broken my glasses	Ho rotto gli occhiali	*O rot-to lyee ok-kya-lee*
I can't see	Non riesco a vedere	*Non ree-es-ko a ve-dair-eh*
A child has fallen in the water	Un bambino/ragazzo è caduto nell'acqua	*Oon bam-bee-no/ra-gat-so eh ka-doo-to nel-lak-wa*
S/he is drowning	Sta annegando	*Sta an-neg-an-do*
S/he can't swim	Non sa nuotare	*Non sa nwo-ta-reh*
There's a fire	C'è un incendio	*Cheh oon een-chen-dyo*
I had an accident	Ho avuto un incidente	*O a-voo-to oon een-chee-den-teh*
The other driver hit my car	L'altro autista ha urtato la mia macchina	*Lal-tro ow-tees-ta a oor-ta-to la mee-a mak-kee-na*
It was my fault/his fault	È stata colpa mia/sua	*Eh sta-ta kol-pa mee-a/soo-a*
I didn't understand the sign	Non ho capito il cartello	*Non o ka-pee-to eel kar-tel-lo*
May I see your insurance certificate?	*Posso vedere il suo certificato d'assicurazione?	*Pos-so ve-dair-eh eel swo chair-tee-fee-ka-to das-see-koo-rat-syo-neh*
driving licence	la patente	*pa-ten-teh*
vehicle registration papers	il libretto di circolazione	*lee-bret-to dee cheer-ko-lat-syo-neh*

What is the owner's name and address	*Qual'è il nome e l'indirizzo del proprietario?	Kwal-eh eel no-meh eh leen-dee-reet-so del prop-rye-tar-yo
Are you willing to act as a witness?	*È disposto a far da testimone?	Eh dees-pos-to a far da tes-tee-mo-neh
Can I have your name and address, please?	Vuol darmi il suo nome e indirizzo, per favore?	Vwol dar-mee eel soo-o no-meh eh een-dee-reet-so, pair fa-vor-eh
You must make a statement/report	*Deve fare denuncia	De-veh fa-reh de-noon-cha
I want a copy of the police report	Voglio una copia del verbale di polizia	Vol-yo oon-a ko-pya del vair-ba-leh dee po-leet-see-a
You were speeding	*Stava andando ad alta velocità	Sta-va an-dan-do ad al-ta ve-lo-chee-ta
How much is the fine?	Quant'è la multa?	Kwant-eh la mool-ta
Apply to the insurance company	*Si rivolga alla compagnia d'assicurazione	See ree-vol-ga al-la kom-pan-yee-a das-see-koo-rat-syo-neh

Lost Property

My luggage	Il mio bagaglio	Eel mee-o ba-ga-lyo
is missing	è andato perso	eh an-da-to pair-so
has been damaged	è stato danneggiato	eh sta-to da-ned-ja-to
Has my luggage been found yet?	È stato trovato il mio bagaglio?	Eh sta-to tro-va-to eel mee-o ba-gal-yo

I have lost	**Ho perso**	*O pair-so*
my luggage	**il mio bagaglio**	*eel mee-o ba-gal-yo*
my passport	**il mio passaporto**	*eel mee-o pas-sa-por-to*
my credit card	**la mia carta di credito**	*la mee-a kar-ta dee kre-dee-to*
my camcorder	**la mia videocamera**	*la mee-a video-ka-mair-a*
my mobile phone	**il mio telefonino**	*eel mee-o te-le-fo-nee-no*
my keys	**le mie chiavi**	*le mee-eh kya-vee*
I've locked myself out	**Mi sono chiuso/ chiusa fuori**	*Mee so-no kyoo-zo/ kyoo-za fwo-ree*
Where is the lost property office?	**Dov'è l'ufficio oggetti smarriti?**	*Dov-eh loof-fee-cho od-jet-tee zmar-ree-tee*
I found this in the street	**Ho trovato questo per la strada**	*O tro-va-to kwes-to pair la stra-da*

Missing Persons

My son/daughter is lost	**Mio figlio/mia figlia si è perso/persa**	*Mee-o feel-yo/mee-a feel-ya see eh pair-so/pair-sa*
He/she is . . . years old, and was wearing a blue shirt and shorts	**(Lui/lei) ha . . . anni, e indossava una maglietta blu e dei pantaloncini**	*(Loo-ee/lay) a . . . an-nee, eh een-dos-sa-va oon-a mal-yet-ta eh day pan-ta-lon-chee-nee*
This is his/her photo	**Questa è la sua foto**	*Kwes-ta eh la soo-a fo-to*
Could you help me find him/her?	**Potreste aiutarmi a trovarlo/la?**	*Pot-res-teh ay-oo-tar-mee a tro-var-lo/tro-var-la*

Have you seen a small girl with brown curly hair?	**Avete visto una bambina con capelli corti ricci?**	*A-ve-teh vee-sto oon-a bam-bee-na kon ka-pel-lee kor-tee ree-chee*
I've lost my wife/husband	**Ho perso mia moglie/mio marito**	*O pair-so mee-a mol-yeh/mee-o ma-ree-to*
Could you please ask for me over the loudspeaker?	**Potrebbe fare l'annuncio (all'autoparlante) da parte mia?**	*Pot-reb-beh fa-reh lan-noon-cho (al-low-to-par-lan-teh) da par-teh mee-a*

Theft

I've been robbed/mugged	**Mi hanno rubato/violato**	*Mee an-no roo-ba-to/vee-o-la-to*
Did you have any jewellery/valuables on you?	***Aveva dei gioielli/cose di valore con sè?**	*A-ve-va day joy-el-lee/ko-zeh dee va-lo-re kon seh*
Were there any witnesses?	***C'erano dei testimoni?**	*Che-ra-no day tes-tee-mo-nee*
My bag/wallet has been stolen	**Mi hanno rubato la borsa/il portafoglio**	*Mee an-no roo-ba-to la bor-sa/eel por-ta-fol-yo*
Some things have been stolen from our car	**Sono state rubate delle cose dalla mia macchina**	*So-no sta-teh roo-ba-teh del-leh ko-zeh dal-la mee-a mak-kee-na*
It was stolen from our room	**È stato rubato dalla nostra camera**	*Eh sta-to roo-ba-to dal-la nos-tra ka-mair-ra*

ENTERTAINMENT

Key Phrases

Is there an entertainment guide?	**C'è una guida degli spettacoli?**	*Cheh oon-a gwee-da del-yee spet-ta-ko-lee*
What is there for children (to do)?	**Cosa c'è (da fare) per bambini?**	*Ko-za cheh (da fa-re) pair bam-bee-nee*
Do you have a programme for the festival?	**Avete un programma del festival?**	*A-ve-teh oon pro-gram-ma del festival*
The cheapest seats please	**I posti meno cari, per favore**	*Ee pos-tee me-no ka-ree, pair fa-vor-eh*

What is there to see/ to do here?	**Che cosa c'è da vedere/fare qui?**	*Ko-za cheh da ve-dair-eh/ fa-reh kwee*
Is the circus on?	**C'è il circo?**	*Cheh eel cheer-ko*
What time is the firework display?	**A che ora fanno i fuochi d'artificio?**	*A keh o-ra fan-no ee fwo-kee dar-tee-fee-cho*
How far is it to the amusement park?	**Quanto dista il parco dei divertimenti?**	*Kwan-to dee-sta eel par-ko day dee-vair-tee- men-tee*
Is there a casino?	**C'è un casinò?**	*Cheh oon ka-zee-no*

Booking Tickets

I want two seats for tonight/the matinée tomorrow	**Due posti per stasera/per il matinée di domani**	*Doo-eh pos-tee pair sta-se-ra/pair eel ma-tee-neh dee do-ma-nee*
I want to book seats for Thursday	**Vorrei riservare dei posti per giovedì**	*Vor-ray ree-zair-var-eh day pos-tee pair jo-ve-dee*
Is the matinée sold out?	**E tutto esaurito per il matinée?**	*Eh toot-to e-zow-ree-to pair eel ma-tee-neh*
Where do you want to sit?	***Dove vuole sedersi?**	*Do-veh vwo-leh sed-er-see*
I'd like seats	**Desidero posti**	*De-zee-dair-o pos-tee*
in the stalls	**in platea**	*een pla-te-a*
in the circle	**in gallería**	*een gal-lair-ee-a*
in the gallery	**in loggione**	*een lod-jo-neh*
at a table at the front	**in un tavolo davanti**	*een oon ta-vo-lo da-van-tee*
The cheapest seats please	**I posti meno cari, per favore**	*Ee pos-tee me-no ka-ree, pair fa-vor-eh*
Are there any concessions?	**Ci sono delle concessioni/degli sconti?**	*Chee sono del-leh kon-ches-syo-nee/del-yee skon-tee*
Are they good seats?	**Sono dei posti buoni?**	*So-no day pos-tee bwo-nee*
Where are these seats?	**Dove si trovano questi posti?**	*Do-veh see tro-va-no kwes-tee pos-tee*
We've sold out (for this performance)	***Tutto esaurito (per questa rappresentazione)**	*Toot-to ez-ow-ree-to (pair kwes-ta rap-pre-zen-tat-syo-neh)*

Everything is sold out	***È tutto venduto**	*Eh toot-to ven-doo-to*
Standing room only	***Solo posti in piedi**	*So-lo po-stee een pye-dee*
Pick the tickets up before the performance	***Prenda i biglietti prima dello spettacolo**	*Pren-da ee beel-yet-tee pree-ma del-lo spet-ta-ko-lo*
This is your seat	***Ecco il suo posto**	*Ek-ko eel swo pos-to*

Cinema, Theatre and Live Music

chamber music	**la musica da camera**	***moo**-see-ka da **ka**-mair-a*
modern dance	**la danza moderna**	*dant-sa mo-dair-na*
play	**lo spettacolo**	*spet-**ta**-ko-lo*
recital	**la recita**	***re**-chee-ta*
Can you recommend	**Può consigliarmi**	*Pwo kon-seel-yar-mee*
a film?	**un film?**	*oon film*
a musical?	**un operetta?**	*oon op-pair-et-ta*
Can you recommend a good show?	**Può raccomandarmi un buon spettacolo?**	*Pwo rak-ko-man-dar-mee oon bwon spet-**ta**-ko-lo*
What's on at the theatre/cinema?	**Cosa danno al teatro/al cinema?**	*Ko-za dan-no al te-at-ro/ al **chee**-ne-ma*
Is it the original version?	**È la versione originale?**	*Eh la ver-syo-neh o-ree-jee-na-leh*
Are there subtitles?	**Ci sono sottotitoli?**	*Chee so-no sot-to-**tee**-to-lee*
Is it dubbed?	**È doppiato?**	*Eh dop-pya-to*

Is there a concert on this evening?	C'è un concerto stasera?	*Cheh oon kon-chair-to sta-se-ra*
Is there a support band?	C'è una banda di accompagnamento?	*Cheh oon-a ban-da dee ak-kom-pan-ya-men-to*
What time does the main band start?	A che ora inizia la banda?	*A keh or-a ee-neet-sya la ban-da*
Who is directing/ conducting?	Chi è il direttore/il maestro?	*Kee eh eel dee-ret-tor-eh/ eel ma-es-tro*
Who is singing?	Chi canta?	*Kee kan-ta*
Who is acting?	Chi recita?	*Kee re-chee-ta*
What time does the performance start?	A che ora comincia lo spettacolo?	*A keh or-a ko-meen-cha lo spet-ta-ko-lo*
What time does it end?	A che ora finisce?	*A keh or-a fee-nee-sheh*
Where is the cloakroom?	Dov'è il guardaroba?	*Dov-eh eel gwar-da-ro-ba*
A programme, please	Un programma, per favore	*Oon pro-gram-ma, pair fa-vor-eh*

Clubs and Discos

Where are the best nightclubs?	Dove sono i migliori locali notturni?	*Do-veh so-no ee meel-yor-ee lo-ka-lee not-toor-nee*
Is there a jazz club here?	C'è un club (di musica) jazz qui (vicino)?	*Cheh oon klab (dee moo-zee-ka) jazz kwee (vee-chee-no)*
Where is the best disco?	Dov'è la discoteca migliore?	*Dov-eh la dees-ko-te-ka meel-yor-eh*

Where can we go dancing?	**Dove si può andare a ballare?**	*Do-veh see pwo an-dar-eh a bal-lar-eh*
Would you like to dance?	**Vuole ballare?**	*Vwo-leh bal-lar-eh*
What time is the floorshow/the cabaret?	**A che ora comincia lo spettacolo/il cabaret?**	*A keh or-a ko-meen-cha lo spet-**ta**-ko-lo/eel ka-bar-eh*

HEALTH

Dentist

Can I make an appointment with the dentist?	**Posso fissare un appuntamento col dentista?**	*Pos-so fees-sar-eh oon ap-poon-ta-men-to kol den-tees-ta*
As soon as possible	**Il più presto possibile**	*Eel pyoo pres-to pos-see-bee-leh*
This tooth hurts	**Questo dente mi fa male**	*Kwes-to den-teh mee fa ma-leh*
I have a broken tooth	**Ho rotto un dente**	*O rot-to oon den-teh*
I have an abscess	**Ho un ascesso**	*O oon a-shes-so*
I've lost a filling	**Mi è caduta l'otturazione**	*Mee eh ka-doo-ta lot-too-rat-syo-neh*

Can you fill it?	**Può otturarlo?**	*Pwo ot-too-rar-lo*
Must you take the tooth out?	**Mi deve togliere il dente?**	*Mee de-veh tol-yair-eh eel den-teh*
I do not want the tooth taken out	**Non voglio togliermi il dente**	*Non vol-yo tol-yair-mee eel den-teh*
Please give me an anaesthetic	**Per favore, mi faccia l'anestesia**	*Pair fa-vor-eh, mee fa-cha lan-es-te-zee-a*
My gums are swollen/keep bleeding	**Le mie gengive sono gonfie/continuano a sanguinare**	*Leh mee-eh jen-jee-veh so-no gon-fyeh/kon-teen-wa-no a san-gwee-nar-eh*
I have broken/ chipped my dentures	**Mi si è rotta/ scheggiata la dentiera**	*Mee see eh rot-ta/ sked-ja-ta la dent-yair-a*
You're hurting me	**Mi fa male**	*Mee fa ma-leh*
Please rinse your mouth	***Si sciacqui la bocca, per favore**	*See shak-wee la bok-ka, pair fa-vor-eh*
I will X-ray your teeth	***Le faccio la radiografia (ai denti)**	*Le fa-cho la ra-dyo-gra-fee-a (a-ee den-tee)*
You have an abscess	***Ha un ascesso**	*A oon a-shes-so*
The nerve is exposed	***Il nervo è scoperto**	*Eel nair-vo eh sko-pair-to*
This tooth will have to come out	***Questo dente bisogna toglierlo**	*Kwes-to den-teh bee-zon-ya tol-yair-lo*
How much do I owe you?	**Quanto le devo?**	*Kwan-to leh de-vo*
When should I come again?	**Quando devo tornare?**	*Kwan-do de-vo tor-nar-eh*

Doctor

Key Phrases

I must see a doctor, can you recommend one?	**Devo vedere un medico. Può raccomandarmene uno?**	*De-vo ve-dair-eh oon me-dee-ko. Pwo rak-ko-man-dar-me-neh oon-o*
Please call a doctor	**Può chiamarmi un medico, per favore?**	*Pwo kya-mar-mee oon me-dee-ko, pair fa-vor-eh*
I suffer from . . .; here is a list of my medication	**Soffro di . . .; ecco la lista delle medicine che prendo**	*Sof-fro dee . . .; ek-ko la lee-sta del-leh me-dee-chee-neh keh pren-do*
I have a heart condition	**Sono ammalato di cuore**	*So-no am-ma-la-to dee kwo-reh*
I am a diabetic	**Sono diabetico**	*So-no dee-a-**be**-tee-ko*
I suffer from asthma	**Soffro d'asma**	*Sof-fro da-sma*
I have a fever	**Ho la febbre**	*O la feb-breh*
I have an upset stomach	**Ho mal di stomaco**	*O mal dee **sto**-ma-ko*

Is there a doctor's surgery near here?	**C'è un ambulatorio medico qui vicino?**	*Cheh oon am-boo-la-tor-yo me-dee-ko kwee vee-chee-no*
When can the doctor come?	**Quando verrà il medico?**	*Kwan-do ver-**ra** eel me-dee-ko*
Does the doctor speak English?	**Parla inglese il medico?**	*Par-la een-gle-zeh eel me-dee-ko*

| Can I make an appointment for as soon as possible? | Mi può fissare un appuntamento il prima possibile? | *Pos-so far-eh oon ap-poon-ta-men-to eel pree-mo pos-see-bee-leh* |
| I'd like to see a paediatrician | Vorrei vedere un pediatra | *Vor-ray ve-dair-eh oon pe-dya-tra* |

Medication

I take daily medication for ...	Prendo delle medicine giornaliere per ...	*Pren-do del-le med-ee-chee-neh jor-nal-yair-eh pair ...*
I suffer from ...; here is a list of my medication	Soffro di ...; ecco la lista delle medicine che prendo	*Sof-fro dee ...; ek-ko la lee-sta del-leh me-dee-chee-neh keh pren-do*
This is a copy of my UK prescription, can you please prescribe ... for me?	Questa è una copia delle medicine che prendo in Gran Bretagna, può prescrivermi ...?	*Kwe-sta eh oon-a ko-pya del-le me-dee-chee-neh keh pren-do een gran bre-ta-nya, pwo pre-skree-vair-mee ...*

Symptoms and conditions

I am ill	Mi sento poco bene	*Mee sen-to po-ko be-neh*
I feel weak	Mi sento debole	*Mee sen-to de-bo-leh*
I have high/low blood pressure	Soffro di pressione alta/bassa	*Sof-fro dee pres-syo-neh al-ta/bas-sa*
I have a heart condition	Sono ammalato di cuore	*So-no am-ma-la-to dee kwo-reh*
I am a diabetic	Sono diabetico	*So-no dee-a-be-tee-ko*
I suffer from asthma	Soffro d'asma	*Sof-fro da-sma*

I have a fever	**Ho la febbre**	*O la feb-breh*
I've had a high temperature since yesterday	**Ho la febbre alta da ieri**	*O la feb-breh al-ta da yair-ee*
I've a pain in my right/left arm	**Ho un dolore al braccio destro/ sinistro**	*O oon do-lor-eh al bra-cho des-tro/see-nees-tro*
It's a sharp pain/a persistent pain	**Ho un dolore acuto/ persistente**	*O oon do-lor-eh a-koo-to/pair-sees-ten-teh*
My wrist hurts	**Ho male al polso**	*O ma-leh al pol-so*
I think I've sprained/ broken my ankle	**Credo di essermi slogata/rotta la caviglia**	*Cre-do dee **es**-sair-mee zlo-ga-ta/rot-ta la ka-veel-ya*
I fell down and hurt my back	**Sono caduto e mi sono fatto male alla schiena**	*So-no ka-doo-to eh mee so-no fat-to ma-leh al-la skye-na*
My feet are swollen	**Ho i piedi gonfi**	*O ee pye-dee gon-fee*
I've burned/cut/ bruised myself	**Mi sono bruciato/ tagliato/ammaccato**	*Mee so-no broo-cha-to/ tal-ya-to/am-mak-ka-to*
I think it is infected	**Credo che sia infetto**	*Kre-do keh see-a een-fet-to*
I've developed a rash/ an inflammation	**Mi è venuto uno sfogo/ un'infiammazione**	*Mee eh ve-nu-to oon-o zfo-go/oon-een-fyam-mat-syo-neh*
I have an upset stomach	**Ho mal di stomaco**	*O mal dee **sto**-ma-ko*
My appetite's gone	**Non ho appetito**	*Non o ap-pe-tee-to*
I think I've got food poisoning	**Credo di aver mangiato del cibo avariato**	*Kre-do dee a-**vair** man-ja-to del chee-bo a-var-ya-to*

I have indigestion/ diarrhoea	Ho preso una indigestione/ho la diarrea	O pre-zo oon-a een-dee-jes-tyo-neh/o la dee-ar-re-a
I keep vomiting	Mi viene spesso da vomitare	Mee vye-neh spes-so da vo-mee-tar-eh
I can't eat/sleep	Non posso mangiare/dormire	Non pos-so man-jar-eh/dor-meer-eh
My nose keeps bleeding	Mi esce sangue dal naso	Mee e-sheh san-gweh dal na-zo
I have earache	Ho mal d'orecchi	O mal dor-ek-kee
I have difficulty in breathing	Provo difficoltà a respirare	Pro-vo dee-fee-kol-**ta** a res-peer-ar-eh
I feel dizzy	Mi gira la testa	Mee jee-ra la tes-ta
I feel sick/shivery	Ho la nausea/mi vengono i brividi	O la **naw**-ze-a/mee **ven**-go-no ee **bree**-vee-dee
I think I've caught 'flu	Credo di aver preso l'influenza	Kre-do dee a-**vair** pre-zo leen-floo-en-za
I've got a heavy cold	Ho un forte raffreddore	O oon for-teh raf-fred-dor-eh
I've had the cold since yesterday	Sono due giorni che ho il raffreddore	So-no doo-eh jor-nee keh o eel raf-fred-dor-eh
I've had it for a few hours	Ce l'ho da alcune ore	Che lo da al-koo-neh or-eh
abscess	l'ascesso *m*	a-shes-so
ache	il dolore	do-lor-eh
allergy	l'allergia *f*	al-lair-jee-a
appendicitis	l'appendicite *f*	ap-pen-dee-chee-teh
asthma	l'asma	as-ma

back pain	**il mal di schiena**	*mal dee skye-na*
blister	**la vescica**	*ve-shee-ka*
boil	**il foruncolo**	*fo-roon-ko-lo*
bruise	**l'ammaccatura** *f*	*am-mak-ka-too-ra*
burn	**la bruciatura**	*broo-cha-too-ra*
cervical arthrosis	**l'artrosi cervicale** *f*	*ar-tro-zee chair-vee-ka-leh*
chill	**il colpo di freddo**	*kol-po dee fred-do*
cold	**il raffreddore**	*raf-fred-dor-eh*
constipation	**la stitichezza**	*stee-tee-ket-sa*
cough	**la tosse**	*tos-seh*
cramp	**il crampo**	*kram-po*
diabetic	**diabetico**	*dee-a-be-tee-ko*
diarrhoea	**la diarrea**	*dee-ar-re-a*
earache	**il mal d'orecchi**	*mal do-rek-kee*
epilepsy	**l'epilessia** *f*	*eh-pee-leh-see-a*
fever	**la febbre**	*feb-breh*
food poisoning	**l'intossicazione da cibo** *f*	*een-tos-see-kat-syo-neh da chee-bo*
fracture	**la frattura**	*frat-too-ra*
hay fever	**la febbre del fieno**	*feb-breh del fye-no*
headache	**il mal di testa**	*mal dee tes-ta*
heart attack	**l'attacco di cuore/ l'infarto** *m*	*at-tak-ko dee kwo-reh/ een-far-to*
high blood pressure	**l'ipertensione** *f*	*ee-pair-ten-syo-neh*

ill, sick	**ammalato**	*am-ma-la-to*
illness	**la malattia**	*ma-lat-tee-a*
indigestion	**l'indigestione**	*een-dee-jes-tyo-neh*
infection	**l'infezione**	*een-fet-syo-neh*
influenza	**l'influenza**	*een-floo-en-za*
insect bite	**la puntura d'insetto**	*poon-too-ra deen-set-to*
insomnia	**l'insonnia**	*een-son-nya*
itch	**il prurito**	*proo-ree-to*
nose bleed	**la emorragia nasale**	*e-mor-ra-jee-a na-za-leh*
pain	**il dolore**	*do-lor-eh*
rheumatism	**il reumatismo**	*re-oo-ma-teez-mo*
sore throat	**il mal di gola**	*mal dee go-la*
sprain	**lo stiramento/la distorsione**	*stee-ra-men-to/ dees-tor-zyo-neh*
sting	**la puntura**	*poon-too-ra*
stomach ache	**il mal di stomaco**	*mal dee sto-ma-ko*
sunburn	**la scottatura da sole**	*skot-ta-too-ra da so-leh*
sunstroke	**il colpo da sole**	*kol-po da so-leh*
swelling	**il gonfiore**	*gon-fyo-reh*
tonsillitis	**la tonsillite**	*ton-see-lee-teh*
toothache	**il mal di denti**	*mal dee den-tee*
ulcer	**l'ulcera** f	*ool-che-ra*
wound	**la ferita**	*fe-ree-ta*

Diagnosis and treatment

Where does it hurt?	*Dove le fa male?	Do-veh leh fa ma-leh
Do you have a pain here?	*Le fa male qui?	Leh fa ma-leh kwee
For how long?	*Da quanto tempo?	Da kwan-to tem-po
Have you taken your temperature?	*Si è misurata la temperatura?	See eh mee-zoo-ra-ta la tem-pair-a-too-ra
Open your mouth	*Apra la bocca, per favore	Ap-ra la bok-ka, pair fa-vor-eh
Put out your tongue	*Mi faccia vedere la lingua	Mee fa-cha ve-dair-eh la leen-gwa
Breathe in	*Inspiri	In-speer-ee
Breathe out	*Espiri	Eh-speer-ee
Cough	*Tossisca	Tos-see-ska
Hold your breath	*Trattenga il respiro	Trat-ten-ga eel res-peer-o
Does that hurt?	*Le fa male?	Leh fa ma-leh
You're hurting me	Mi fa male	Mee fa ma-leh
A lot or a little?	*Tanto o poco?	Tan-to o po-ko
How long have you had the pain/been suffering from ...?	Da quanto tempo ha questo dolore/soffre di ...?	Da kwan-to tem-po a kwes-to do-lor-eh/ sof-freh dee ...
Please lie down	*Si sdrai, per favore	See zdra-ee, pair fa-vor-eh
I will need a blood/ urine specimen	*Mi occorre un campione del sangue/delle urine	Mee ok-kor-reh oon kam-pyo-neh del san-gweh/del-leh oor-ee-neh

What medicines are you taking?	*Che medicine prende?	Keh me-dee-chee-neh pren-deh
I am pregnant	Sono incinta	So-no een-cheen-ta
I am allergic to . . .	Sono allergico a . . .	So-no al-lair-jee-ko a . . .
Are you being treated for these symptoms?	*È stato curato per questi sintomi?	Eh sta-to koo-ra-to pair kwes-tee seen-to-mee
Can you please prescribe a sleeping pill?	Mi può prescrivere dei sonniferi, per favore?	Mee pwo pre-skree-vair-eh day son-nee-fair-ee, pair fa-vor-eh
I will give you an antibiotic/a sedative/a painkiller	*Le ordinerò degli antibiotici/ un calmante/un antidolorifico	Le or-deen-air-o del-yee an-tee-byo-tee-chee/ oon kal-man-teh/oon an-tee-do-lo-ree-fee-ko
Take this prescription to the chemist	*Porti questa ricetta alla farmacia	Por-tee kwes-ta ree-chet-ta al-la far-ma-chee-a
Take this three times a day	*Prenda questa medicina tre volte al giorno	Pren-da kwes-ta me-dee-chee-na treh vol-teh al jor-no
I'll give you an injection	*Le faccio una iniezione	Le fa-cho oon-a een-yet-syo-neh
Roll up your sleeve	*Si tiri su la manica	See tee-ree soo la ma-nee-ka
You should follow a diet for a few days	*Deve stare a dieta per alcuni giorni	De-veh star-eh a dye-ta pair al-koo-nee jor-nee
You must go to hospital	*Deve ricoverarsi in ospedale	De-veh ree-ko-vair-ar-see een os-pe-da-leh
Your leg must be X-rayed	*Deve farsi fare i raggi X a questa gamba	De-veh far-see far-eh ee rad-jee eeks a kwes-ta gam-ba

You've pulled a muscle	*Ha stirato un muscolo	*A stee-ra-to oon moos-ko-lo*
You have a fracture/sprain	*Ha una frattura/stiratura	*A oon-a frat-too-ra/stee-ra-too-ra*
You need a few stitches	*Ha bisogno di qualche punto	*A bee-zon-yo dee kwal-keh poon-to*
You must stay in bed for a few days	*Deve rimanere a letto per alcuni giorni	*De-veh ree-ma-nair-eh a let-to pair al-koo-nee jor-nee*
Come and see me again in two days' time	*Torni da me tra due giorni	*Tor-nee da meh tra doo-eh jor-nee*
Will you come and see me again?	Tornerà di nuovo a farmi una visita?	*Tor-nair-a dee nwo-vo a far-mee oon-a vee-zee-ta*
Is it serious/contagious?	È serio/contagioso?	*Eh sair-yo/kon-ta-jo-zo*
Nothing to worry about	*Niente di preoccupante	*Nyen-teh dee pre-ok-koo-pan-teh*
I feel better now	Adesso mi sento meglio	*A-des-so mee sen-to mel-yo*
When do you think I can leave?	Quando crede che possa partire?	*Kwan-do kre-deh keh pos-sa par-teer-eh*
You should not travel for at least ... days	*Non si metta in viaggio per almeno ... giorni	*Non see met-ta een vyad-jo pair al-me-no ... jor-nee*
How much do I owe you?	Quanto le devo?	*Kwan-to leh de-vo*
I'd like a receipt for the health insurance	Vorrei una ricevuta per l'assicurazione	*Vor-ray oon-a ree-che-voo-ta pair las-see-koo-rat-syo-neh*

ambulance	l'ambulanza *f*	*am-boo-lant-sa*
anaesthetic	l'anestetico *m*	*an-es-te-tee-ko*
aspirin	l'aspirina *f*	*as-pee-ree-na*
bandage	la fascia	*fa-sha*
chiropodist	il pedicure	*pe-dee-koo-reh*
first aid station	il reparto di pronto soccorso	*eel re-par-to dee pron-to sok-kor-so*
hospital	l'ospedale *m*	*os-pe-da-leh*
injection	l'iniezione *f*	*een-yet-syo-neh*
laxative	il lassativo	*las-sa-tee-vo*
nurse	l'infermiera *f*	*een-fair-mye-ra*
operation	l'operazione *f*	*o-pair-at-syo-neh*
optician	l'ottico *m*	*ot-tee-ko*
ophtalmologist	l'oculista	*o-koo-lee-sta*
osteopath	l'osteopata	*o-ste-o-pa-ta*
paediatrician	il/la pediatra	*pe-dya-tra*
pill	la pastiglia	*pas-teel-ya*
plaster (adhesive)	il cerotto	*chair-ot-to*
prescription	la ricetta	*ree-chet-ta*
X-ray	raggi X	*rad-jee eeks*

Optician

Key Phrases

I have broken my glasses. Can you repair them?	**Ho rotto gli occhiali. Me li può riparare?**	*O rot-to lyee ok-kya-lee. Meh lee pwo ree-pa-rar-eh*
Can you give me a new pair of glasses to the same prescription?	**Posso avere degli occhiali nuovi con la stessa prescrizione?**	*Pos-so a-vair-eh del-yee ok-kya-lee nwo-vee kon la stes-sa pres-kreet-syo-neh*
Please test my eyes	**Potrebbe misurarmi la vista?**	*Pot-reb-beh mee-zoo-rar-mee la vees-ta*
short-sighted	**miope**	*myo-peh*
long-sighted	**presbite**	***prez**-bee-teh*

I have broken the frame/the arm	**Ho rotto la montatura/la stecchetta**	*O rot-to la mon-ta-too-ra/la stek-ket-ta*
When will they be ready?	**Quando saranno pronti?**	*Kwan-do sa-ran-no pron-tee*
I have difficulty with reading/with long-distance vision	**Mi risulta difficile leggere/vedere da lontano**	*Mee ree-zool-ta deef-**fee**-chee-leh **led**-jair-eh/ve-dair-eh da lon-ta-no*
Please test my eyes	**Potrebbe misurarmi la vista?**	*Pot-reb-beh mee-zoo-rar-mee la vees-ta*
I have lost one of my contact lenses	**Ho perso una delle mie lenti a contatto**	*O pair-so oon-a del-leh mee-eh len-tee a kon-tat-to*
I should like to have contact lenses	**Desidero delle lenti a contatto**	*De-**zee**-dair-o del-leh len-tee a kon-tat-to*

| My vision is blurred | **La vista mi si è offuscata** | *La vee-sta mee see eh of-foo-ska-ta* |
| I can't see clearly | **Non ci vedo bene** | *Non chee ve-do be-ne* |

Parts of the Body

ankle	**la caviglia**	*ka-veel-ya*
arm	**il braccio**	*bra-cho*
artery	**l'arteria** *f*	*ar-tair-ya*
back	**la schiena**	*skye-na*
bladder	**la vescica**	*ve-shee-ka*
blood	**il sangue**	*san-gweh*
body	**il corpo**	*kor-po*
bone	**l'ossa**	*os-sa*
bowels	**l'intestino** *m*	*een-tes-tee-no*
brain	**il cervello**	*chair-vel-lo*
breast (women)	**il seno**	*se-no*
breast (men)	**il petto**	*pet-to*
cheek	**la guancia**	*gwan-cha*
chest	**il petto**	*pet-to*
chin	**il mento**	*men-to*
collar-bone	**la clavicola**	*kla-**vee**-ko-la*
ear	**l'orecchio** *m*	*or-rek-kyo*
elbow	**il gomito**	***go**-mee-to*

eye	l'occhio *m*	*ok-kyo*
eyelid	la palpebra	*pal-peb-ra*
face	la faccia	*fa-cha*
finger	il dito	*dee-to*
foot	il piede	*pye-deh*
forehead	la fronte	*fron-teh*
gall bladder	la cistifellea	*chee-stee-fel-le-a*
gum	la gengiva	*jen-jee-va*
hand	la mano	*ma-no*
head	la testa	*tes-ta*
heart	il cuore	*kwor-eh*
heel	il tallone	*tal-lo-neh*
hip	il fianco/l'anca *f*	*fyan-ko/an-ka*
jaw	la mascella	*ma-shel-la*
joint	l'articolazione/la giuntura	*ar-tee-ko-lat-syo-neh/ joon-too-ra*
kidney	il rene	*re-neh*
knee	il ginocchio	*jee-nok-kyo*
knee-cap	la rotula	*ro-too-la*
leg	la gamba	*gam-ba*
lip	il labbro	*lab-bro*
liver	il fegato	*fe-ga-to*
lung	il polmone	*pol-mo-neh*
mouth	la bocca	*bok-ka*

muscle	il muscolo	*moos*-ko-lo
nail	l'unghia *f*	*oon-gya*
neck	il collo	*kol-lo*
nerve	il nervo	*nair-vo*
nose	il naso	*na-zo*
pelvis	la pelvi	*pel-vee*
pulse	il polso	*pol-so*
rib	la costola	*kos*-to-la
shoulder	la spalla	*spal-la*
skin	la pelle	*pel-leh*
spine	la colonna vertebrale/ spina dorsale	*ko-lon-na vair-te-bra-leh/ spee-na dor-sa-leh*
stomach	lo stomaco	*sto-ma-ko*
temple	la tempia	*tem-pya*
thigh	la coscia	*ko-sha*
throat	la gola	*go-la*
thumb	il pollice	*pol*-lee-cheh
toe	il dito	*dee-to*
tongue	la lingua	*leen-gwa*
tonsils	le tonsille	*ton-seel-leh*
tooth	il dente	*den-teh*
vein	la vena	*ve-na*
wrist	il polso	*pol-so*

MEETING PEOPLE

Key Phrases

Glad to meet you	**Lieto di conoscerla**	*Lye-to dee ko-no-shair-la*
How are you?	**Come sta (state *pl*)?**	*Ko-meh sta (sta-teh)*
My name is . . .	**Mi chiamo . . .**	*Mee kya-mo . . .*
I'm on holiday/a business trip	**Sono in vacanza/ in giro d'affari**	*So-no een va-kant-sa/ een jee-ro daf-far-ee*
Would you give me your telephone number?	**Vuol darmi il suo numero di telefono?**	*Vwol dar-mee eel swo noo-mair-o dee te-le-fo-no*
Thank you for the invitation	**Grazie dell'invito**	*Grat-syeh del-leen-vee-to*
I'd like to come	**Sarei lieto di venire**	*Sa-ray lye-to dee ve-neer-eh*
I'm sorry, I can't come	**Mi dispiace, non posso venire**	*Mee dees-pya-cheh, non pos-so ve-neer-eh*

Introductions

May I introduce . . .?	**Posso presentarle . . .?**	*Pos-so pre-zen-tar-leh . . .*
May I introduce myself?	**Posso presentarmi?**	*Pos-so pre-zen-tar-mee*
Have you met . . .?	**Conosce . . .?**	*Ko-no-sheh . . .*

How are things?	**Come va?**	*Ko-meh va*
Fine, thank you; and you?	**Bene, grazie; e lei?**	*Be-neh, grat-syeh; eh lay*
What is your name?	**Come si chiama?**	*Ko-meh see kya-ma*
This is . . .	**Questo/questa è . . .**	*Kwes-to/Kwes-ta eh . . .*
Am I disturbing you?	**La disturbo?**	*La dees-toor-bo*
Sorry to have troubled you	**Mi scusi per il disturbo**	*Mee skoo-zee pair eel dees-toor-bo*
Go away	**Se ne vada**	*Seh neh va-da*
Leave me alone	**Mi lasci in pace**	*Mee la-shee een pa-cheh*

Getting Acquainted

Are you on holiday?	**È qui in vacanza?**	*Eh kwee een va-kant-sa*
Do you travel a lot?	**Viaggia molto?**	*Vyad-ja mol-to*
We've been here a week	**Siamo qui da una settimana**	*Sya-mo kwee da oon-a set-tee-ma-na*
Do you live/are you staying here?	**Vive/sta qui?**	*Vee-veh/sta kwee*
Is this your first time here?	**È la prima volta che lei è qui?**	*Eh la pree-ma vol-ta keh lay eh kwee*
Do you like it here?	**Le piace da queste parti?**	*Leh pya-cheh da kwes-teh par-tee*
Where do you come from?	**Di dov'è?**	*Dee dov-eh*
Which part of Italy do you come from?	**Da che parte d'Italia viene?**	*Da keh par-teh dee-tal-ya vye-neh*

I come from ...	**Vengo da.../ Sono di ...**	*Ven-go da.../ So-no dee ...*
Have you been to England/America?	**È stato in Inghilterra/America?**	*Eh sta-to een een-geel-ter-ra/a-me-ree-ka*
Are you on your own?	**È solo/sola?**	*Eh so-lo/so-la*
I am travelling alone	**Viaggio da solo/sola**	*Vyad-jo da so-lo/so-la*
It's been a pleasure talking to you	**È stato un piacere parlare con lei**	*Eh sta-to oon pya-chair-eh par-lar-eh kon lay*
Can we meet again?	**Possiamo vederci di nuovo?**	*Pos-sya-mo ve-dair-chee dee nwo-vo*

Personal Information

I am with	**Sono qui con**	*So-no kwee kon*
my husband	**mio marito**	*mee-o ma-ree-to*
my wife	**mia moglie**	*mee-a mol-yeh*
my parents	**i miei genitori**	*ee myay je-nee-tor-ee*
my family	**la famiglia**	*la fa-meel-ya*
a friend	**un amico/amica**	*oon a-mee-ko/a-mee-ka*
a colleague	**un/una collega**	*oon/oon-a kol-le-ga*
I have a boyfriend/ girlfriend	**Ho un ragazzo/una ragazza**	*O oon ra-gat-so/oon-a ra-gat-sa*
I live with my partner	**Vivo con il mio compagno/la mia compagna**	*Vee-vo kon eel mee-o kom-pan-yo/la mee-a kom-pan-ya*
I am separated/ divorced	**Sono separato/ separata/divorziato/ divorziata**	*So-no se-pa-ra-to/ se-pa-ra-ta/dee-vort-sya-to/dee-vort-sya-ta*

I am a widower/widow	**Sono vedovo/vedova**	*So-no **ve**-do-vo/**ve**-do-va*
Are you married?	**È sposato?**	*Eh spo-za-to*
Do you have children/ grandchildren?	**Ha dei bambini/ nipoti?**	*A day bam-bee-nee/ nee-po-tee*
What do you do?	**Che lavoro fa?**	*Keh la-vo-ro fa?*
I work for . . .	**Lavoro per . . .**	*La-vo-ro pair . . .*
I am a	**Sono**	*So-no*
student	**studente/ studentessa**	*stoo-den-teh/ stoo-den-tes-sa*
nurse	**infermiere/ infermiera**	*een-fair-mye-reh/ een-fair-mye-ra*
accountant	**ragioniere/ ragioniera**	*ra-jo-nye-reh/ ra-jo-nye-ra*
I work freelance	**Lavoro come freelance**	*La-vo-ro ko-meh freelance*
I'm a consultant	**Sono consulente**	*So-no kon-soo-len-teh*
We're retired	**Siamo pensionati**	*Sya-mo pen-syo-na-tee*
What are you studying?	**Cosa studia?**	*Ko-za stoo-dya*
What do you do in your spare time?	**Cosa fa nel tempo libero?**	*Ko-za fa nel tem-po **lee**-bair-o*
I (don't) like sailing/ swimming/walking/ cycling/tennis	**(Non) mi piace fare vela/nuotare/ camminare/andare in bici/il tennis**	*(Non) mee pya-cheh fa-re ve-la/nwo-ta-reh/ kam-mee-na-reh/ an-da-reh een bee-chee/ eel tennis*
I'm interested in art/ music	**M'interessa l'arte/la musica**	*Meen-tair-es-sa lar-teh/la **moo**-zee-ka*

Going Out

English	Italian	Pronunciation
Could we have coffee/a drink together?	**Potremmo prendere un caffè/bere qualcosa insieme?**	*Pot-rem-mo **pren**-dair-eh oon kaf-**feh**/be-reh kwal-ko-za een-sye-meh*
Can I get you a drink?	**Posso offrirle qualcosa da bere?**	*Pos-so of-freer-leh kwal-ko-za da be-reh*
I'd like a . . . please	**Prenderei volentieri un . . .**	*Pren-dair-**ay** vo-len-tyair-eh oon . . .*
Cheers!	**Salute!/Cin cin!**	*Sa-loo-teh/cheen cheen*
Would you like to have lunch tomorrow?	**Ci incontriamo per pranzo domani?**	*Chee een-kon-trya-mo pair prand-zo do-ma-nee*
Can you come to dinner/for a drink?	**Può venire a cena/per un drink?**	*Pwo ve-neer-eh a che-na/pair oon drink?*
We are giving a party, would you like to come?	**Noi diamo un ricevimento, vuol venire?**	*Noy dya-mo oon ree-che-vee-men-to, vwol ve-neer-eh*
May I bring a friend?	**Posso portare anche un amico *m*/un' amica *f*?**	*Pos-so por-tar-eh an-keh oon a-mee-ko/oon-a-mee-ka*
Shall we go	**Vogliamo andare**	*Vol-ya-mo an-dar-eh*
to the cinema?	**al cinema?**	*al **chee**-ne-ma*
to the theatre?	**al teatro?**	*al te-at-ro*
for a walk?	**a fare una camminata?**	*a fa-reh oon-a kam-mee-na-ta*
Would you like to go dancing?	**Vuole andare a ballare?**	*Vwol-eh an-dar-eh a bal-lar-eh*
Would you like to go for a drive?	**Vuole fare un giro in macchina?**	*Vwol-eh far-eh oon jee-ro een **mak**-kee-na*

| Do you know a good disco/restaurant? | **Conosce una buona discoteca/un buon ristorante?** | *Ko-no-sheh oon-a bwo-na dees-ko-te-ka/oon bwon rees-tor-an-teh* |
| Let's go to a gay bar | **Andiamo in un bar gay** | *An-dya-mo een oon bar gay* |

Arrangements

Where shall we meet?	**Dove ci troviamo?**	*Do-veh cee tro-vya-mo*
What time shall I/we come?	**A che ora devo/ dobbiamo venire?**	*A keh or-a de-vo/dob-bya-mo ve-neer-eh*
I could pick you up at your hotel	**Potrei venire a prenderti all'albergo**	*Pot-**ray** ve-nee-reh a pren-dair-tee al-lal-bair-go*
Could you meet me at . . . ?	**Possiamo trovarci a . . . ?**	*Pos-sya-mo tro-var-chee a . . .*
May I see you home?	**Posso accompagnarla a casa?**	*Pos-so ak-kom-pan-yar-la a ka-za*
Can we give you a lift home/to your hotel?	**Possiamo darle un passaggio fino a casa/all'albergo?**	*Pos-sya-mo dar-leh oon pas-sad-jo fee-no a ka-za/ al-lal-bair-go*
Where do you live?	**Dove abita?**	*Do-veh **a**-bee-ta*
Would you give me your telephone number?	**Vuol darmi il suo numero di telefono?**	*Vwol dar-mee eel soo-o **noo**-mair-o dee te-**le**-fo-no*
I hope to see you again soon	**Spero di rivederla presto**	*Spair-o dee ree-ve-dair-la pres-to*
See you soon/later/ tomorrow	**A presto/a più tardi/a domani**	*A pres-to/a pyoo tar-dee/ a do-ma-nee*

| Are you free at the weekend? | **Sei libero/libera questo fine settimana?** | *Say lee-bair-o/lee-bair-a kwes-to fee-neh set-tee-ma-na* |

Accepting and declining

I'd like to come	**Sarei lieto di venire**	*Sa-ray lye-to dee ve-neer-eh*
Thank you for the invitation	**Grazie dell'invito**	*Grat-syeh del-leen-vee-to*
Did you enjoy it?	**Ti è piaciuto?**	*Tee-eh pya-choo-to*
I've enjoyed myself very much	**Mi sono divertito/divertita molto**	*Mee so-no dee-vair-tee-to/dee-vair-tee-ta mol-to*
It was interesting/funny/fantastic/lovely	**È stato interessante/divertente/fantastico/bello**	*Eh sta-to een-tair-es-san-teh/dee-vair-ten-teh/fan-tas-tee-ko/bel-lo*
Thank you for a pleasant evening	**Grazie per la bellissima serata**	*Grat-syeh pair la bel-lees-see-ma se-ra-ta*
a drink	**un drink**	*oon drink*
a ride	**un giro**	*oon jee-ro*
I'm sorry, I can't come	**Mi dispiace, non posso venire**	*Mee dees-pya-cheh, non pos-so ve-neer-eh*
Maybe another time	**Forse un'altra volta**	*For-seh oon-al-tra vol-ta*
No thanks, I'd rather not	**Grazie, ma preferisco di no**	*Grat-syeh, ma pre-fe-ree-sko dee no*
Go away	**Se ne vada**	*Seh neh va-da*
Leave me alone	**Mi lasci in pace**	*Mee la-shee een pa-cheh*

MONEY[1]

Key Phrases

Where is the nearest ATM?	**Dov'è il bancomat più vicino?**	*Do-**veh** eel **ban**-ko-mat pyu vee-chee-no*
Do you take credit cards?	**Accetta una carta di credito?**	*A-chet-ta oon-a kar-ta dee **kre**-dee-to*
Is there a bank that changes money/an exchange bureau near here?	**C'è una banca/ un'ufficio cambi qui vicino?**	*Cheh oon-a ban-ka/oon oof-fee-cho kam-bee kwee vee-chee-no*
Can you give me some small change?	**Può darmi degli spiccioli?**	*Pwo dar-mee del-yee spee-cho-lee*
I want to open a bank account	**Vorrei aprire un conto in banca**	*Vor-**ray** ap-reer-eh oon kon-to een ban-ka*

Credit and Debit Cards

I'd like to get/ withdraw some cash from my debit/credit card	**Vorrei avere/ prelevare dei contanti dal mio bancomat/dalla mia carta di credito**	*Vor-**ray** a-vair-eh/ pre-le-va-re day kon-tan-tee dal mee-o **ban**-ko-mat/da-la mee-a kar-ta dee **kre**-dee-to*
Enter your pin number	**Inserisca il suo numero pin**	*Een-sair-ee-ska eel swo **noo**-mair-o-pia*

1. In Italy, banks are usually open from 09.00 to 13.00, closed Saturday.

The ATM has swallowed my card	**Lo sportello del bancomat ha trattenuto la mia carta**	*Lo spor-tel-lo del **ban**-ko-mat a trat-ten-oo-to la mee-a kar-ta*

Exchange

Do you cash travellers' cheques?	**Può cambiare dei travellers' cheques?**	*Pwo kam-byar-eh day travellers' cheques*
Where can I cash travellers' cheques?	**Dove posso cambiare dei travellers' cheques?**	*Do-veh pos-so kam-byar-eh day travellers' cheques*
I want to change some pounds/dollars	**Vorrei cambiare delle sterline/dei dollari**	*Vor-**ray** kam-byar-eh del-le ster-lee-neh/day **dol**-la-ree*
(Your) passport please	***(Il suo) passaporto, prego**	*(Eel soo-o) pas-sa-por-to, pre-go*
Where do I sign?	**Dove devo firmare?**	*Do-veh de-vo feer-mar-eh*
Sign here, please	***Vuol firmare qui, per favore**	*Vwol feer-mar-eh kwee, pair fa-vor-eh*
Go to the cashier	***Si accomodi alla cassa**	*See ak-**ko**-mo-dee al-la kas-sa*
What is the exchange rate?	**Quant' è il cambio oggi?**	*Kwan-teh eel kam-byo od-jee*

How much is your commission?	**Quanto è la commissione?**	*Kwan-teh la kom-mee-syo-neh?*
Can you give me some small change?	**Può darmi degli spiccioli?**	*Pwo dar-mee del-yee spee-cho-lee*
I'd like small notes please	**Vorrei banconote di taglio piccolo, per favore**	*Vor-ray ban-ko-no-teh dee ta-lyo pee-ko-lo, pair fa-vo-reh*

General Banking

I arranged for money to be transferred from the UK. Has it arrived yet?	**Ho dato istruzioni di trasferire del denaro dal Regno Unito. È arrivato?**	*O da-to is-troot-syo-nee dee tras-fe-reer-eh del de-na-ro dal ren-yo oo-nee-to. Eh ar-ree-va-to*
I want to open a bank account	**Vorrei aprire un conto in banca**	*Vor-ray ap-reer-eh oon kon-to een ban-ka*
Please credit this to my account	**Vuol versare questo sul mio conto**	*Vwol vair-sar-eh kwes-to sool mee-o kon to*
I would like to make a transfer	**Vorrei fare un bonifico**	*Vor-ray fa-re oon bo-nee-fee-ko*
balance	**il saldo**	*sal-do*
bank card	**la carta bancaria**	*kar-ta ban-kar-ya*
cheque book	**il libretto (degli assegni)**	*leeb-ret-to del-yee as-sen-yee*
current account	**il conto corrente**	*kon-to kor-ren-teh*
deposit account	**il conto deposito**	*kon-to de-po-zee-to*
foreign currency	**la valuta estera**	*va-loo-ta e-ste-ra*
statement	**l'estratto conto**	*es-trat-to kon-to*

SHOPS[1] AND SERVICES

Where to Go

antique shop	**il negozio d'antiquariato**	*ne-got-syo dan-tee-kwa-rya-to*
audio equipment shop	**il negozio di dischi**	*ne-got-syo dee dee-skee*
bakery	**il panettiere**	*pa-net-tyair-eh*
bank	**la banca**	*ban-ka*
barber (see p. 192)	**il barbiere**	*bar-byair-eh*
beauty and spa treatments (see p. 181)	**l'estetista**	*es-te-tee-sta*
bicycle repair shop (see p. 46)	**il negozio di biciclette**	*ne-got-syo dee bee-chee-klet-teh*
books, newspapers and stationery (see p. 181)	**la libreria**	*lee-brair-ee-a*
building supplies (see p. 77)	**il costruttore edile**	*kos-troot-tor-eh e-dee-leh*
butcher (see p. 190)	**la macelleria**	*ma-chel-lair-ee-a*
cake shop (see p. 126)	**la pasticceria**	*pas-tee-chair-ee-a*

1. Shops generally close at 13.00 in Italy, and re-open between 16.00 and 17.00. The length of the lunch break varies considerably from region to region, but is usually longer in the south than in the north.

camping equipment (see p. 194)	**l'attrezzatura da campeggio** *f*	*at-tret-sa-toor-a da kam-ped-jo*
carpenter	**il carpentiere**	*kar-pen-tye-reh*
chemist (see p. 183)	**la farmacia**	*far-ma-chee-a*
consulate (see p. 132)	**il consolato**	*kon-so-la-to*
craft shop	**il negozio d'artigianato**	*ne-got-syo dar-tee-ja-na-to*
dairy	**la latteria**	*lat-tair-ee-a*
decorator/painter	**il pittore**	*peet-to-reh*
delicatessen	**la salumeria**	*sa-loo-mair-ee-a*
dentist (see p. 144)	**il dentista**	*den-tees-ta*
department stores	**i grandi magazzini**	*gran-dee ma-gad-zee-nee*
D.I.Y./hardware shop (see p. 194)	**il negozio di ferramenta**	*ne-got-syo dee fer-ra-men-ta*
doctor (see p. 146)	**il medico/dottore**	*me-dee-ko/dot-tor-eh*
dry cleaner (see p. 196)	**la pulitura a secco**	*poo-lee-too-ra a sek-ko*
electrical appliances	**gli elettrodomestici**	*e-let-tro-do-mes-tee-chee*
electrician	**l'elettricista** *m*	*e-let-tree-chees-ta*
fishmonger (see p. 120)	**il pescivendolo**	*pe-shee-ven-do-lo*
florist	**il fioraio**	*fyo-ra-yo*
furniture shop(see p. 79)	**il negozio di mobili**	*ne-got-syo dee mo-bee-lee*

garden centre	il vivaio	vee-va-yo
gardener	il giardiniere	jar-dee-nye-reh
gift shop	il negozio di articoli da regalo	ne-got-syo dee ar-**tee**-ko-lee da re-ga-lo
greengrocer (see pp 124 and 127)	il fruttivendolo	froot-tee-**ven**-do-lo
grocery (see p. 190)	la drogheria	dro-gair-ee-a
haberdashery (for fabrics see p. 178)	la merceria	mer-chair-ee-a
hairdresser (see p. 192)	il parrucchiere/la parrucchiera	par-rook-**kyair**-eh/ par-rook-**kyair**-a
health food shop	il negozio di alimenti macrobiotici	ne-got-syo dee a-lee-men-tee ma-kro-bee-**o**-tee-chee
hypermarket	l'ipermercato m	ee-pair-mair-ka-to
interior design shop	il negozio di design degli interni	ne-got-syo dee design del-yee een-tair-nee
jeweller (see p. 200)	la gioielleria	jo-yel-lair-ee-a
kitchen shop (see p. 82)	il negozio di cucine	ne-got-syo dee koo-chee-neh
launderette/laundry (see p. 196)	la lavanderia	la-van-dair-ee-a
lighting shop	il negozio di lampadari	ne-got-syo dee lam-pa-da-ree
market (see p. 198)	il mercato	mair-ka-to
mobile/cell phone shop (see p. 91)	il negozio di telefonini	ne-got-syo dee te-le-fo-nee-nee

newsagent (see p. 181)	il giornalaio/ l'edicola *f*	*jor-na-la-yo/e-**dee**-ko-la*
notary	il notaio	*no-ta-yo*
optician (see p. 156)	l'ottico *m*	***ot**-tee-ko*
outdoor equipment shop (see p. 194)	il negozio di attrezzature	*ne-got-syo dee at-tret-sa-too-reh*
pastry shop/ patisserie (see p. 126)	la pasticceria	*pas-tee-chair-ee-a*
photographer	il fotografo	*fo-**to**-gra-fo*
photographic equipment (see p. 198)	attrezzature fotografiche	*at-tret-sa-too-reh fo-to-**gra**-fee-keh*
plasterer	l'intonacatore *m*	*een-to-na-ka-tor-eh*
plumber	l'idraulico *m*	*eed-**row**-lee-ko*
police (see p. 132)	la polizia/i carabinieri	*pol-eet-see-a/ ka-ra-been-yair-ee*
post office (see p. 89)	l'ufficio postale *m*	*oof-fee-cho pos-ta-leh*
shoe repairs (see p. 200)	il calzolaio	*kalt-so-la-yo*
shoe shop (for sizes see p. 189)	il negozio di calzature	*ne-got-syo dee kalt-sa-too-reh*
shopping centre	il centro commerciale	*chen-tro kom-mair-cha-leh*
souvenir shop	il negozio di souvenir	*ne-got-syo dee souvenir*
sports shop	il negozio sportivo	*ne-got-syo spor-tee-vo*

stationer (see p. 181)	**la cartoleria**	*kar-to-lair-ee-a*
supermarket (see p. 190)	**il supermercato**	*soo-pair-mair-ca-to*
sweet shop	**il negozio di dolciumi**	*ne-got-syo dee dol-choo-mee*
tobacconist	**la tabaccheria**	*ta-bak-kair-ee-a*
tourist information office	**l'ufficio informazioni turistiche**	*oof-fee-cho een-for-mat-syo-nee too-**ree**-stee-keh*
toy shop	**il negozio di giocattoli**	*ne-got-syo dee jo-**kat**-to-lee*
travel agency	**l'agenzia (di) viaggi** *f*	*a-jen-tsee-a (dee) vyad-jee*
travel goods shop	**il negozio di attrezzature da viaggio**	*ne-got-syo dee at-tret-sa-too-reh da vyad-jo*
wine merchant	**la rivendita di vino/ la enoteca**	*ree-**ven**-dee-ta dee vee-no/ee-no-te-ka*
Which is the best …?	**Qual'è il/la miglior …?**	*Kwal-**eh** eel/la meel-yor*
Where is the nearest …?	**Dov'è il/la … più vicino/vicina…?**	*Dov-**eh** eel/la … pyoo vee-chee-no/vee-chee-na …*
Can you recommend a …?	**Mi può consigliare un …?**	*Mee pwo kon-see-lya-reh …*
Where is the market?	**Dov'è il mercato?**	*Dov-**eh** eel mair-ka-to*
Is there a market every day?	**C'è mercato ogni giorno?**	*Cheh mair-ka-to on-yee jor-no*

Where can I buy...?	**Dove posso comprare...?**	*Do-veh pos-so kom-prar-eh...*
When do the shops open/close?	**A che ora aprono/ chiudono i negozi?**	*A keh or-a ap-ro-no/ **kyoo**-do-no ee ne-got-see*
Where are the best department stores?	**Dove sono i migliori magazzini?**	*Do-veh so-no ee meel-yor-ee ma-gad-zee-nee*

In the Shop

check out/cash desk	***cassa**	*kas-sa*
manager	**direttore**	*dee-ret-tor-eh*
self-service	***self-service**	*self-service*
sale (*clearance*)	***la svendita**	*sven-dee-ta*
shop assistant	**commesso/ commessa**	*ko-mes-so/ko-mes-sa*
Where are the trolleys?	**Dove sono i carrelli?**	*Do-ve so-no ee kar-rel-lee*
Can I help you?	***In cosa posso servirla?**	*Een ko-za pos-so sair-veer-la*
I would like to buy...	**Vorrei comprare...**	*Vor-**ray** kom-prar-eh...*
Do you sell...?	**Vende...?**	*Ven-deh...*
I just want to look round	**Vorrei solo dare un'occhiata in giro**	*Vor-**ray** solo dar-eh oon-ok-kya-ta een jee-ro*
I'm not buying anything now	**Non compro niente adesso**	*Non kom-pro nyen-teh a-des-so*

Could you show me ...?	Può farmi vedere ...?	Pwo far-mee ve-dair-eh ...
I don't like this	Questo non mi piace	Kwes-to non mee pya-cheh
I'll have this	Prendo pure questo	Pren-do poo-reh kwes-to
Could you wrap the gift please?	Potrebbe incartare il regalo?	Pot-reb-beh een-kar-ta-reh eel re-ga-lo
You'll find them at the counter	*Li troverà a quel banco	Lee tro-vair-a a kwel ban-ko
We've sold out but we'll have more tomorrow	*Sono finiti ma li riceveremo domani	So-no fee-nee-tee ma lee ree-che-ve-re-mo do-ma-nee
Anything else?	*Nient'altro?	Nyen-tal-tro
That will be all	Questo è tutto	Kwes-to eh toot-to
Will you take it with you?	*Lo prende adesso?	Lo pren-deh a-des-so
Please send them to this address/X hotel	Per favore li mandi a questo indirizzo/all'albergo X	Pair fa-vor-eh lee man-dee a kwes-to een-dee-reet-so/al-lal-bair-go X

Choosing

I like the one in the window	Mi piace quello in vetrina	Mee pya-cheh kwel-lo een vet-ree-na
Could I see that one, please?	Posso vedere quello, per favore?	Pos-so ve-dair-eh kwel-lo, pair fa-vor-eh
Is it handmade?	È fatto a mano?	Eh fat-to a ma-no
What's it made of?	Di cosa è fatto?	Dee ko-za eh fat-to

I like the colour but I want a different style	Il colore va bene ma vorrei uno stile diverso	*Eel ko-lor-eh va be-neh ma vor-**ray** oon-o stee-leh dee-vair-so*
I want a darker/lighter shade	Vorrei una tinta più scura/più chiara	*Vor-**ray** oon-a teen-ta pyoo skoo-ra/pyoo kya-ra*
Do you have it in another colour/size?	Ne ha in un colore diverso/di un'altra taglia?	*Neh a een oon ko-lor-eh dee-vair-so/dee oon-al-tra tal-ya*
It's for a three-year old	È per un bambino di tre anni	*Eh pair oon bam-bee-no dee treh an-nee*
Do you have anything better/cheaper?	Vorrei qualcosa di meglio/meno costoso	*Vor-**ray** kwal-ko-za dee mel-yo/me-no kos-to-zo*
How much is this?	Quanto costa?	*Kwan-to kos-ta*
That is too expensive for me	È troppo caro per me	*Eh trop-po ka-ro pair meh*

Colours

beige	beige	*beige*
black	nero	*ne-ro*
blue	blu	*bloo*
brown	marrone	*mar-ro-neh*
golden	dorato	*dor-a-to*
green	verde	*vair-deh*
grey	grigio	*gree-jo*
mauve	malva	*mal-va*

orange	arancione	*a-ran-cho-neh*
pink	rosa	*ro-za*
purple	porpora	*por-por-a*
red	rosso	*ros-so*
silver	argento	*ar-jen-to*
white	bianco	*byan-ko*
yellow	giallo	*jal-lo*

Materials

canvas	la tela	*te-la*
cotton	il cotone	*ko-to-neh*
glass	il vetro	*ve-tro*
lace	il merletto	*mair-let-to*
leather	la pelle	*pel-leh*
linen	il lino	*lee-no*
plastic	la plastica	*plas-tee-ka*
silk	la seta	*se-ta*
suede	la pelle scamosciata	*pel-leh ska-mo-sha-ta*
synthetic	sintetico	*seen-te-tee-ko*
velvet	il velluto	*vel-loo-to*
wood	il legno	*len-yo*
wool	la lana	*la-na*

Paying

How much is this?	**Quanto costa questo?**	*Qwun-lo ko-sta kwes-to*
That will be ...	***Fa .../Sono ...**	*Fa .../So-no ...*
That's ... euros	***Costa ... euro**	*Kos-ta ... e-oo-ro*
They are ... euros each	***Costano ... euro l'uno**	***Kos**-ta-no ... e-oo-ro loo-no*
It's too expensive	**È troppo caro**	*Eh trop-po ka-ro*
Is that your best price?	**Questo è il suo miglior prezzo?**	*Kwes-to eh eel soo-o meel-**yor** pret-so*
Can you give me a discount?	**Mi può fare uno sconto?**	*Mee pwo fa-re oon-o skon-to*
How much does that come to?	**Quanto è in tutto?**	*Kwan-to eh in toot-to*
How would you like to pay?	***Come vuole pagare?**	*Ko-me vwo-leh pa-ga-re*
Cash only	***Solo contanti**	*So-lo kon-tan-tee*
Will you take English/ American currency?	**Posso pagare in sterline/in dollari?**	*Pos-so pa-gar-eh een stair-lee-neh/een **dol**-lar-ee*
Do you take credit cards?	**Accetta carte di credito?**	*A-chet-ta kar-teh dee **kre**-dee-to*
Do I have to pay VAT?	**Devo pagare l'IVA?**	*De-vo pa-gar-eh lee-va*
Please pay at the cash desk/check out	***Si accomodi alla cassa, per favore**	*See ak-**ko**-mo-dee al-la kas-sa, pair fa-vor-eh*

| May I have a receipt, please? | Mi può rilasciare una ricevuta, per favore? | Mee pwo ree-la-shar-eh oon-a ree-che-voo-ta, pair fa-vor-eh |
| You've given me too little/too much change | Mi ha dato meno di resto/mi ha dato troppo | Mee a da-to me-no dee res-to/mee a da-to trop-po |

Complaints

I would like to see the manager	Vorrei vedere il direttore	Vor-**ray** ve-dair-eh eel dee-ret-tor-eh
I bought this yesterday	L'ho comprato ieri	Lo kom-pra-to yair-ee
It doesn't work	Non funziona	Non foont-syo-na
It doesn't fit	Non è la misura giusta	Non eh la mee-zoo-ra joos-ta
This is	È	Eh
dirty	sporco	spor-ko
stained	macchiato	mak-kya-to
torn	strappato	strap-pa-to
broken	rotto	rot-to
cracked	spaccato	spak-ka-to
I want to return this	Voglio restituire questo	Vol-yo res-tee-twee-reh kwes-to
Will you change it, please?	Lo può cambiare, per favore?	Lo **pwo** kam-byar-eh, pair fa-vor-eh
Will you refund my money?	Mi può restituire il denaro?	Mee pwo res-tee-twee-reh eel de-na-ro
Here is the receipt	Ecco la ricevuta	Ek-ko la ree-che-voo-ta

Beauty and Spa Treatments

I'd like a manicure/ pedicure	**Vorrei una manicure/un pedicure**	*Vor-ray oon-a ma-nee- koo-reh/oon pe-dee- koo-reh*
I'd like a (facial) massage	**Vorrei un massaggio (al viso)**	*Vor-ray oon mas-sad-jo (al vee-so)*
Do you do waxing?	**Fate la ceretta?**	*Fa-teh la che-ret-ta*
I'd like my eyebrows shaped	**Vorrei fare le sopracciglia**	*Vor-ray fa-reh leh sopra-chee-lya*
Do you do aromatherapy?	**Praticate l'aromaterapia?**	*Pra-tee-ka-teh la-ro-ma- te-ra-pee-a*
Is there a sauna/ steam room?	**C'è una sauna?**	*Cheh oon sow-na*
What spa packages are available?	**Che pacchetti/ offerte avete nel centro benessere?**	*Keh pak-ket-tee/of-fair- teh a-vet-eh nel chen-tro ben-es-se-reh*

Books, Newspapers and Stationery

Do you sell English/American newspapers/ magazines?	**Vende giornali/ riviste inglesi/ americani?**	*Ven-deh jor-na-lee/ree- vee-steh een-gle-zee/a- me-ree-ka-nee*
Can you get this magazine for me?	**Può ordinare questa rivista per me?**	*Pwo or-dee-nar-eh kwes- ta ree-vees-ta pair meh*
I want a map of the city/road map	**Vorrei una cartina della città/stradale**	*Vor-ray oon-a kar-tee-na del-la cheet-ta/stra-da-leh*

I'd like a guide to the city in English	**Vorrei una guida della città in inglese**	*Vor-ray oon-a gwee-da del-la chee-ta een een-gle-zeh*
I'd like an entertainment/ amusements guide	**Vorrei una guida delle attrazioni/dei divertimenti**	*Vor-ray oon-a gwee-da del-leh at-trat-syo-nee/ day dee-vair-tee-men-tee*
Do you have any English books?	**Vende libri inglesi?**	*Ven-deh lee-bree een-gle-zee*
Do you have any novels by . . .?	**Ha qualche romanzo di . . .?**	*A kwal-keh ro-man-zo dee . . .*
I want some picture postcards	**Vorrei delle cartoline**	*Vor-ray del-leh kar-to-lee-neh*
Do you sell souvenirs/toys?	**Vende dei ricordi/ giocattoli?**	*Ven-deh day ree-kor-dee/ jo-kat-to-lee*
ballpoint pen	**il biro**	*bee-ro*
calculator	**la calcolatrice**	*kal-ko-la-tree-cheh*
card	**il bigliettino**	*beel-yet-tee-no*
dictionary	**il dizionario**	*deet-syo-nar-yo*
drawing paper	**la carta da disegno**	*kar-ta da dee-zen-yo*
drawing pin	**la puntina da disegno**	*poon-tee-na da dee-zen-yo*
elastic band	**l'elastico** *m*	*e-las-tee-ko*
envelope	**la busta**	*boos-ta*
felt-tip pen	**il pennarello**	*pen-na-rel-lo*
fountain pen	**la penna stilografica**	*pen-na stee-lo-gra-fee-ka*
glue	**la colla**	*kol-la*

greeting card	il biglietto d'auguri	*beel-yet-to dow-goo-ree*
guide book	la guida	*gwee-da*
ink	l'inchiostro *m*	*een-kyos-tro*
notebook	il taccuino	*tak-kwee-no*
paperclip	il fermaglio	*fair-mal-yo*
pen	la penna	*pen-na*
(coloured) pencil	la matita (colorata)	*ma-tee-ta (ko-lo-ra-ta)*
pencil sharpener	il temperino	*tem-pe-ree-no*
postcard	la cartolina	*kar-to-lee-na*
rubber/eraser	la gomma	*gom-ma*
sellotape	il nastro adesivo/lo scotch	*nas-tro a-de-zee-vo/ skotch*
sketch pad	il quadernetto (da disegno)	*kwa-der-net-to (da dee-zen-yo)*
string	lo spago	*spa-go*
wrapping paper	la carta da regalo	*kar-ta da re-ga-lo*
writing paper	la carta da scrivere	*kar-ta da **skree**-vair-eh*

Chemist[1]

| Can you make up this prescription for me, please? | Mi può preparare questa ricetta, per favore? | *Mee pwo pre-par-ar-eh kwes-ta ree-chet-ta, pair fa-vor-eh* |
| Do you have a small first-aid kit? | Ha una valigetta di pronto soccorso? | *Ha oon-a va-lee-jet-ta dee pron-to sok-kor-so* |

1. See also Doctor (p. 146).

A packet of aspirin, please	**Una scatola di aspirine, per favore**	*Oon-a ska-to-la dee as-pee-ree-neh, pair fa-vor-eh*
A packet of adhesive plasters	**Un pacchetto di cerotti**	*Oon pak-ket-to dee chair-ot-tee*
Suncream for children	**Crema solare per bambini**	*Kre-ma so-la-reh pair bam-bee-nee*
Can you suggest something for	**Mi può indicare qualcosa contro**	*Mee pwo ee-dee-kar-eh kwal-ko-za kon-tro*
constipation?	**la stitichezza?**	*la stee-tee-ket-sa*
diarrhoea?	**la diarrea?**	*la dee-ar-re-a*
indigestion?	**l'indigestione?**	*leen-dee-jes-tyo-neh*
an upset stomach	**mal di stomaco**	*mal dee **sto**-ma-ko*
I want something for insect bites	**Voglio qualcosa contro i morsi degli insetti**	*Vol-yo kwal-ko-za kon-tro ee mor-see del-yee een-set-tee*
Do you sell contraceptives?	**Vende te dei contraccettivi?**	*Ven-de-te day kon-tra-che-tee-vee*
I want	**Desidero**	*De-**zee**-dair-o*
a disinfectant	**del disinfettante**	*del dee-zeen-fet-tan-teh*
a mouthwash	**un colluttorio**	*oon kol-loot-tor-yo*
some nose drops	**delle gocce per il naso**	*del-leh go-cheh pair eel na-zo*
an antiseptic cream	**della crema antisettica**	*del-la kre-ma an-tee-**set**-tee-ka*
lipsalve	**della pomata per le labbra**	*del-la po-ma-ta pair le lab-bra*

Can you give me something for sunburn?	**Mi può dare qualcosa contro le bruciature di sole?**	*Mee pwo dar-eh kwal-ko-za kon-tro leh broo-cha-too-reh dee so-leh*
I want some throat/cough lozenges	**Vorrei delle pasticche per la gola/per la tosse**	*Vor-ray del-leh pas-teek-keh pair la go-la/pair la tos-seh*
Do you have	**Avete**	*A-ve-teh*
cotton wool?	**dei batuffolini di cotone?**	*day bat-toof-fo-lee-nee dee ko-to-neh*
sanitary towels?	**degli assorbenti?**	*del-yee as-sor-ben-tee*
tampons?	**dei tamponi?**	*day tam-po-nee*
I need something for a headache/sea sickness	**Vorrei qualcosa contro il mal di testa/il mal di mare**	*Vor-**ray** kwal-ko-za kon-tro eel mal dee tes-ta/eel mal dee mar-eh*

Clothes, Shoes[1] and Accessories

I want a hat/sunhat	**Vorrei un cappello/un cappello da sole**	*Vor-**ray** oon kap-pel-lo/oon kap-pel-lo da so-leh*
Where are the beach clothes?	**Dove sono gli abiti da spiaggia?**	*Do-veh so-no lyee a-bee-tee da spyad-ja*
The men's department is on the second floor	***Le confezioni per uomo sono al secondo piano**	*Le kon-fet-syo-nee pair wo-mo so-no al se-kon-do pya-no*

1. For sizes see (p. 191).

I want a short-/ long-sleeved shirt, collar size . . .	**Voglio una camicia a maniche corte/ lunghe, colletto numero . . .**	*Vol-yo oon-a ka-mee-cha a ma-nee-keh kor-teh/loon-geh, kol-let-to noo-mair-o . . .*
Where can I find	**Dov'è che vendono**	*Dov-eh keh ven-do-no*
stockings?	**calze?**	*kalt-seh*
socks?	**calzini?**	*kalt-see-nee*
tights?	**collant?**	*kol-lan*
I am looking for	**Cerco**	*Chair-ko*
a blouse	**una blusa**	*oon-a bloo-za*
a bra	**un reggiseno**	*oon red-jee-se-no*
a dress	**un vestito**	*oon ves-tee-to*
a sweater	**una maglietta**	*oon-a mal-yet-ta*
I need	**Ho bisogno di**	*O bee-zon-yo dee*
a coat	**un soprabito**	*oon sop-ra-bee-to*
a raincoat	**un impermeabile**	*oon eem-pair-mee-a-bee-leh*
a jacket	**una giaccha**	*oon-a jak-a*
a pair of trousers	**un paio di calzoni**	*oon pa-yo dee kalt-so-nee*
Do you have other colours?	**Avete altri colori?**	*A-ve-teh al-tree ko-lo-ree*
I need it to match this	**Voglio che vada bene con questo**	*Vol-yo keh va-da be-neh kon kwes-to*
What size is this?	**Di che misura è questo?**	*Dee keh mee-zoo-ra eh kwes-to*

I want size . . .	**Voglio la misura . . .**	*Vol-yo la mee-zoo-ra . . .*
I don't know the Italian size	**Non conosco le misure italiane**	*Non ko-nos-ko leh mee-zoo-reh ee-tal-ya-neh*
Can you measure me?	**Può prendermi le misure?**	*Pwo **pren**-dair-mee leh mee-zoo-reh*
Can I try it on?	**Posso provarlo?**	*Pos-so pro-var-lo*
Is there a mirror?	**C'è uno specchio?**	*Cheh oon-o spek-kyo*
This doesn't fit	**Non va bene**	*Non va be-neh*
It's too	**È troppo**	*Eh trop-po*
short	**corto**	*kor-to*
long	**lungo**	*loon-go*
tight	**stretto**	*stret-to*
loose	**largo**	*lar-go*
Do you have a larger/smaller one?	**Ne ha uno più grande/più piccolo?**	*Neh a oon-o pyoo gran-deh/pyoo **peek**-ko-lo*
I need something warmer/thinner	**Vorrei qualcosa di più pesante/più leggero**	*Vor-**ray** kwal-ko-za dee pyoo pe-zan-teh/pyoo led-je-ro*
Is it colourfast?	**È di colore solido?**	*Eh dee ko-lor-eh **so**-lee-do*
Is it machine washable?	**È lavabile in lavatrice?**	*Eh la-**va**-bee-leh een la-va-tree-cheh*
Will it shrink?	**Si restringerà?**	*See res-treen-jair-**a***
I need a pair of walking shoes	**Ho bisogno di un paio di scarpe da passeggio**	*O bee-zon-yo dee oon pa-yo dee skar-peh da pas-sed-jo*

I want a pair of	**Voglio un paio di**	*Vol-yo oon pa-yo dee*
boots	**stivali**	*stee-va-lee*
trainers	**scarpe da tennis**	*skar-peh da tennis*
beach sandals	**sandali da mare**	*san-da-lee da ma-re*
black shoes	**scarpe nere**	*skar-peh ne-reh*
These heels are too high/too low	**Questi tacchi sono troppo alti/troppo bassi**	*Kwes-tee tak-kee so-no trop-po al-tee/trop-po bas-see*
Do you sell	**Vende**	*Ven-deh*
buttons?	**bottoni?**	*bot-to-nee*
elastic?	**elastico?**	*e-las-tee-ko*
zips?	**cerniere?**	*chair-nyair-eh*
What colour do you want?	***Che colore desidera?**	*Keh ko-lor-eh de-zee-dair-a*
I don't like this colour	**Non mi piace questo colore**	*Non mee pya-cheh kwes-to ko-lor-eh*
I am sorry, that's too much	**Mi dispiace, costa troppo**	*Mee dees-pya-cheh, kos-ta trop-po*
How long is the guarantee?	**Per quanto tempo è garantito?**	*Pair kwan-to tem-po eh ga-ran-tee-to*
The English/American size is ...	**La misura inglese/americana è ...**	*La mee-zoo-ra een-gle-zeh/a-me-ree-ka-na eh ...*
The collar size is ...	**Il numero di colletto è ...**	*Eel noo-mair-o dee ko-let-to eh ...*
My chest measurement is ...	**Il mio numero di petto è ...**	*Eel mee-o noo-mair-o dee pet-to eh ...*
My waist measurement is ...	**Il mio numero di cintura è ...**	*Eel mee-o noo-mair-o dee cheen-toor-a eh ...*

Clothing Sizes
WOMEN'S CLOTHING
coats, dresses, skirts, tops, trousers

UK/Australia	8	10	12	14	16	18
USA/Canada	6	8	10	12	14	16
Europe	38	40	42	44	46	48

shoes

UK	4	5	6	7	8	9	10
USA/Canada	$5\frac{1}{2}$	$6\frac{1}{2}$	$7\frac{1}{2}$	$8\frac{1}{2}$	$9\frac{1}{2}$	$10\frac{1}{4}$	$11\frac{1}{4}$
Europe	37	38	39/40	41	42	43	44

MEN'S CLOTHING
suits and coats

UK/USA/Canada	36	38	40	42	44	46
Europe	46	48	50	52	54	56

shirts

UK/USA/Canada	14	$14\frac{1}{2}$	15	$15\frac{1}{2}$	16	$16\frac{1}{2}$	17
Europe	36	37	38	39	40	41	42

shoes

UK	$9\frac{1}{2}$	10	$10\frac{1}{2}$	11	$11\frac{1}{2}$
USA/Canada	10	$10\frac{1}{2}$	11	$11\frac{1}{2}$	12
Europe	43	44	44	45	45

Food[1]

A kilo/half a kilo of . . . , please	Vuol darmi un chilo/ mezzo chilo di . . . , per favore	Vwol dar-mee oon kee-lo/med-zo kee-lo dee . . . , pair fa-vor-eh
I want some sweets, please	Vorrei dei dolciumi, per favore	Vor-ray day dol-choo-mee, pair fa-vor-eh
A litre of semi-skimmed/full milk	Un litro di latte parzialmente scremato/intero	Oon lee-tro dee lat-teh part-syal-men-teh skre-ma-to/een-te-ro
A carton of plain yogurt	Un vasetto di yogurt naturale	Oon va-zet-to dee yo-**goort** na-too-ra-leh
A dozen eggs	Una dozzina di uova	Oon-a dod-zee-na dee wo-va
A bottle of mineral water	Una bottiglia di acqua minerale	Oon-a bot-teel-ya dee ak-wa mee-nair-a-leh
A litre/half a litre of wine	Un litro/mezzo litro di vino	Oon leet-ro/med-zo leet-ro dee vee-no
A bottle of beer	Una bottiglia di birra	Oon-a bot-teel-ya dee beer-ra
I want	Vorrei	Vor-**ray**
a jar of . . .	un barattolo di . . .	oon ba-**rat**-to-lo dee
a can of . . .	una scatola di . . .	oon-a **ska**-to-la dee
a packet of . . .	un pacchetto di . . .	oon pak-ket-to dee . . .
. . . slices of ham/ Parma ham, please	. . . fette di prosciutto cotto/ crudo, per favore	. . . fet-teh dee pro-shoot-to kot-to/ kroo-do, pair fa-vor-eh
300g of cheese, please	300 grammi di formaggio, per favore	treh chen-to gram-mee dee for-mad-jo, pair fa-vor-eh

1. See also Eating Out (p. 99), The Menu (p. 116) and Weights and Measures, p. 241.

Do you sell frozen food?	**Vende cibi surgelati?**	*Ven-deh chee-bee soor-je-la-tee*
Is it fresh or frozen?	**È fresco o surgelato?**	*Eh fres-ko o soor-je-la-to*
These pears are too hard/soft	**Queste pere non sono ancora mature/ sono troppo mature**	*Kwes-teh pe-reh non so-no an-kor-a ma-too-reh/so-no trop-po ma-too-reh*
Is it fresh?	**È fresco?**	*Eh fres-ko*
Are they ripe?	**Sono mature?**	*So-no ma-too-reh*
This is bad/stale	**Questa è marcia/ andata a male**	*Kwes-ta eh mar-cha/ an-da-ta a ma-leh*
A loaf of (wholemeal) bread, please	**Un filone di pane (integrale), per favore**	*Oon fee-lo-neh dee pa-neh (een-teg-ra-leh), pair fa-vor-eh*
Six rolls	**Sei panini**	*say pa-nee-nee*
How much a kilo/ a litre?	**Quanto costa al chilo/al litro?**	*Kwan-to kos-ta al kee-lo/ al leet-ro*
A kilo of sausages	**Un chilo di salsicce**	*Oon kee-lo dee sal-see-che*
Four pork chops	**Quattro bistecche di maiale**	*Kwat-tro bee-stek-keh dee ma-ya-leh*
Could you mince it/ bone it?	**Me lo potrebbe tritare/disossare (meat)/spinare (fish)?**	*Me lo pot-reb-beh tree-tar-eh/dees-os-sar-eh/ spee-nar-eh*
Could you clean the fish?	**Mi potrebbe pulire il pesce?**	*Mee pot-reb-beh poo-leer-eh eel pe-sheh*
Please fillet the fish	**Mi potrebbe filettare il pesce?**	*Mee po-treb-beh fee-let-tar-eh eel pe-sheh*

I'll take the bones	**Mi dia le ossa, per favore**	*Mee dee-a leh os-sa, pair fa-vor-eh*
Is there any shellfish?	**Ci sono dei frutti di mare?**	*Chee so-no day froot-tee dee ma-reh*
Shall I help myself?	**Mi posso servire?**	*Mee pos-so sair-veer-eh*

Hairdresser and Barber

May I make an appointment for tomorrow/this afternoon?	**Posso fissare un appuntamento per domani/per questo pomeriggio?**	*Pos-so fees-sar-eh oon ap-poon-ta-men-to pair do-ma-nee/pair kwes-to po-mair-eed-jo*
What time?	**A che ora?**	*A keh or-a*
I want my hair cut/trimmed	**Mi vuol tagliare/spuntare i capelli, per favore**	*Mee vwol tal-yar-eh/spoon-tar-eh ee ka-pel-lee, pair fa-vor-eh*
I want my hair trimmed just a little	**Vorrei solo una spuntatina**	*Vor-**ray** so-lo oon-a spoon-ta-tee-na*
Not too short at the sides	**Non troppo corti ai lati**	*Non trop-po kor-tee ay la-tee*
I'll have it shorter at the back, please	**Può farmeli un po' più corti sul collo?**	*Pwo **far**-me-lee oon po pyoo kor-tee sool kol-lo*
Shorter on top	**Più corti in cima**	*Pyoo kor-tee een chee-ma*
That's fine	**Va bene così**	*Va be-neh ko-**zee***
No shorter	**Basta così**	*Bas-ta ko-**zee***
Shave and hair cut	**Barba e capelli**	*Bar-ba eh ka-pel-lee*

Please trim my beard/my moustache	**Vuole spuntarmi la barba/i baffi, per favore**	*Vwo-leh spoon-tar-mee la bar-ba/ee baf-fee, pair fa-vor-eh*
My hair is greasy/dry/normal	**Ho i capelli grassi/secchi/normali**	*O ee ka-pel-lee gras-see/sek-kee/nor-ma-lee*
I want a shampoo	**Vorrei uno shampoo**	*Vor-ray oon-o sham-poo*
Please use conditioner	**Vorrei del balsamo, per favore**	*Vor-ray del bal-sa-mo, pair fa-vor-eh*
I want my hair washed, styled and blow-dried	**Vorrei lo shampoo, il taglio e la piega a phon**	*Vor-ray lo sham-poo, eel tal-yo eh la pye-ga a fon*
I'd like to see a colour chart	**Vorrei vedere la gamma delle tinte**	*Vor-ray ve-dair-eh la gam-ma del-leh teen-teh*
I want my hair tinted	**Vorrei farmi tingere i capelli**	*Vor-ray far-mee teen-jair-eh ee ka-pel-lee*
highlights	**i colpi di sole**	*kol-pee dee so-leh*
I'd like a darker/lighter shade	**Vorrei una tinta più scura/più chiara**	*Vor-ray oon-a teen-ta pyoo skoo-ra/pyoo kya-ra*
The water is too cold	**L'acqua è troppo fredda**	*Lak-wa eh trop-po fred-da*
The dryer is too hot	**Il casco è troppo caldo**	*Eel kas-ko eh trop-po kal-do*
I want a manicure	**Vorrei la manicure**	*Vor-ray la ma-nee-koo-reh*
Thank you, I like it very much	**Grazie, mi piace moltissimo**	*Grat-syeh, mee pya-cheh mol-tees-see-mo*

Hardware and Outdoors[1]

Where is the camping equipment?	**Dove sono le attrezzature da campeggio?**	*Do-veh so-no leh at-tret-sa-too-reh da kam-ped-jo*
Do you have a battery for this?	**Ha una batteria per questo?**	*A oon-a bat-tair-ee-a pair kwes-to*
Where can I get butane gas?	**Dove posso trovare del gas butano?**	*Do-veh pos-so tro-var-eh del gaz boo-ta-no*
I need	**Mi occorre**	*Mee ok-kor-reh*
a bottle-opener	**un apribottiglie**	*oon ap-ree-bot-teel-yeh*
a corkscrew	**un cavatappi**	*oon ka-va-tap-pee*
a tin-opener	**un apriscatole**	*oon ap-ree-**ska**-to-leh*
I'd like some candles and a box of matches	**Vorrei delle candele ed una scatola di fiammiferi**	*Vor-**ray** del-leh kan-de-leh ed oon-a **ska**-to-la dee fyam-**mee**-fair-ee*
I want	**Vorrei**	*Vor-**ray***
a torch/flashlight	**una torcia elettrica**	*oon-a tor-cha e-**let**-tree-ka*
a knife	**un coltello**	*oon kol-tel-lo*
a pair of scissors	**un paio di forbici**	*oon pa-yo dee **for**-bee-chee*
a small/large screwdriver	**un cacciavite grande/piccolo**	*oon ka-cha-vee-teh gran-deh/**peek**-ko-lo*
Do you sell string/rope?	**Vende dello spago/della corda?**	*Ven-deh del-lo spa-go/del-la kor-da*

1. See also Camping (p. 67) and Apartments and Villas (p. 75).

Where can I find washing-up liquid/soap?	**Dove posso trovare un detersivo per i piatti/del sapone?**	*Do-veh pos-so tro-var-eh oon de-tair-see-vo pair ee pyat-tee/del sa-po-neh*
Do you have a dishcloth/broom?	**Ha uno strofinaccio/una scopa?**	*A oon-o stro-fee-na-cho/oon-a sko-pa*
I need	**Ho bisogno di**	*O bee-zo-nyo dee*
a groundsheet	**un telone impermeabile**	*oon te-lo-neh eem-pair-me-**a**-bee-leh*
a brush	**una scopa**	*oon-a sko-pa*
a bucket	**un secchiello**	*oon sek-kyel-lo*
I want to buy a barbecue	**Vorrei comprare una griglia**	*Vor-**ray** kom-prar-eh oon-a greel-ya*
Do you sell charcoal?	**Vende il carbone di legno?**	*Ven-deh eel kar-bo-neh dee len-yo*
adaptor	**la presa multipla**	*pre-za **mool**-tee-pla*
basket	**il cestino**	*ches-tee-no*
duster	**lo straccio**	*stra-cho*
electrical flex	**il cordoncino elettrico**	*kor-don-chee-no e-**let**-tree-ko*
extension lead	**una prolunga**	*pro-loon-ga*
fuse	**la valvola fusibile**	***val**-vo-la foo-**zee**-bee-leh*
fuse wire	**il fusibile**	*foo-**zee**-bee-leh*
insulating tape	**il nastro isolante**	*nas-tro ee-zo-lan-teh*
lightbulb	**una lampadina**	*lam-pa-dee-na*
penknife	**il temperino**	*tem-pe-ree-no*
(electric) plug	**la presa (elettrica)**	*pre-za (e-**let**-tree-ka)*

Laundry and Dry Cleaning

Where is the nearest launderette/dry cleaner?	Dov'è la lavanderia automatica/ lavanderia a secco più vicina?	Dov-**eh** la la-van-dair-ee-a ow-to-**ma**-tee-ka/ la-van-dair-ee-a a sek-ko pyoo vee-chee-na
I want to have these things washed/ cleaned	Vorrei far lavare/ pulire a secco queste cose	Vor-**ray** far la-var-eh/ poo-leer-eh a sek-ko kwes-teh ko-zeh
Can you get this stain out?	Può togliere questa macchia?	Pwo **tol**-yair-eh kwes-ta mak-kya
It is	È	Eh
coffee	caffè	kaf-**feh**
wine	vino	vee-no
grease	grasso	gras-so
These stains won't come out	*Queste macchie non vanno via	Kwes-teh mak-kyeh non van-no vee-a
It only needs to be pressed	Ha solo bisogno di essere stirato	A so-lo bee-zon-yo dee **es**-se-reh stee-ra-to
This is torn. Can you mend it?	Questo è rotto. Può rammendarlo?	Kwes-to eh rot-to. Pwo ram-men-dar-lo
There's a button missing	Ci manca un bottone	Chee man-ka oon bot-to-neh
Can you sew on a button here, please?	Può attaccare un bottone qui, per favore?	Pwo at-tak-kar-eh oon bot-to-neh kwee, pair fa-vor-eh
Do you do invisible mending?	Può fare un rammendo invisibile?	Pwo far-eh oon ram-men-do een-vee-**zee**-bee-leh

When will they be ready?	**Quando saranno pronti?**	*Kwan-do sa-ran-no pron-tee*
I need them by this evening/tomorrow	**Ne ho bisogno per questa sera/domani**	*Neh o bee-zon-yo pair kwes-ta se-ra/do-ma-nee*
Call back at five o'clock	***Torni alle cinque**	*Tor-nee al-leh cheen-kweh*
We can do it by Tuesday	***Possiamo farlo per martedì**	*Pos-sya-mo far-lo pair mar-te-dee*
It will take three days	***Ci vorranno tre giorni**	*Chee vor-ran-no treh jor-nee*
This isn't mine	**Questo non è mio**	*Kwes-to non eh mee-o*
I've lost my ticket	**Ho perso il mio biglietto**	*O pair-so eel mee-o beel-yet-to*

Household laundry

bath towel	**il telo da bagno**	*te-lo da ban-yo*
blanket	**la coperta**	*ko-pair-ta*
napkin	**il tovagliolo**	*to-val-yo-lo*
pillow case	**la federa**	*fe-dair-a*
sheet	**il lenzuolo**	*lend-zwo-lo*
table cloth	**la tovaglia**	*to-val-ya*
tea towel	**il canovaccio per asciugare i piatti**	*ka-no-va-cho pair a-shoo-gar-eh ee pyat-tee*
towel	**l'asciugamano** *m*	*a-shoo-ga-ma-no*

Markets

Which day is the market?	**In che giorno fanno il mercato?**	*Een keh jor-no fan-no eel mair-ka-to*
Where is the market held?	**Dove fanno il mercato?**	*Do-veh fan-no eel mair-ka-to*
Is it a permanent/ covered market?	**È un mercato permanente/al coperto?**	*Eh oon mair-ka-to per-ma-nen-teh/ al ko-per-to*
What time does it open/close?	**A che ora apre/ chiude?**	*A keh o-ra ap-reh/ kyoo-deh*
Is there a market today in a nearby town?	**Oggi c'è un mercato in una città vicina?**	*Od-jee che oon mair-ka-to een oon-a cheet-ta vee-chee-na*

Photography

I'd like to buy a ... camera	**Vorrei comprare una macchina fotografica ...**	*Vor-ray kom-prar-eh oon-a mak-kee-na fo-to-gra-fee-ka ...*
digital	**digitale**	*dee-jee-ta-leh*
disposable	**usa e getta**	*oo-sa eh jet-ta*
Do you have a memory card for this camera?	**Avete una memory card per questa macchina fotografica?**	*A-ve-teh oon-a memory card pair kwe-sta mak-kee-na fo-to-gra-fee-ka*
Can you print photos from this card/ disk/USB?	**È possible sviluppare delle foto da questa card/questo disco/ questa pennina (USB)**	*Eh pos-see-bee-leh svee-loo-pa-reh del-leh fo-to da kwes-ta card/kwe-sto dee-sko/kwe-sta pen-nee-na (oo es-se bee)*

I'd like ... prints/ enlargements of this image/photo	**Vorrei ... stampe/ ingrandimenti di questa immagine/ foto**	*Vor-**ray** ... stam-peh/ een-gran-dee-men-tee dee kwes-ta eem-**ma**-jee- neh/fo-to*
I'd like the express service	**Vorrei un sevizio espresso**	*Vor-**ray** oon sair-veet-syo es-pres-so*
When will they be ready?	**Quando saranno pronte?**	*Kwan-do sa-ran-no pron-teh*
Will they be done tomorrow?	**Saranno pronte per domani?**	*Sa-ran-no pron-teh pair do-ma-nee*
My camera's not working. Can you mend it?	**La mia macchina non funziona. Può accomodarla?**	*La mee-a mak-kee-na non foont-syo-na. Pwo ak-ko-mo-dar-la*
You will have to leave the camera for a few days/hours	***Deve lasciare la macchina fotografica per alcuni giorni/alcune ore**	*De-ve la-sha-reh la mak-kee-na fo-to-**gra**- fee-ka pair al-koo-nee jor-nee/al-koo-neh o-reh*
battery	**la batteria**	*bat-tair-ee-a*
camcorder	**l'apparecchio video** *m*	*ap-pa-rek-kyo **vee**-de-o*
camera case	**la custodia per macchina fotografica**	*koo-sto-dya pair **mak**-kee-na fo-to-**gra**-fee-ka*
filter	**il filtro**	*feel-tro*
glossy	**la foto lucida**	*fo-to **loo**-chee-da*
lens	**la lente**	*len-teh*
lens cap	**il copriobiettivo**	*kop-ree-ob-yet-tee-vo*
light meter	**l'esposimetro** *m*	*e-spo-**zee**-me-tro*
matt	**appannato**	*ap-pan-na-to*

Repairs

This is broken	**Questo è rotto**	*Kwes-to eh rot-to*
Can you repair it?	**Può ripararlo?**	*Pwo ree-pa-rar-lo*
How much will it cost?	**Quanto costerà?**	*Kwan-to kos-te-ra*
Can you do it while I wait?	**Può farlo mentre aspetto?**	*Pwo far-lo men-tre as-pet-to*
When should I pick them up?	**Quando devo venire a ritirarli?**	*Kwan-do de-vo ve-neer-eh a ree-teer-ar-lee*
I want these shoes soled (with leather)	**Vorrei far risuolare queste scarpe (in cuoio)**	*Vor-ray far ree-swo-lar-eh kwes-teh skar-peh (een kwo-yo)*
Can you heel these shoes (with rubber)?	**Può mettere dei tacchi (di gomma) a queste scarpe?**	*Pwo met-tair-eh day tak-kee (dee gom-ma) a kwes-teh skar-peh*
Do you sell shoelaces?	**Vendete lacci per scarpe?**	*Ven-de-teh la-chee pair skar-peh*
My watch is broken	**Mi si è rotto l'orologio**	*Mee see eh rot-to lo-ro-lo-jo*
I have broken	**Ho rotto**	*O rot-to*
the glass	**il vetro**	*eel vet-ro*
the strap	**la cinghia**	*la cheen-gya*
the spring	**lo scatto**	*lo skat-to*
My watch is always fast/slow	**Il mio orologio va sempre avanti/indietro**	*Eel mee-o o-ro-lo-jo va sem-preh a-van-tee/een-dye-tro*

Could you mend this bag for me, please?	**Potrebbe aggiustarmi questa borsa, per favore?**	*Pot-reb-beh ad-joo-star-mee kwe-sta bor-sa, pair fa-vo-reh*
Could you put in a new zip?	**Potrebbe mettere una nuova cerniera?**	*Pot-reb-beh met-tair-eh oon-a nwo-va chair-nye-ra*
The charm has come loose	**Il ciondolo si è allentato**	*Eel chon-do-lo see eh al-len-ta-to*
The stone is loose	**La gemma non è ben fissa**	*La jem-ma non eh ben fees-sa*
The fastener/clip/chain is broken	**La chiusura/la molletta/la catena è rotta**	*La kyoo-zoo-ra/la mol-let-ta/la ka-te-na eh rot-ta*
It can't be repaired	***Non si può riparare**	*Non see pwo ree-pa-rar-eh*
You need a new one	***Deve comprarne uno nuovo**	*De-veh kom-prar-neh oon o nwo-vo*
How much will a new one cost?	**Quanto costerebbe nuovo?**	*Kwan-to kos-te-reb-beh nwo-vo*

Toiletries

A packet of razor blades, please	**Un pacchetto di lamette da barba, per favore**	*Oon pak-ket-to dee la-met-teh da bar-ba, pair fa-vor-eh*
Do you have some after-shave?	**Ha una lozione de barba?**	*A oon-a lot-syo-neh de bar ba*
How much is this lotion?	**Quanto costa questa lozione?**	*Kwan-to kos-ta kwes-ta lot-syo-neh*
A tube of toothpaste, please	**Un dentifricio, per favore**	*Oon den-tee-free-cho, pair fa-vor-eh*

A box of paper handkerchiefs, please	Una scatola di fazzoletti di carta, per favore	*Oon-a **ska**-to-la dee fat-so-let-tee dee kar-ta, pair fa-vor-eh*
I want some eau-de-cologne/perfume	Vorrei dell'acqua di colonia/un profumo	*Vor-**ray** del-lak-wa dee ko-lon-ya/oon pro-foo-mo*
A bottle of shampoo for normal/dry/greasy hair	Una bottiglia di shampoo per capelli normali/secchi/grassi	*Oon-a bot-teel-ya dee sham-poo pair kap-pel-lee nor-ma-lee/sek-kee/gras-see*
Do you sell sanitary towels/tampons/cotton wool?	Vende assorbenti igienici/tamponi/cotone?	*Ven-deh as-sor-ben-tee ee-**jen**-ee-chee/tam-po-nee/ko-to-neh*
Do you have suntan oil/cream?	Ha qualche lozione/crema abbronzante?	*A kwal-keh lot-syo-neh/kre-ma ab-brond-zan-teh*
I'd like some	Vorrei	*Vor-**ray***
cleansing cream/lotion	una crema/lozione detergente	*oon-a kre-ma/lot-syo-neh de-tair-jen-teh*
conditioner	un balsamo	*oon **bal**-sa-mo*
hand cream	una crema per le mani	*oon-a kre-ma pair le ma-nee*
moisturizer	una crema idratante	*oon-a kre-ma eed-ra-tan-teh*
soap	una saponetta	*oon-a sa-po-net-ta*
sun cream for children	crema solare per ragazzi	*kre-ma so-lar-eh pair ra-gat-see*
toilet paper	carta igienica	*kar-ta ee-**jen**-ee-ka*

SIGHTSEEING[1]

Key Phrases

Where is the tourist office?	**Dov'è l'ufficio turistico?**	*Dov-**eh** loof-fee-cho too-**rees**-tee-ko*
We want to take a sightseeing tour of the city	**Vogliamo fare un giro turistico della città**	*Vol-ya-mo far-eh oon jeer-o toor-**ees**-tee-ko del-la cheet-**ta***
Is there a walking tour of the town?	**C'è un giro turistico da fare a piedi?**	*Cheh oon jee-ro toor-**ees**-tee-ko da fa-reh a pye-dee*
How much does the tour cost?	**Quanto costa il giro?**	*Kwan-to kos-ta eel jee-ro*
Is there a map/plan of the places to visit?	**C'è una mappa/una pianta con le cose da vedere?**	*Cheh oon-a map-pa/ oon-a pyan-ta kon leh ko-zeh da ve-dair-eh*
I want a good guidebook	**Vorrei una buona guida**	*Vor-**ray** oon-a bwo-na gwee-da*
Is there access for wheelchairs?	**Ci si può entrare con le sedie a rotelle?**	*Chee see pwo en-trar-eh kon le se-dyeh a ro-tel-leh*
Is there an audio guide in English?	**C'è una guida audio in inglese?**	*Cheh oon-a gwee-da ow-dyo een een-gle-zeh*

1. See also Getting Around (p. 12) and Directions (p. 53).

What should we see here?	**Cosa c'è di interessante da vedere qui?**	*Ko-za cheh dee een-tair-es-san-teh da ve-dair-eh kwee*
Is there a good sightseeing tour?	**C'è un bel giro turistico?**	*Cheh oon bel jee-ro too-rees-tee-ko*
Can you suggest an interesting half-day excursion?	**Potrebbe consigliarmi un'escursione interessante di mezza giornata?**	*Pot-reb-beh kon-seel-yar-mee oo-nes-koor-syo-neh dee med-za jor-na-ta*
Can we take	**Possiamo fare**	*Pos-sya-mo fa-re*
a cruise?	**una crociera?**	*oon-a kro-che-ra*
a balloon flight?	**un giro in mongolfiera?**	*oon jee-ro een mon-gol-fye-ra*
We want to go hiking	**Vogliamo fare delle escursioni**	*Vol-ya-mo fa-re del-le es-koor-syo-nee*
Do we need a guide?	**Abbiamo bisogno di una guida?**	*Ab-bya-mo bee-zon-yo dee oon-a gwee-da*
It's beautiful	**È bellissimo**	*Eh bel-lees-see-mo*
amusing/funny	**divertente/buffo**	*dee-vair-ten-teh/ boof-fo*
impressive	**impressionante**	*eem-pres-syo-nan-teh*
romantic	**romantico**	*ro-man-tee-ko*
stunning	**spettacolare**	*spet-ta-ko-la-reh*
unusual	**insolito**	*een-so-lee-to*

Exploring

Where is the old part of the city?	**Dov'è il centro storico?**	*Dov-eh eel chen-tro sto-ree-ko*
I'd like to walk around the old town	**Vorrei fare un giro per il centro storico**	*Vor-ray far-eh oon jee-ro pair eel chen-tro sto-ree-ko*
Is there a good street plan showing the buildings?	**C'è una bella pianta con gli edifici indicati?**	*Cheh oon-a bel-la pyan-ta kon lyee e-dee-fee-chee een-dee-ka-tee*
We want to visit	**Vogliamo visitare**	*Vol-ya-mo vee-zee-tar-eh*
the cathedral	**la cattedrale**	*la kat-te-dra-leh*
the cloister	**il convento**	*eel kon-ven-to*
the fortress	**la fortezza**	*la for-tet-sa*
the library	**la biblioteca**	*la beeb-lyo-te-ka*
the monastery	**il monastero**	*eel mo-nas-te-ro*
the palace	**il palazzo**	*eel pa-lat-so*
the ruins	**le rovine**	*leh ro-vee-neh*
May we walk around the walls/go up the tower?	**Si può fare il giro delle mura a piedi/ salire la torre?**	*See pwo far-eh eel jee-ro del-leh moo-ra a pye-dee/ sa-leer-eh la tor-reh*
What is this building?	**Cos'è quest'edificio?**	*Koz-eh kwes-te-dee-fee-cho*
Where is	**Dov'è**	*Dov-eh*
the house of …?	**la casa di …?**	*la ka-za dee …*
the church of …?	**la chiesa di …?**	*la kye-za dee …*
the cemetery of …?	**il cimitero di …?**	*eel chee-mee-te-ro dee …*

| Where is the antiques/flea market? | Dov'è il mercato delle antichità/delle pulci? | Dov-*eh* eel mair-ka-to del-leh an-tee-kee-*ta*/del-leh pool-chee |

Gardens, Parks and Zoos

Where is the botanical garden/zoo?	Dov'è il giardino botanico/lo zoo?	Dov-*eh* eel jar-dee-no bo-*ta*-nee-ko/lo zoo
How do I get to the park?	Qual'è la strada per il parco?	Kwal-*eh* la stra-da pair eel par-ko
Can we walk there?	Si può fare una passeggiata lì?	See pwo far-eh oon-a pas-sed-ja-ta lee
Can we drive through the park?	Si può girare a macchina nel parco?	See pwo jee-rar-eh a *mak*-kee-na nel par-ko
Are the gardens open to the public?	Il giardino è aperto al pubblico?	Eel jar-dee-no eh a-pair-to al *poob*-blee-ko
What time do the gardens close?	A che ora chiude il giardino?	A keh or-a kyoo-deh eel jar-dee-no
Is there a plan of the gardens?	C'è una pianta dei giardini?	Cheh oon-a pyan-ta day jar-dee-nee
Who designed the gardens?	Chi creò i giardini?	Kee kre-*o* ee jar-dee-nee
Where is the tropical plant house/lake?	Dov'è la serra delle piante tropicali/il lago?	Dov-*eh* la ser-ra del-leh pyan-teh tro-pee-ka-lee/eel la-go

Historic Sites

We want to visit . . .; can we get there by car?	**Vogliamo visitare . . .; ci si arriva in macchina?**	*Vol-ya-mo vee-zee-tar-eh . . .; chee see ar-ree-va een **mak**-kee-na*
Is it far to walk?	**È lungo a piedi?**	*Eh loon-go a pye-dee*
Is it an easy walk?	**È facile arrivarci a piedi?**	*Eh **fa**-chee-leh ar-ree-var-chee a pye-dee*
Is there access for wheelchairs?	**Ci si può entrare con le sedie a rotelle?**	*Chee see pwo en-trar-eh kon le se-dyeh a ro-tel-leh*
Is it far to	**È distante**	*Eh dees-tan-teh*
the aqueduct?	**l'acquedotto?**	*lak-weh-dot-to*
the castle?	**il castello?**	*eel kas-tel-lo*
the fort?	**la fortezza?**	*la for-tet-sa*
the fortifications?	**le fortificazioni?**	*leh for-tee-fee-cat-syo-nee*
the fountain?	**la fontana?**	*la fon-ta-na*
the gate?	**il cancello?**	*eel kan-chel-lo*
the walls?	**le mura?**	*leh moo-ra*
When was it built?	**Quando fu costruito?**	*Kwan-do foo kost-rwee-to*
Who built it?	**Chi lo costruì?**	*Kee lo kost-**rwee***

Museums and Art Galleries

When does the museum open/close?	**A che ora apre/ chiude il museo?**	*A keh or-a ap-reh/kyoo-deh eel moo-ze-o*
Is it open every day?	**È aperto ogni giorno?**	*Eh a-pair-to on-yee jor-no*

The gallery is closed on Mondays	*La galleria è chiusa il lunedì	*La gal-lair-ee-a eh kyoo-za eel loo-ne-**dee**
Is there wheelchair access?	C'è l'accesso per la sedia a rotelle?	Cheh la-ches-so pair la se-dya a ro-tel-leh
How much does it cost?	Quanto costa l'ingresso?	Kwan-to kos-ta leen-gres-so
Are there reductions for	Ci sono riduzioni per	Chee so-no ree-doot-syo-nee pair
children?	(i) ragazzi?	ra-gat-see
students?	(gli) studenti?	stoo-den-tee
seniors?	(gli) anziani?	lyee an-zya-nee
Are admission fees lower some days?	Ci sono prezzi ridotti certi giorni?	Chee so-no pret-see ree-dot-tee chair-tee jor-nee
Admission free	*Ingresso libero	Een-gres-so **lee**-bair-o
Have you got a ticket?	*Ha il biglietto?	A eel beel-yet-to
Where do I buy a ticket?	Dove si comprano i biglietti?	Do-veh see **kom**-pra-no ee beel-yet-tee
Is there a family ticket?	C'è un biglietto famiglia?	Cheh oon beel-yet-to fa-meel-ya
Are there guided tours of the museum?	Ci sono giri organizzati del museo?	Chee so-no jee-ree or-ga-neet-sa-tee del moo-ze-o
Does the guide speak English?	Parla inglese la guida?	Par-la een-gle-zeh la gwee-da
Is there an audio guide in English?	C'è una guida audio in inglese?	Cheh oon-a gwee-da ow-dyo een een-gle-zeh

We don't need a guide	**Non abbiamo bisogno di una guida**	*Non ab-bya-mo bee-zon-yo dee oon-a gwee-da*
I would prefer to go round alone; is that all right?	**Preferisco girare da solo; va bene?**	*Pre-fe-rees-ko jee-rar-eh da so-lo; va be-neh*
Where is the . . . collection/exhibition?	**Dov'è la collezione/ l'esposizione . . .?**	*Dov-eh la kol-let-syo-neh/ les-po-zeet-syo-neh . . .*
It's over there	***È da quella parte**	*Eh da kwel-la par-teh*
Please leave your bag in the cloakroom	***Lasci la cartella nel guardaroba, per favore**	*La-shee la kar-tel-la nel gwar-da-ro-ba, pair fa-vor-eh*
Can I take photographs?	**Si possono fare delle fotografie?**	*See pos-so-no far-eh del-leh fo-to-gra-fee-eh*
Can I use a tripod?	**Posso servirmi del cavalletto?**	*Pos-so sair-veer-mee del ca-val-let-to*
Photographs are not allowed	***Vietato fotografare**	*Vye-ta-to fo-to-gra-far-eh*
I want to buy a catalogue	**Vorrei comprare un catalogo**	*Vor-ray kom-prar-eh oon ka-ta-lo-go*

Places of Worship

Is there	**C'è**	*Cheh*
a Catholic church?	**una chiesa cattolica?**	*oon-a kye-za kat-to-lee-ka*
a Protestant church?	**una chiesa protestante?**	*oon-a kye-za pro-tes-tan-teh*
a mosque?	**una moschea?**	*oon-a mos-ke-a*
a synagogue?	**una sinagoga?**	*oon-a see-na-go-ga*

What time is mass/the service?	**A che ora è la messa/la funzione?**	*A keh or-a eh la mes-sa/la foont-syo-neh*
I'd like to look round the church	**Vorrei fare il giro della chiesa**	*Vor-**ray** far-eh eel jee-ro del-la kye-za*
When was the church built?	**Quando fu costruita la chiesa?**	*Kwan-do foo kost-rwee-ta la kye-za*

Tours

We want to take a sightseeing tour of the city	**Vogliamo fare un giro turistico della città**	*Vol-ya-mo far-eh oon jeer-o toor-**ees**-tee-ko del-la cheet-**ta***
Is there a sightseeing tour (of the city)?	**C'è un giro turistico (della città)?**	*Cheh oon jee-ro toor-**ees**-tee-ko (del-la cheet-**ta**)*
Is there a walking tour of the town?	**C'è un giro turistico da fare a piedi?**	*Cheh oon jee-ro toor-**ees**-tee-ko da fa-reh a pye-dee*
Is there an excursion to …?	**C'è una escursione per …?**	*Cheh oon-a es-koor-syo-neh pair …*
How long does the tour take?	**Quanto tempo dura il giro?**	*Kwan-to tem-po doo-ra eel jee-ro*
When does it leave/return?	**A che ora parte/ritorna?**	*A keh o-ra par-teh/ree-tor-na?*
Does the bus/coach call at our hotel?	**Questo autobus/pullman passa dal nostro albergo?**	*Kwes-to **ow**-to-bus/pool-man pas-sa dal nos-tro al-bair-go*
How much does the tour cost?	**Quanto costa il giro?**	*Kwan-to kos-ta eel jee-ro*
Are all admission fees included?	**Sono compresi tutti gli ingressi?**	*So-no kom-pre-zee toot-tee lyee een-gres-see*

Does it include lunch?	**È compreso il pranzo?**	*Eh kom-pre-zo eel prand-zo*
Could we stop here to	**Possiamo fermarci qui per**	*Pos-sya-mo fair-mar-chee kwee pair*
take photographs?	**fare foto?**	*fa-re fo-to*
buy souvenirs?	**comprare souvenir?**	*kom-pra-reh souvenir*
get a bottle of water?	**prendere una bottiglia d'acqua?**	*pren-dair-eh oon-a bot-teel-ya dak-wa*
How long do we stay here?	**Quanto dobbiamo stare qui?**	*Kwan-to dob-bya-mo sta-reh kwee*

SPORTS AND LEISURE[1]

Where is the nearest tennis court/golf course?	Dov'è il più vicino campo da tennis/ campo di golf?	Dov-*eh* eel pyoo vee-chee-no kam-po da tennis/ kam-po dee golf
Is there	C'è	Cheh
a gym?	una palestra?	oon-a pa-les-tra
a running track?	un campo da corsa?	oon kam-po da kor-sa
What is the charge per	Quanto si paga	Kwan-to see pa-ga
game?	per partita?	pair par-tee-ta
hour?	all'ora?	al-lor-a
day?	a giornata?	a jor-na-ta
Is it a club?	È un'associazione?	Eh oon-as-so-chat-syo-neh
Do I need temporary membership?	Ci vuole un'iscrizione provvisoria?	Chee vwo-leh oon-ees-kreet-syo-neh prov-vee-zor-ya
Where can we go swimming/fishing?	Dove si può andare per fare il bagno/per pescare?	Do-veh see pwo an-dar-eh pair far-eh eel ban-yo/ pair pes-kar-eh
Can I hire	Si può noleggiare	See pwo no-led-jar-eh
a racket?	una racchetta?	oon-a rak-ket-ta
golf clubs?	mazze da golf?	mat-seh da golf
fishing tackle?	arnesi da pesca?	ar-ne-zee da pes-ka

1. See also By Bike or Moped (p. 46)

Do I need a permit?	**Occorre un permesso speciale?**	*Ok-kor-reh oon pair-mes-so spe-cha-leh*
Where do I get a permit?	**Chi rilascia questo permesso?**	*Kee ree-la-sha kwes-to pair-mes-so*
Is there a skating rink?	**C'è una pista per pattinaggio?**	*Cheh oon-a pees-ta pair pat-tee-nad-jo*
Can I hire skates?	**Posso noleggiare i pattini?**	*Pos-so no-led-jar-eh ee pat-tee-nee*
I'd like to ride	**Vorrei andare a cavallo**	*Vor-ray an-dar-eh a ka-val-lo*
Is there a riding stable nearby?	**C'è una scuderia qui vicino?**	*Cheh oon-a skoo-de-ree-a kwee vee-chee-no*
Do you give lessons?	**Si danno lezioni?**	*See dan-no let-syo-nee*
I am an inexperienced rider	**Non ho molta esperienza**	*Non o mol-ta es per-yen-sa*
I am a good rider	**Cavalco bene**	*Ka-val-ko be-neh*

Winter Sports

Can I hire skis/ ski boots?	**Posso noleggiare degli sci/scarponi da sci?**	*Pos-so no-led-jar-eh del-yee shee/skar-po-nee da shee*
Can I take lessons here?	**Danno anche lezioni?**	*Dan-no an-keh let-syo-nee*
I've never skied before	**Non ho mai sciato**	*Non o my shee-a-to*
Are there ski runs for beginners/average skiers?	**Ci sono delle piste per principianti/ sciatori medii?**	*Chee so-no del-leh pees-teh pair preen-chee-pyan-tee/shee-a-tor-ee me-dee*

I'd like to go cross-country skiing	**Vorrei fare lo sci di fondo**	*Vor-**ray** far-eh lo shee dee fon-do*
Are there ski lifts?	**Vi sono sciovie?**	*Vee so-no sho-vee-eh*
Can we go snowboarding?	**Possiamo fare snowboarding?**	*Pos-sya-mo fa-reh snowboarding*
Can I buy a lift pass?	**Posso comprare un lift pass?**	*Pos-so kom-prar-eh oon lift pass*

At the Beach

Where are the best beaches?	**Dove sono le migliori spiagge?**	*Do-veh so-no leh meel-yor-ee spyad-jeh*
Is there a quiet beach near here?	**C'è una spiaggia tranquilla qui vicino?**	*Cheh oon-a spyad-ja tran-kweel-la kwee vee-chee-no*
Can we walk or is it too far?	**Ci si può andare a piedi o è troppo lontana?**	*Chee see pwo an-dar-eh a pye-dee o eh trop-po lon-ta-na*
Is there a bus to the beach?	**C'è un autobus per andare alla spiaggia?**	*Cheh oon **ow**-to-bus pair an-dar-eh al-la spyad-ja*
Is the beach sand or shingle?	**La spiaggia è in sabbia o ghiaia?**	*La spyad-ja eh een sab-bya o gya-ya*
Is it dangerous to bathe here?	**È pericoloso fare bagni qui?**	*Eh pair-ee-ko-lo-zo far-eh ban-yee kwee*
Is it safe for swimming?	**Si può nuotare senza pericolo?**	*See pwo nwo-tar-eh send-za pair-**ee**-ko-lo*
Is there a lifeguard?	**C'è un bagnino?**	*Cheh oon ban-yee-no*

Is it safe for small children?	**Questa spiaggia è sicura per i bambini?**	*Kwes-ta spyad-ja eh see-koo-ra pair ee bam-bee-nee*
Bathing prohibited	***Vietato fare bagni**	*Vye-ta-to far-eh ban-yee*
Diving prohibited	***Vietato tuffarsi**	*Vye-ta-to toof-far-see*
It's dangerous	***È pericoloso**	*Eh pair-ee-ko-lo-zo*
What time is high/ low tide?	**A che ora arriva la bassa/l'alta marea?**	*A keh or-a ar-ree-va la bas-sa/lal-ta ma-re-a*
I'd like a beach hut for	**Vorrei una cabina per**	*Vor-**ray** oon-a ka-bee-na pair*
the day	**oggi soltanto**	*od-jee sol-lan-to*
the morning	**stamani**	*sta-ma-nee*
two hours	**due ore**	*doo-eh or-eh*
I'd like to hire a deckchair/sunshade	**Vorrei noleggiare una sedia a sdraio/ un ombrellone**	*Vor-**ray** no-led-jar-eh oon-a se-dya a zdra-yo/ oon om-brel-lo-neh*
Where can I buy	**Dove posso comprare**	*Do-veh pos-so kom-prar-eh*
a snorkel?	**un boccaglio?**	*oon bok-kal-yo*
flippers?	**delle pinne?**	*del-leh peen-neh*
a bucket and spade?	**un secchiello e una paletta?**	*oon sek-kyel-lo ed oon-a pa-let-ta*
ball	**il pallone/palla**	*pal-lo-neh/pal-la*
bat	**il bastone**	*bas-to-neh*
beach bag	**il borsone da spiaggia**	*bor-so-neh da spyad-ja*

boat	la barca	bar-ka
sailing	a vela	a ve-la
motor	a motore	a mo-tor-eh
rowing	a remi	a re-mee
cliffs	gli scogli	skol-yee
crab	il granchio	gran-kyo
first aid	il pronto soccorso	pron-to sok-kor-so
jellyfish	la medusa	me-doo-za
lifebelt/vest	la cintura/il giubbotto/il di salvataggio	cheen-too-ra/ joob-bot-to/dee sal-va-tad-jo
lighthouse	il faro	fa-ro
rock	la roccia	ro-cha
sand	la sabbia	sab-bya
sandbank	la banchina di sabbia	ban-kee-na dee sab-bya
sandcastle	il castello di sabbia	kas-tel-lo dee sab-bya
shell	la conchiglia	kon-kee-lya
sun	il sole	so-leh
sunglasses	gli occhiali da sole	ok-kya-lee da so-leh
sunshade	l'ombrellone m	om-brel-lo-neh
swimsuit/swimming trunks	il costume da bagno	kos-too-meh da ban-yo
towel	asciugamano m	a-shoo-ga-ma-no
waves	le onde	on-deh

Swimming

Is there an indoor/outdoor swimming pool?	C'è una piscina coperta/all'aperto?	Cheh oon-a pee-shee-na ko-pair-ta/al-la-pair-to
Is it heated?	È riscaldata?	Eh rees-kal-da-ta
How's the water? Cold?	Com'è l'acqua? Fredda?	Kom-eh lak-wa. Fred-da
It's warm	È tiepida	Eh tye-pee-da
Is it salt or fresh water?	È acqua salata o dolce?	Eh ak-wa sa-la-ta o dol-cheh
Can we swim in the lake/river?	Si può fare un bagno nel lago/nel fiume?	See pwo far-eh oon ban-yo nel la-go/nel fyoo-meh
There's a strong current here	*C'è una forte corrente qui	Cheh oon-a for-teh kor-ren-teh kwee
Are you a strong swimmer?	*Nuota bene lei?	Nwo-ta be-neh lay
Is it deep?	È profonda l'acqua qui?	Eh pro-fon-da lak-wa kwee
Are there showers?	Ci sono docce?	Chee so-no do-cheh
No lifeguard on duty	*Non ci sono bagnini in servizio	Non chee so-no ban-yee-nee een sair-veet-syo
armbands	i braccioli	bra-cho-lee
goggles	gli occhialini	ok-kya-lee-nee
rubber ring	l'anello di gomma *m*	a-nel-lo dee gom-ma
swimsuit	il costume da bagno	kos-too-meh da ban-yo
towel	l'asciugamano *m*	a-shoo-ga-ma-no
trunks	il costume da bagno	kos-too-meh da ban-yo

Watersports

I'd like to try waterskiing	**Vorrei fare dello sci nautico**	*Vor-ray far-eh del-lo shee now-tee-ko*
I haven't waterskied before	**Non ho mai fatto lo sci nautico**	*Non o my fat-to lo shee now-tee-ko*
Can I hire a wetsuit?	**Posso noleggiare una muta subacquea?**	*Pos-so no-led-jar-eh oon-a moo-ta soob-ak-we-a*
Should I wear a life jacket?	**Dovrei mettermi un giubbotto di salvataggio?**	*Dov-ray met-tair-mee oon joob-bot-to dee sal-va-tad-jo*
Do you have a course on windsurfing for beginners?	**Avete un corso di windsurf per principianti?**	*A-ve-teh oon kor-so dee windsurf pair preen-chee-pyan-tee*
Can I hire	**Si possono noleggiare**	*See pos-so-no no-led-jar-eh*
a rowing boat?	**una barca a remi?**	*oon-a bar-ka a re-mee*
a motor boat?	**una barca a motore?**	*oon-a bar-ka a mo-tor-eh*
a wind surfer?	**un windsurf?**	*oon windsurf*
a surf board?	**una tavola da surf?**	*oon-a ta-vo-la da surf*
waterskis?	**degli sci d'acqua?**	*shee dak-wa*
diving equipment?	**attrezzatura subacquea?**	*at-tret-sa-too-ra soob-ak-we-a*
Is there a map of the river?	**C'è una mappa del fiume?**	*Cheh oon-a map-pa del fyoo-meh*
Are there many locks to pass?	**Ci sono tante serrande da chiusa?**	*Chee so-no tan-teh ser-ran-deh da kyoo-za*
Can we get fuel here?	**Si può comprare il carburante qui?**	*See pwo kom-prar-eh eel kar-boo-ran-teh kwee*

Where's the harbour?	**Dov'è il porto?**	*Dov-eh eel por-to*
Can we go out in a fishing boat?	**Si può andare in un battello da pesca?**	*See pwo an-dar-eh een oon bat-tel-lo da pes-ka*
We want to go fishing	**Vorremmo andare a pescare**	*Vor-rem-mo an-dar-eh a pes-kar-eh*
What does it cost by the hour?	**Quanto costa all'ora?**	*Kwan-to kos-ta al-lor-a*

Walking[1]

I'd like a map of the area showing walking trails	**Vorrei una cartina che mostri percorsi da fare a piedi**	*Vor-**ray** oon-a kar-tee-nu keh mos-tree pair-kor-see da fa-reh a pye-dee*
Can we walk?	**Ci si arriva a piedi?**	*Chee see ar-ree-va a pye-dee*
How far is the next village?	**Quanto dista il prossimo paese?**	*Kwan-to dees-ta eel **pros**-see-mo pa-e-zeh*
How long is the walk to . . .?	**Quanto dura la camminata?**	*Kwan-to doo-ra la kam-mee-na-ta*
It's an hour's walk to . . .*	**È un'ora a piedi per . . .**	*Eh oo-no-ra a pye-dee pair . . .*
Which way is	**In quale direzione è**	*Een kwa-leh dee-ret-syo-neh eh*
the nature reserve?	**la riserva naturale?**	*la ree-zair-va na-too-ra-leh*
the lake?	**il lago?**	*eel la-go*
the waterfall?	**la cascata?**	*la kas-ka-ta*

1. See also Directions (p. 53).

Is there a scenic walk to...	C'è una camminata panoramica per ...	*Cheh oon-a kam-mee-na-ta pa-no-ra-mee-ka pair ...*
Is it steep/far/difficult?	È ripida/lontana/difficile?	*Eh ree-pee-da/lon-ta-na/deef-fee-chee-leh*
Is there a footpath to ...?	C'è un sentiero per ...?	*Cheh oon sen-tyair-o pair ...*
Is it possible to go across country?	Ci si può arrivare per i campi?	*Chee see pwo ar-ree-var-eh pair ee kam-pee*
Is there a shortcut?	C'è una scorciatoia?	*Cheh oon-a skor-cha-toy-a*
Is this a public footpath?	È questo un sentiero autorizzato?	*Eh kwes-to oon sen-tyair-o ow-to-reet-sa-to*
Is there a bridge across the stream?	C'è un ponte sul torrente?	*Cheh oon pon-teh sool tor-ren-teh*
Can you give me a lift to ...?	Può darmi un passaggio per ...?	*Pwo dar-mee oon pas-sad-jo pair ...*

Spectator Sports and Indoor Games

We want to go to a football match/the tennis tournament	Vogliamo andare ad una partita di calcio/al torneo di tennis	*Vol-ya-mo an-dar-eh ad oon-a par-tee-ta dee kal-cho/al tor-ne-o dee tennis*
Where is the stadium?	Dov'è lo stadio?	*Dov-eh lo sta-dyo*
Can you get us tickets?	Può procurarci dei biglietti?	*Pwo pro-koo-rar-chee day beel-yet-tee*

Are there any seats left in the grandstand?	Ci sono ancora posti in tribuna?	*Chee so-no an-kor-a pos-tee een tree-boon-a*
How much are the cheapest seats?	Quanto costano i posti meno cari?	*Kwan-to kos-ta-no ee pos-tee me-no ka-ree*
Which are the cheapest seats?	Quali sono i posti meno costosi?	*Kwal-ee so-no ee pos-tee me-no kos-to-zee*
Are the seats in the sun/shade?	Questi posti sono al sole/all'ombra?	*Kwes-tee pos-tee so-no al so-leh/al-lom-bra*
Who's playing?	Chi gioca?	*Kee jo-ka*
When does it start?	Quando comincia?	*Kwan-do ko-meen-cha*
What is the score?	Qual'è il punteggio?	*Kwal-eh eel poon-ted-jo*
Who's winning?	Chi vince?	*Kee veen-cheh*
Where's the racecourse?	Dove sono le corse di cavalli?	*Do-veh so-no le kor-seh dee ka-val-lee*
When's the next meeting?	Quando sarà il prossimo incontro?	*Kwan-do sa-ra eel pros-see-mo een-kon-tro*
Which is the favourite?	Chi è il favorito?	*Kee eh eel fa-vo-ree-to*
Who's the jockey?	Chi è il fantino?	*Kee eh eel fan-tee-no*
Where can I place a bet?	Dove posso puntare delle scommesse?	*Do-veh pos-so poon-ta-reh del-le scom-mes-seh?*
Do you play cards?	Gioca a carte?	*Jo-ka a kar-teh*
Would you like a game of chess?	Ha voglia di fare una partita a scacchi?	*A vol-ya dee far-eh oon-a par-tee-ta a skak-kee*
I'll give you a game of checkers, if you like	Posso fare una partita a dama, se vuole	*Pos-so far-eh oon-a par-tee-ta a da-ma, seh vwo-leh*

TRAVELLING WITH CHILDREN

Key Phrases

Are children allowed?	**I bambini possono entrare?**	*Ee bam-bee-nee pos-so-no en-tra-reh*
Is there a discount for children?	**C'è uno sconto per i bambini?**	*Cheh oon-o skon-to pair ee bam-bee-nee*
Are there any organized activities for children?	**Ci sono delle attività organizzate per bambini?**	*Chee so-no del-le at-tee-vee-ta or-ga-neet-sa-teh pair bam-bee-nee*
Can you put a child's bed/cot in our room?	**Può mettere un letto da bambino/una culla nella nostra stanza?**	*Pwo met-tair-eh oon let-to da bam-bee-no/oon-a kool-la nel-la nos-tra stan-za*
Where can I feed/change my baby?	**Dove posso allattare il bimbo/cambiare il pannolino al bimbo?**	*Do-veh pos-so al-lat-tar-eh eel beem-bo/kam-byar-eh eel pan-no-lee-no al beem-bo*
My son/daughter is missing	**Mio figlio/mia figlia è sparito/sparita**	*Mee-o feel-yo/mee-a feel-ya eh spa-ree-to/spa-ree-ta*

Out and About[1]

Is there	C'è	*Cheh*
an amusement park	**un parco dei divertimenti**	*oon par-ko day dee-vair-tee-men-tee*
a park	**un parco**	*oon par-ko*
a zoo	**uno zoo**	*oon-o zoo*
a toyshop nearby?	**un negozio di giocattoli qui vicino?**	*oon ne-got-syo dee jo-**kat**-to-lee kwee vee-chee-no*
Where is the aquarium?	**Dov'è l'acquario?**	*Dov-**eh** la-kwa-ryo*
Is there	C'è	*Cheh*
a paddling pool?	**una piscina per bambini?**	*oon-a pee-shee-na pair bam-bee-nee*
a playground?	**un campo di ricreazione?**	*oon kam-po dee ree-kre-at-syo-neh*
a games room?	**una stanza dei giochi?**	*oon-a stan-za day jo-kee*
Is the beach safe for children?	**È una spiaggia sicura per bambini?**	*Eh oon-a spyad-ja see-koo-ra pair bam-bee-nee*
Can we hire a paddle boat?	**Possiamo noleggiare un pedalò?**	*Pos-sya-mo no-led-jar-eh oon pe-da-**lo***

1. See also At the Beach (p. 214)

I'd like	Vorrei	*Vor-ray*
a doll	**una bambola**	*oon-a bam-bo-la*
some playing cards	**delle carte da gioco**	*del-leh kar-teh da jo-ko*
He has lost his toy	**Ha perso il suo giocattolo**	*A pair-so eel soo-o jo-kat-to-lo*
I'm sorry if they have bothered you	**Mi scusa se l' hanno infestidita**	*Mee skoo-za seean-no een-fes-tee-dee-tah*

Everyday Needs

Can you put a child's bed/cot in our room?	**Può mettere un letto da bambino/una culla nella nostra stanza?**	*Pwo met-tair-eh oon let-to da bam-bee-no/ oon-a kool-la nel-la nos-tra stan-za*
Can you give us adjoining rooms?	**Può darci stanze contigue?**	*Pwo dar-chee stan-zeh kon-tee-gweh*
Does the hotel have a baby-sitting service?	**C'è un servizio baby-sitting nell'albergo?**	*Cheh oon sair-veet-syo baby-sitting nel-lal-bair-go*
Can you find me a baby-sitter?	**Può trovarmi un/ una baby-sitter?**	*Pwo tro-var-mee oon/ oon-a baby-sitter*
We shall be out for a couple of hours	**Usciamo per un paio d'ore**	*Oo-sha-mo pair oon pa-yo dor-eh*
We shall be back at …	**Torneremo alle …**	*Tor-ne-re-mo al-leh …*
You can reach me at …	**Mi trova al …**	*Mee tro-va al*
This is my mobile (cell) number	**Questo è il mio numero (di cellulare)**	*Kwes-to eh eel mee-o noo-mair-o (dee chel-loo-la-reh)*

Is there a children's menu?	**C'è un menù per bambini?**	*Cheh oon me-noo pair bam-bee-nee*
Do you have (half) portions for children?	**Si fanno porzioni per bambini?**	*See fan-no port-syo-nee pair bam-bee-nee*
Have you got a high chair?	**Ha un seggiolone?**	*A oon sed-jo-lo-neh*
Where can I feed/ change my baby?	**Dove posso allattare il bimbo/cambiare il pannolino al bimbo?**	*Do-veh pos-so al-lat-tar-eh eel beem-bo/kam-byar-eh eel pan-no-lee-no al beem-bo*
Can you heat this bottle for me?	**Mi potrebbe riscaldare questo poppatoio?**	*Mee pot-reb-beh rees-kal-dar-eh kwes-to pop-pa-to-yo*
I want	**Voglio**	*Vol-yo*
some baby wipes	**delle salviette per bambini**	*del-leh sal-vyet-teh pair bam-bee-nee*
a bib	**un bavaglino**	*oon ba-val-yee-no*
some disposable nappies	**dei pannolini usa e getta**	*day pan-no-lee-nee oo-za eh jet-ta*
a feeding bottle	**un biberon per neonati**	*oon bee-ber-on pair ne-o-na-tee*
some baby food	**del cibo per neonati**	*del chee-bo pair ne-o-na-tee*

Health and Emergencies[1]

| My daughter suffers from travel/car/train/ air/sea sickness | **Mia figlia soffre di mal di viaggio d'auto/di treno/ d'aria/di mare** | *Mee-a feel-ya sof-freh dee mal dee vyad-jo/dow-to/ dee tre-no/dar-ya/dee mar-reh* |

She has hurt herself	**Si è fatta male**	*See eh fat-ta ma-leh*
My son is ill	**Mio figlio è malato**	*Mee-o feel-yo eh ma-la-to*
He/she is allergic to ...	**Lui/lei è allergico/allergica a ...**	*Loo-ee/lay eh al-**lair**-jee-ko/al-lair-jee-ka a*
My son/daughter is missing	**Mio figlio/mia figlia è sparito/sparita**	*Mee-o feel-yo/mee-a feel-ya eh spa-ree-to/spa-ree-ta*
He/she is ... years old	**(Lui/lei) ha ... anni**	*(Loo-ee/lay) a ... an-nee*
He/she was wearing ...	**(Lui/lei) indossava ...**	*(Loo-ee/lay) een-dos-sa-va*

1. See also Doctor (p. 146).

WORK[1]

I'm here on business	**Sono qui per affari**	*So-no kwee pair af-far-ee*
Where is the conference centre?	**Dov'è il centro conferenze?**	*Dov-eh eel chen-tro kon-fair-ent-seh*
I'm here for the . . . trade fair	**Sono qui per la . . . fiera del commercio**	*So-no kwee pair la . . . fye-ra del kom-mair-cho*
I've come for/to	**Sono venuto/ venuta per/a**	*So-no ven-oo-to/ ven-oo-ta pair/a*
a conference	**una conferenza**	*oon-a kon-fair-ent-sa*
a seminar	**un seminario**	*oon se-mee-na-ryo*
This is my colleague	**Questo/questa è il mio/la mia collega**	*Kwes-to/kwes-ta eh eel mee-o/la mee-a col-le-ga*
I have an appointment with . . .	**Ho un appuntamento con . . .**	*O oon ap-poon-ta-men-to kon . . .*
My name is . . .	**Mi chiamo . . .**	*Mee kya-mo . . .*
Here is my card	**Ecco il mio bigliettino (da visita)**	*Ek-ko eel mee-o beel-yet-tee-no (da **vee**-zee-ta)*
Can you provide an interpreter?	**Potrebbe farmi avere un interprete?**	*Pot-reb-beh far-mee a-vair-eh oon een-**tair**-pre-teh*

1. See also Telephones, Mobiles and SMS (p. 91).

TIME AND DATES

Time

What time is it?	**Che ore sono?**	*Keh or-eh so-no*
It's one o'clock	**È l'una**	*Eh loon-a*
It's two o'clock	**Sono le due**	*So-no le doo-eh*
It's quarter to ten	**Sono le dieci meno un quarto**	*So-no le dye-chee me-no oon kwar-to*
It's twenty to three	**Sono le tre meno venti**	*So-no le treh me-no ven-tee*
It's quarter past five	**Sono le cinque e un quarto**	*So-no leh cheen-kweh eh oon kwar-to*
It's half past four	**Sono le quattro e mezza**	*So-no leh kwat-tro eh med-za*
It's five past eight	**Sono le otto e cinque**	*So-no leh ot-to eh cheen-kweh*
It's 7 a.m./7 p.m. (07.00/19.00)	**Sono le sette di mattina/di sera (or le sette/le diciannove)**	*So-no leh set-teh dee mat-tee-na/dee se-ra (leh set-teh/lee dee-chan-no-veh)*
second	**il secondo**	*se-kon-do*
minute	**il minuto**	*mee-noo-to*
hour	**l'ora** f	*or-a*
It's early/late	**È presto/tardi**	*Eh pres-to/tar-dee*

| My watch is slow/is fast/has stopped | Il mio orologio va indietro/va avanti/è fermo | *Eel mee-o o-ro-lo-jo va een-dye-tro/va a-van-tee/ eh fair-mo* |
| Sorry I'm late | Mi scusi per il ritardo | *Mee skoo-zee pair eel ree-tar-do* |

Days

Sunday	**domenica**	*do-**me**-nee-ka*
Monday	**lunedì**	*loo-ne-**dee***
Tuesday	**martedì**	*mar-te-**dee***
Wednesday	**mercoledì**	*mair-ko-le-**dee***
Thursday	**giovedì**	*jo-ve-**dee***
Friday	**venerdì**	*ven-air-**dee***
Saturday	**sabato**	*sa-ba-to*

Months

January	**gennaio**	*jen-na-yo*
February	**febbraio**	*feb-bra-yo*
March	**marzo**	*mart-so*
April	**aprile**	*ap-ree-leh*
May	**maggio**	*mad-jo*
June	**giugno**	*joon-yo*
July	**luglio**	*lool-yo*

August	**agosto**	*a-gos-to*
September	**settembre**	*set-tem-breh*
October	**ottobre**	*ot-to-breh*
November	**novembre**	*no-vem-breh*
December	**dicembre**	*dee-chem-breh*

Seasons

spring	**la primavera**	*pree-ma-vair-a*
summer	**l'estate** *f*	*es-ta-teh*
autumn	**l'autunno** *m*	*ow-toon-no*
winter	**l'inverno** *m*	*een-vair-no*

Periods of Time

day	**giono**	*joor-no*
morning	**la mattina**	*mat-tee-na*
this morning	**stamani**	*sta-ma-nee*
in the morning	**di mattina**	*dee mat-tee-na*
midday, noon	**mezzogiorno**	*med-zo-jor-no*
afternoon	**il pomeriggio**	*po-mair-eed-jo*
yesterday afternoon	**ieri pomeriggio**	*yair-ee po-mair-eed-jo*
evening	**la sera**	*se-ra*
tomorrow evening	**domani sera**	*do-ma-nee se-ra*

midnight	**mezzanotte**	*med-za-not-teh*
night	**notte**	*not-teh*
tonight	**stanotte**	*sta-not-teh*
day	**il giorno**	*jor-no*
today	**oggi**	*od-jee*
yesterday	**ieri**	*yair-ee*
day before yesterday	**l'altro ieri**	*lal-tro yair-ee*
four days ago	**quattro giorni fa**	*kwat-tro jor-nee fa*
tomorrow	**domani**	*do-ma-nee*
day after tomorrow	**dopodomani**	*do-po do-ma-nee*
in ten days' time	**fra dieci giorni**	*fra dye-chee jor-nee*
on Tuesday	**martedì**	*mar-te-**dee***
on Sundays	**la domenica**	*la do-**me**-nee-ku*
week	**la settimana**	*set-tee-ma-na*
weekend	**il fine settimana**	*fee-neh set-tee-ma-na*
on weekdays	**nei giorni feriali**	*nay jor-nee fer-ya-lee*
every week	**ogni settimana**	*on-yee set-tee-ma-na*
once a week	**una volta alla settimana**	*oon-a vol-ta al-la set-tee-ma-na*
fortnight	**quindici giorni**	***kween**-dee-chee jor-nee*
month	**il mese**	*me-zeh*
in January	**a/in gennaio**	*a/een jen-na-yo*
since March	**da marzo**	*da mart-so*
this year	**quest'anno**	*kwest-an-no*

next year	l'anno prossimo	*lan-no pros-see-mo*
last year	l'anno scorso	*lan-no skor-so*
in spring	a/in primavera	*a/een pree-ma-vair-a*
during the summer	durante l'estate	*doo-ran-teh les-ta-teh*
sunrise, dawn	l'alba *f*	*al-ba*
sunset	il tramonto	*tra-mon-to*
twilight, dusk	il crepuscolo	*kre-poos-ko-lo*

Dates

What's the date today?	Quanto ne abbiamo oggi?	*Kwan-to neh ab-bya-mo od-jee*
It's 9th December[1]	È il nove dicembre	*Eh eel no-veh dee-chem-breh*
We got here on 27th July	Siamo arrivati qui il ventisette luglio	*Sya-mo ar-ree-va-tee kwee eel ven-tee-set-teh lool-yo*
We're leaving on 5th January	Partiamo il cinque gennaio	*Par-tya-mo eel cheen-kweh jen-na-yo*

1. In Italian cardinal numbers are used for dates except for *first*, **primo**.

Public Holidays

1 January	**Capodanno**
6 January (Epiphany)	**Epifania**
Easter (variable)	**Pasqua**
Easter Monday (variable)	**Lunedì dell'angelo/Pasquetta**
25 April (Liberation Day)	**Anniversario della Liberazione**
1 May (Labour Day)	**Festa del lavoro**
2 June (Republic Day)	**Festa della Repubblica**
15 August (Assumption)	**Assunzione/Ferragosto**
1 November (All Saints' Day)	**Tutti i Santi**
2 November (All Souls' Day)	**Commemorazione dei defunti**
8 December (Conception of the Virgin)	**Immacolata Concezione**
25 December (Christmas)	**Natale**
26 December (Bank Holiday)	**Santo Stefano**

WEATHER

What is the weather forecast?	**Come sono le previsioni del tempo?**	*Ko-meh so-no le pre-vee-zyo-nee del tem-po*
What is the temperature?	**Com'è la temperatura?**	*Ko-meh la tem-pe-ra-too-ra*
Is it usually as hot as this?	**Fa sempre caldo così?**	*Fa sem-preh kal-do ko-zee*
It's going to be hot/cold today	**Farà caldo/freddo oggi**	*Fa-ra kal-do/fred-do od-jee*
It's windy	**C'è vento**	*Cheh ven-to*
It's foggy	**C'è la nebbia**	*Cheh la neb-bya*
The mist will clear later	**La nebbia scomparirà più tardi**	*La neb-bya skom-pa-ree-ra pyoo tar-dee*
Will it be fine tomorrow?	**Farà bel tempo domani?**	*Fa-ra bel tem-po do-ma-nee*
What lovely/awful weather	**Che bel/brutto tempo**	*Keh bel/broot-to tem-po*
Do you think it will rain/snow?	**Pensa che pioverà/nevicherà?**	*Pen-sa keh pyo-vair-a/ne-vee-kair-a*
It's clear/cloudy/humid/frosty/unstable	**È sereno/nuvoloso/umido/ghiacciato/instabile**	*Eh se-re-no/noo-vo-lo-zo/oo-mee-do/gya-cha-to/een-sta-bee-leh*
There is:	**C'è**	*Cheh*
hail	**della grandine**	*del-la gran-dee-neh*
ice	**del ghiaccio**	*del gya-cho*
a storm	**una tempesta**	*oon-a tem-pes-ta*

OPPOSITES

before/after	**prima/dopo**	*pree-ma/do-po*
early/late	**presto/tardi**	*pres-to/tar-dee*
first/last	**primo/ultimo**	*pree-mo/**ool**-tee-mo*
now/later, then	**ora/dopo, poi**	*or-a/do-po, poy*
far/near	**lontano/vicino**	*lon-ta-no/vee-chee-no*
here/there	**qui/lì**	*kwee/lee*
in/out	**dentro/fuori**	*den-tro/fwo-ree*
inside/outside	**dentro/fuori**	*den-tro/fwo-ree*
under/over	**sotto/sopra**	*sot-to/sop-ra*
big, large/small	**grande/piccolo**	*gran-de/**peek**-ko-lo*
deep/shallow	**profondo/basso**	*pro-fon-do/bas-so*
empty/full	**vuoto/pieno**	*vwo-to/pye-no*
fat/lean	**grasso/magro**	*gras-so/mag-ro*
heavy/light	**pesante/leggero**	*pe-zan-teh/led-je-ro*
high/low	**alto/basso**	*al-to/bas-so*
long, tall/short	**lungo, alto/breve, basso**	*loon-go, al-to/bre-veh, bas-so*
narrow/wide	**stretto/largo**	*stret-to/lar-go*
thick/thin	**spesso, grosso/sottile, fine, magro**	*spes-so, gros-so/sot-tee-leh, fee-neh, mag-ro*
least/most	**minimo/massimo**	*mee-nee-mo/**mas**-see-mo*

many/few	molti/pochi	mol-tee/po-kee
more/less	più/meno	pyoo/me-no
much/little	molto/poco	mol-to/po-ko
beautiful/ugly	bello/brutto	bel-lo/broot-to
better/worse	meglio/peggio	mel-yo/ped-jo
cheap/expensive	a buon mercato/costoso, caro	a bwon mair-ka-to/kos-to-zo, kar-o
clean/dirty	pulito/sporco	poo-lee-to/spor-ko
cold/hot, warm	freddo, fresco/caldo, tiepido	fred-do, fres-ko/kal-do, tye-pee-do
easy/difficult	facile/difficile	fa-chee-leh/deef-fee-chee-leh
fresh/stale	fresco/stantio, andato a male	fres-ko/stan-tee-o, an-da-to a ma-leh
good/bad	buono/cattivo	bwo-no/kat-tee-vo
new, young/old	nuovo, giovane/vecchio	nwo-vo, jo-va-neh/vek-kyo
nice/nasty	buono/cattivo, disgustoso	bwon-o/kat-tee-vo, deez-goos-to-zo
right/wrong	giusto/sbagliato	joos-to/zbal-ya-to
vacant/occupied	libero/occupato	lee-bair-o/ok-koo-pa-to
open/closed, shut	aperto/chiuso	a-pair-to/kyoo-zo
quick/slow	rapido/lento	ra-pee-do/len-to
quiet/noisy	quieto, silenzioso/rumoroso	kye-to, see-lent-syo-zo/roo-mo-ro-zo
sharp/blunt	affilato/non taglia	af-fee-la-to/non tal-ya

NUMBERS

Cardinal

0	**zero**	*dze-ro*
1	**uno**	*oon-o*
2	**due**	*doo-eh*
3	**tre**	*treh*
4	**quattro**	*kwat-tro*
5	**cinque**	*cheen-kweh*
6	**sei**	*say*
7	**sette**	*set-teh*
8	**otto**	*ot-to*
9	**nove**	*no-veh*
10	**dieci**	*dye-chee*
11	**undici**	***oon**-dee-chee*
12	**dodici**	***do**-dee-chee*
13	**tredici**	***tre**-dee-chee*
14	**quattordici**	*kwat-**tor**-dee-chee*
15	**quindici**	***kween**-dee-chee*
16	**sedici**	*se-dee-chee*
17	**diciassette**	*dee-chas-set-teh*
18	**diciotto**	*dee-chot-to*

19	**diciannove**	*dee-chan-no-veh*
20	**venti**	*ven-tee*
21	**ventuno**	*ven-toon-o*
22	**ventidue**	*ven-tee-doo-eh*
30	**trenta**	*tren-ta*
31	**trentuno**	*tren-toon-o*
40	**quaranta**	*kwa-ran-ta*
50	**cinquanta**	*cheen-kwan-ta*
60	**sessanta**	*ses-san-ta*
70	**settanta**	*set-tan-ta*
80	**ottanta**	*ot-tan-ta*
90	**novanta**	*no-van-ta*
100	**cento**	*chen-to*
101	**cento uno**	*chen-to oon-o*
200	**duecento**	*doo-eh-chen-to*
1,000	**mille**	*meel-leh*
2,000	**duemila**	*doo-eh mee-la*
1,000,000	**un milione**	*meel-yo-neh*

Ordinal

1st	**primo**	*pree-mo*
2nd	**secondo**	*se-kon-do*
3rd	**terzo**	*tairt-so*

4th	quarto	*kwar-to*
5th	quinto	*kween-to*
6th	sesto	*ses-to*
7th	settimo	*set-tee-mo*
8th	ottavo	*ot-ta-vo*
9th	nono	*no-no*
10th	decimo	*de-chee-mo*
11th	undicesimo	*oon-dee-che-zee-mo*
12th	dodicesimo	*do-dee-che-zee-mo*
13th	tredicesimo	*tre-dee-che-zee-mo*
14th	quattordicesimo	*kwat-tor-dee-che-zee-mo*
15th	quindicesimo	*kween-dee-che-zee-mo*
16th	sedicesimo	*se-dee-che-zee-mo*
17th	diciassettesimo	*dee-chas-set-te-zee-mo*
18th	diciottesimo	*dee-chot-te-zee-mo*
19th	diciannovesimo	*dee-chan-nov-ve-zee-mo*
20th	ventesimo	*ven-te-zee-mo*
30th	trentesimo	*tren-te-zee-mo*
40th	quarantesimo	*kwa-ran-te-zee-mo*
50th	cinquantesimo	*cheen-kwan-te-zee-mo*
60th	sessantesimo	*ses-san-te-zee-mo*
70th	settantesimo	*set-tan-te-zee-mo*
80th	ottantesimo	*ot-tan-te-zee-mo*

90th	**novantesimo**	*no-van-te-zee-mo*
100th	**centesimo**	*chen-te-zee-mo*
half	**un mezzo**	*med-zo*
quarter	**un quarto**	*kwar-to*
three quarters	**tre quarti**	*treh kwar-tee*
a third	**un terzo**	*oon tairt-so*
two thirds	**due terzi**	*doo-eh tairt-see*

WEIGHTS AND MEASURES

Distance

Kilometres – miles

km	miles or km	miles	km	miles or km	miles
1.6	1	0.6	14.5	9	5.6
3.2	2	1.2	16.1	10	6.2
4.8	3	1.9	32.2	20	12.4
6.4	4	2.5	40.2	25	15.5
8	5	3.1	80.5	50	31.1
9.7	6	3.7	160.9	100	62.1
11.3	7	4.4	804.7	500	310.7
12.9	8	5			

A rough way to convert from miles to km: divide by 5 and multiply by 8; from km to miles, divide by 8 and multiply by 5.

Length and Height

Centimetres – inches

cm	inch or cm	inch
2.5	1	0.4
5.1	2	0.8
7.6	3	1.2
10.2	4	1.6
12.7	5	2
15.2	6	2.4

cm	inch or cm	inch
17.8	7	2.8
20.3	8	3.2
22.9	9	3.5
25.4	10	3.9
50.8	20	7.9
127	50	19.7

A rough way to convert from inches to cm: divide by 2 and multiply by 5; from cm to inches, divide by 5 and multiply by 2.

Metres – feet

m	ft or m	ft
0.3	1	3.3
0.6	2	6.6
0.9	3	9.8
1.2	4	13.1
1.5	5	16.4
1.8	6	19.7
2.1	7	23

m	ft or m	ft
2.4	8	26.2
2.7	9	29.5
3	10	32.8
6.1	20	65.6
15.2	50	164
30.5	100	328.1

A rough way to convert from ft to m: divide by 10 and multiply by 3; from m to ft, divide by 3 and multiply by 10.

Metres – yards

m	yds or m	yds	m	yds or m	yds
0.9	1	1.1	7.3	8	8.7
1.8	2	2.2	8.2	9	9.8
2.7	3	3.3	9.1	10	10.9
3.7	4	4.4	18.3	20	21.9
4.6	5	5.5	45.7	50	54.7
5.5	6	6.6	91.4	100	109.4
6.4	7	7.7	457.2	500	546.8

A rough way to convert from yds to m: subtract 10 per cent from the number of yds; from m to yds, add 10 per cent to the number of metres.

Liquid Measures

Litres – gallons

litres	galls or litres	galls	litres	galls or litres	galls
4.6	1	0.2	36.4	8	1.8
9.1	2	0.4	40.9	9	2
13.6	3	0.7	45.5	10	2.2
18.2	4	0.9	90.9	20	4.4
22.7	5	1.1	136.4	30	6.6
27.3	6	1.3	181.8	40	8.8
31.8	7	1.5	227.3	50	11

1 pint = 0.6 litre   1 litre = 1.8 pints

A rough way to convert from galls to litres: divide by 2 and multiply by 9; from litres to galls, divide by 9 and multiply by 2.

Weight

Kilogrammes – pounds

kg	lb or kg	lb	kg	lb or kg	lb
0.5	1	2.2	3.2	7	15.4
0.9	2	4.4	3.6	8	17.6
1.4	3	6.6	4.1	9	19.8
1.8	4	8.8	4.5	10	22
2.3	5	11	9.1	20	44.1
2.7	6	13.2	22.7	50	110.2

A rough way to convert from lb to kg: divide by 11 and multiply by 5; from kg to lb, divide by 5 and multiply by 11.

Grammes – ounces

grammes	oz	oz	grammes
100	3.5	2	56.7
250	8.8	4	114.3
500	17.6	8	228.6
1000 (1 kg)	35	16 (1 lb)	457.2

Temperature

Centigrade (°C) – fahrenheit (°F)

°C	°F
− 10	14
− 5	23
0	32
5	41
10	50
15	59
20	68
25	77
30	86
35	95
37	98.4
38	100.5
39	102
40	104
100	212

To convert °F to °C: deduct 32, divide by 9, multiply by 5; to convert °C to °F: divide by 5, multiply by 9, and add 32.

BASIC GRAMMAR

Nouns
All Italian nouns are either masculine or feminine. Almost all nouns ending in **-o** are *masculine* (e.g. ragazzo – boy, biglietto – ticket). Most nouns ending in **-a** are *feminine* (e.g. ragazza – girl, cartolina – postcard). Those ending in **-e** are masculine or feminine (e.g. melone *m* – melon, stazione *f* – station).

Plural
Nouns ending in **-o** change to **-i** in the plural (e.g. ragazzi – boys, biglietti – tickets).

Nouns ending in **-a** change to **-e** (e.g. ragazze – girls, cartoline – postcards).

Nouns ending in **-e** change to **-i** whether they are masculine or feminine (e.g meloni – melons, stazioni – stations).

N.B. An exception: the plural of uomo (man) is uomini (men).

The articles
The articles change form to match the gender of the noun, and the definite article has a plural as well as a singular form.

'A' before a *masculine noun* is **un** unless the noun begins with **s** followed by a consonant, or **z**, when it is **uno** (e.g. un uomo – a man, un giornale – a newspaper, but uno zio – an uncle, uno specchio – a mirror).

'A' before a *feminine noun* is **una** unless the noun begins with a vowel, when it is shortened to **un'** (e.g. una donna – a woman, but un'avventura – an adventure).

'The' with *masculine singular nouns* is usually **il** (e.g. il ragazzo – the boy). But it is **lo** before a word beginning with **s** + consonant, or **z** (e.g. lo specchio – the mirror, lo zio – the uncle). It becomes **l'** before a vowel (e:g. l'anno – the year).

'The' before a *masculine plural noun* is generally **i** (e.g. i giorni – the days). But it is **gli** before a word beginning with **s** + consonant, **z** or a vowel (e.g. gli specchi – the mirrors, gli uomini – the men).

'The' before a *feminine singular noun* is **la**, shortened to **l'** if the noun begins with a vowel (e.g. la madre – the mother, l'opera – the opera). With *feminine nouns in the plural* 'the' is **le** (e.g. le case – the houses).

Adjectives
Adjectives end either in **-o** or in **-e**. Those ending in **-o** form the feminine by changing to **-a**; those ending in **-e** are the same in both genders.

All adjectives form their plural in the same way as nouns: **-o** changes to **-i**; **-a** to **-e**; **-e** to **-i**.

	Sing	Pl			sing	pl	
m	rosso	rossi	*red*	*m*	verde	verdi	*green*
f	rossa	rosse		*f*	verde	verdi	

Adjectives have the same gender and number as the nouns they qualify, and they sometimes follow the noun (e.g. un ragazzo intelligente – due ragazzi intelligenti).

Possessive adjectives

Sing			Pl	
m	*f*		*m*	*f*
mio	mia	*my*	miei	mie
tuo	tua	*your*	tuoi	tue
suo	sua	*his, her, its*	suoi	sue
nostro	nostra	*our*	nostri	nostre
vostro	vostra	*your*	vostri	vostre
loro	loro	*their*	loro	loro

Possessive adjectives are usually preceded by the definite article (e.g. la mia macchina – my car, la nostra casa – our house, i suoi fratelli – his/her brothers), except for members of the family in the singular form: e.g. my mum = mia mamma.

You
The polite form of address in Italian is in the third person. 'You' is translated by **Lei** if addressing one person. **Loro** is also used when addressing more than one person, but nowadays this is very unusual, and the form **voi** tends to be used instead. 'Your' is **suo** (sing.) and **loro** (plu.), e.g. Come sta? How are you? Come stanno i suoi figli? How are your children? **Tu** is used to a close friend, a child and often to people of the same age.

Verbs
Personal pronouns (io, tu, etc.) tend to be used only for emphasis.

ESSERE – *to be*

Present			Future	
(io)	sono	*I am*	sarò	*I shall be*
(tu)	sei	*you are*	sarai	*you will be*
(lui/lei)	è	*s/he/it is*	sarà	*s/he/it will be*
(Lei)	è	*you are (formal)*	sarà	*you will be (formal)*
(noi)	siamo	*we are*	saremo	*we will be*
(voi)	siete	*you are*	sarete	*you will be*
(loro)	sono	*they are*	saranno	*they will be*

Past	
sono stato	*I was* or *I have been, etc.*
sei stato	*you were*
è stato/a	*s/he/It was*
è stato/a	*you were (formal)*
siamo stati/e	*we were*
siete stati/e	*you were*
sono stati/e	*they were*

AVERE – *to have*

Present			Future	
(io)	ho	*I have*	avrò	*I shall have*
(tu)	hai	*you have*	avrai	*you will have*
(lui/lei)	ha	*s/he/it has*	avrà	*s/he/it will have*

Present			Future	
(Lei)	ha	*you have (formal)*	avrà	*you will have (formal)*
(noi)	abbiamo	*we have*	avremo	*we shall have*
(voi)	avete	*you have*	avrete	*you will have*
(loro)	hanno	*they have*	avranno	*they will have*

Past

ho avuto	*I had or I have had, etc.*
hai avuto	*you had*
ha avuto	*s/he/it had*
ha avuto	*you had (formal)*
abbiamo avuto	*we had*
avete avuto	*you had*
hanno avuto	*they had*

Regular verbs

Italian regular verbs fall into three conjugations, determined by the ending of the infinitive.

1st conjugation	infinitives ending in **-are**	e.g.	parlare – to speak, comprare – to buy
2nd conjugation	infinitives ending in **-ere**	e.g.	vedere – to see, vendere – to sell
3rd conjugation	infinitives ending in **-ire**	e.g.	sentire – to hear, capire – to understand

PRESENT TENSE

	1st conj.	*2nd conj.*	*3rd conj.*
(io)	parl-**o**	vend-**o**	sent-**o**
(tu)	parl-**i**	vend-**i**	sent-**i**
(lui/lei)	parl-**a**	vend-**e**	sent-**e**
(Lei)	parl-**a**	vend-**e**	sent-**e**
(noi)	parl-**iamo**	vend-**iamo**	sent-**iamo**
(voi)	parl-**ate**	vend-**ete**	sent-**ite**
(loro)	parl-**ano**	vend-**ono**	sent-**ono**

Some 3rd conjugation verbs add **-isc** before the normal
present tense endings in the singular and in the third person
plural, e.g. io capisco, from capire – to understand.

FUTURE TENSE

The future tense of almost all Italian verbs is formed from the
infinitive in the following way:

(io)	parl-er-**ò**	vend-er-**ò**	sent-ir-**ò**
(tu)	parl-er-**ai**	vend-er-**ai**	sent-ir-**ai**
(lui/lei)	parl-er-**à**	vend-er-**à**	sent-ir-**à**
(Lei)	parl-er-**à**	vend-er-**à**	sent-ir-**à**
(noi)	parl-er-**emo**	vend-er-**emo**	sent-ir-**emo**
(voi)	parl-er-**ete**	vend-er-**ete**	sent-ir-**ete**
(loro)	parl-er-**anno**	vend-er-**anno**	sent-ir-**anno**

Note that in the 1st conjugation **-are** changes to **-ere** before the future endings are added.

PAST TENSE

The form of the past tense given in this book can be used to translate the English 'I did (something)' as well as 'I have done (something)'. It is formed by using the present tense of **avere**, or sometimes **essere**, with the past participle of the verb.

When **essere** – to be – is used to form the past tense, past participles agree with the subject of the verb in number and gender, using the same endings as adjectives ending in -o (e.g. Maria è venut**a** – Maria has come; I miei amici sono andat**i** a Roma – My friends have gone to Rome).

The past participle of 1st conjugation verbs ends in **-ato**, e.g. parlato.

The past participle of 2nd conjugation verbs usually ends in **-uto**, e.g. venduto.

The past participle of 3rd conjugation verbs usually ends in **-ito**, e.g. sentito.

The past tense is formed as follows:

(io) ho parlato, etc.	ho venduto, etc.	ho sentito, etc.

Some common irregular verbs
ANDARE – *to go*

Present		Future	
(io) vado	*I go, etc.*	andrò	*I shall go, etc.*
(tu) vai		andrai	
(lui/lei) va		andrà	
(Lei)		andrà	
(noi) andiamo		andremo	
(voi) andate		andrete	
(loro) vanno		andranno	

Past

sono andato/a	*I went/have been, etc.*

DIRE – *to say*

Present		Future	
(io) dico	*I say, etc.*	dirò	*I shall say, etc.*
(tu) dici		dirai	
(lui/lei) dice		dirà	
(Lei) dice		dirà	
(noi) diciamo		diremo	
(voi) dite		direte	
(loro) dicono		diranno	

Past

ho detto	*I said/have said, etc.*

DOVERE – *to have to, must*

Present		Future	
(io) devo	*I have to, etc.*	dovrò	*I shall have to, etc.*
(tu) devi		dovrai	
(lui/lei) deve		dovrà	
(Lei) deve		dovrà	
(noi) dobbiamo		dovremo	
(voi) dovete		dovrete	
(loro) devono		dovranno	

Past

ho dovuto	*I had to/have had to, etc.*

FARE – *to do, to make*

Present		Future	
(io) faccio	*I do, etc.*	farò	*I shall do, etc.*
(tu) fai		farai	
(lui/lei) fa		farà	
(Lei) fa		farà	
(noi) facciamo		faremo	
(voi) fate		farete	
(loro) fanno		faranno	

Past

ho fatto	*I did/have done, etc.*

POTERE – *to be able to, can*

Present		*Future*	
(io) posso	*I can, etc.*	potrò	*I shall be able to, etc.*
(tu) puoi		potrai	
(lui/lei) può		potrà	
(Lei) può		potrà	
(noi) possiamo		potremo	
(voi) potete		potrete	
(loro) possono		potranno	

Past	
ho potuto	*I could/was able to, etc.*

VENIRE – *to come*

Present		*Future*	
(io) vengo	*I come, etc.*	verrò	*I shall come, etc.*
(tu) vieni		verrai	
(lui/lei) viene		verrà	
(Lei) viene		verrà	
(noi) veniamo		verremo	
(voi) venite		verrete	
(loro) vengono		verranno	

Past	
sono venuto/a	*I came/have come, etc.*

VOLERE – *to want*

Present		*Future*	
(io) voglio	*I want, etc.*	vorrò	*I shall want, etc.*
(tu) vuoi		vorraí	
(lui/lei) vuole		vorrà	
(Lei) vuole		vorrà	
(noi) vogliamo		vorremo	
(voi) volete		vorrete	
(loro) vogliono		vorranno	

Past

ho voluto	*I wanted/have wanted, etc.*

Prepositions

There are nine Italian prepositions, and they are all used very frequently. *Tra* and *fra* have the same meaning.

di	*of*	a	*at, to*	da	*from*
in	*in, to*	con	*with*	su	*on, over*
per	*for*	tra	*between, among*	fra	*between, among*

Five prepositions can be combined with the definite articles as follows:

	il	*lo*	*l'*	*la*	*i*	*gli*	*le*
a	al	allo	all'	alla	ai	agli	alle
di	del	dello	dell'	della	dei	degli	delle
da	dal	dallo	dall'	dalla	dai	dagli	dalle
in	nel	nello	nell'	nella	nei	negli	nelle
su	sul	sullo	sull'	sulla	sui	sugli	sulle

e.g. al mercato – to the market; nel giardino – in the garden; dall'Italia – from Italy; sulla tavola – on the table. Con, per, tra, fia remain separate, e.g. con la famiglia – with the family.

VOCABULARY

Various groups of specialized words are given elsewhere in this book and these words are usually not repeated in the Vocabulary:

A

a, an	**un, una**	*oon, oon-a*
abbey	**l'abbazia** *f*	*ab-bat-see-a*
able (to be)	**potere**	*po-tair-eh*
about	**circa**	*cheer-ka*
above	**sopra**	*sop-ra*
abroad	**all'estero**	*al-les-tair-o*
accept (to)	**accettare**	*a-chet-tar-eh*
accident	**l'incidente** *m*	*een-chee-den-teh*
accommodation	**l'alloggio** *m*	*al-lod-jo*

account	il conto	kon-to
ache (to)	dolere	do-lair-eh
acquaintance	il conoscente	ko-no-shen-teh
across	attraverso	at-tra-vair-so
act (to)	agire	a-jeer-eh
add (to)	aggiungere	ad-**joon**-jair-eh
address	l'indirizzo m	een-dee-reet-so
admire (to)	ammirare	am-meer-ar-eh
admission	l'ingresso m/l'entrata f	een-gres-so/en-tra-ta
adventure	l'avventura f	av-ven-too-ra
advertisement	l'annunzio m	an-noont-syo
advice	il consiglio	kon-seel-yo
aeroplane	l'aeroplano m	a-air-o-pla-no
afford (to)	permettersi (di)	pair-**met**-tair-see (dee)
afraid (to be)	(aver) paura	(a-vair) pa-oo-ra
after	dopo	do-po
afternoon	il pomeriggio	po-mair-eed-jo
again	ancora	an-kor-a
against	contro	kon-tro
age	l'età f	e-ta
ago	(tempo) fa	(tem-po) fa
agree (to)	essere d'accordo	es-se-reh dak-kor-do
air	l'aria f	ar-ya

air-conditioning	**il condizionatore (d'aria)**	*kon-deet-syo-na-tor-eh (dar-ya)*
alarm clock	**la sveglia**	*zvel-ya*
alcoholic *drink*	**alcolico**	*al-ko-lee-ko*
alive	**vivo**	*vee-vo*
all	**tutto**	*toot-to*
all right	**va bene**	*va be-neh*
allow (to)	**permettere**	*pair-met-tair-eh*
almost	**quasi**	*kwa-zee*
alone	**solo**	*so-lo*
along	**lungo**	*loon-go*
already	**già**	*ja*
also	**anche**	*an-keh*
alter (to)	**modificare**	*mo-dee-fee-kar-eh*
alternative	**l'alternativa** *f*	*al-tair-na-tee-va*
although	**benchè**	*ben-keh*
always	**sempre**	*sem-preh*
ambulance	**l'ambulanza** *f*	*am-boo-lant-sa*
America	**America** *f*	*a-me-ree-ka*
American	**americano**	*a-me-ree-ka-no*
amuse (to)	**divertire**	*dee-vair-teer-eh*
amusement park	**parco dei divertimenti**	*par-ko day dee-vair-tee-men-tee*
amusing	**divertente**	*dee-vair-ten-teh*

ancient	**vecchio**	*vek-kyo*
and	**e**	*eh*
angry	**arrabbiato**	*ar-rab-bya-to*
animal	**l'animale** *m*	*a-nee-ma-leh*
anniversary	**l'anniversario** *m*	*an-nee-vair-sar-yo*
annoyed	**seccato**	*sek-ka-to*
another	**un altro**	*oon al-tro*
answer	**la risposta**	*rees-pos-ta*
answer (to)	**rispondere**	*rees-**pon**-dair-eh*
antique	**antico**	*an-tee-ko*
any	**qualche/qualunque**	*kwal-keh/kwal-oon-kweh*
anyone	**qualcuno/chiunque**	*kwal-koo-no/* *kee-oon-kweh*
anything	**qualchecosa**	*kwal-keh-ko-za*
anywhere	**dovunque**	*do-voon-kweh*
apartment	**l'appartamento** *m*	*ap-par-ta-men-to*
apologize (to)	**scusarsi**	*skoo-zar-see*
appetite	**l'appetito** *m*	*ap-pe-tee-to*
appointment	**l'appuntamento** *m*	*ap-poon-ta-men-to*
architect	**l'architetto** *m*	*ar-kee-tet-to*
architecture	**l'architettura** *f*	*ar-kee-tet-too-ra*
area	**la zona/la regione**	*tso-na/re-jo-neh*
area code	**il prefisso**	*pre-fees-so*
arm	**il braccio**	*bra-cho*

armchair	**la poltrona**	*pol-tro-na*
army	**l'esercito** *m*	*e-**zair**-chee-to*
arrange (to)	**combinare**	*kom-bee-nar-eh*
arrival	**l'arrivo** *m*	*ar-ree-vo*
arrive (to)	**arrivare**	*ar-ree-var-eh*
art	**l'arte** *f*	*ar-teh*
art gallery	**la galleria d'arte**	*ga-lair-ee-a dar-teh*
artificial	**sintetico**	*seen-**te**-tee-ko*
artist	**l'artista**	*ar-tees-ta*
as	**come**	*ko-meh*
as much as	**tanto quanto**	*tan-to kwan-to*
as soon as	**appena che**	*ap-pe-na keh*
as well	**in più/come pure**	*een pyoo/ko-meh poo-reh*
ashtray	**il portacenere**	*por-ta-**che**-nair-eh*
ask (to)	**chiedere**	***kye**-dair-eh*
asleep	**addormentato**	*ad-dor-men-ta-to*
at	**a**	*a*
at last	**finalmente**	*fee-nal-men-teh*
at once	**subito**	***soo**-bee-to*
atmosphere	**l'atmosfera** *f*	*at-mos-fair-a*
attention	**l'attenzione** *f*	*at-tent-syo-neh*
attractive	**attraente**	*at-tra-en-teh*
auction	**l'asta**	*as-ta*

audience	**il pubblico**	*eel **poob**-lee-ko*
aunt	**la zia**	*tsee-a*
Australia	**Australia** *f*	*ow-**stra**-lya*
Australian	**australiano**	*ow-stra-lya-no*
author	**l'autore** *m*	*ow-tor-eh*
autumn	**l'autunno** *m*	*ow-toon-no*
available	**disponibile**	*dees-po-**nee**-bee-leh*
avalanche	**la valanga**	*va-lan-ga*
avenue	**il viale**	*vya-leh*
average	**la media**	*med-ya*
avoid (to)	**evitare**	*e-vee-tar-eh*
awake	**sveglio**	*zvel-yo*
away	**via**	*vee-a*

B

baby	**il bambino**	*bam-bee-no*
baby food	**il cibo per bambini**	*chee-bo pair bam-bee-nee*
baby sitter	**il/la baby sitter**	*baby sitter*
bachelor	**il celibe**	*__che__-lee-beh*
back *adv*	**indietro**	*een-dye-tro*
backpack	**la bisaccia**	*bee-za-cha*
bad	**cattivo**	*kat-tee-vo*
bad *food*	**guasto**	*gwas-to*

bag	**la borsa**	*bor-sa*
baggage	**i bagagli**	*ba-gal-yee*
baggage cart	**il carello**	*ka-rel-lo*
bait	**lo spuntino**	*spoon-tee-no*
balcony	**il balcone**	*bal-ko-neh*
ball *sport*	**la palla**	*pal-la*
ballet	**il balletto**	*bal-let-to*
balloon	**il palloncino**	*pal-lon-chee-no*
band *music*	**l'orchestra** *f*	*or-kes-tra*
bank	**la banca**	*ban-ka*
bank account	**il conto in banca**	*kon-to een ban-ka*
barn	**la stalla**	*stal-la*
basket	**il cesto**	*ches-to*
bath	**il bagno**	*ban-yo*
bath essence	**l'estratto per il bagno**	*es-trat-to pair eel ban-yo*
bathe (to)	**fare un bagno**	*fa-reh oon ban-yo*
bathing cap	**la cuffia da bagno**	*koof-fya da ban-yo*
bathing suit	**il costume da bagno**	*kos-too-meh da ban-yo*
bathing trunks	**i calzoncini da bagno**	*kalt-son-chee-nee da ban-yo*
bathroom	**la stanza da bagno**	*stan-za da ban-yo*
battery	**la batteria**	*bat-tair-ee-a*
bay *sea*	**la baia**	*ba-ya*
be (to)	**essere**	***es**-se-reh*

beach	la spiaggia	*spyad-ja*
beard	la barba	*bar-ba*
beautiful	bello	*bel-lo*
because	perché	*pair-keh*
become (to)	divenire	*dee-ve-neer-eh*
bed	il letto	*let-to*
bed and breakfast	l'alloggio e prima collazione	*al-lod-jo eh pree-ma kol-lat-syo-neh*
bedroom	la camera	*ka-mair-a*
before *space*	davanti a	*da-van-tee a*
time	prima di	*pree-ma dee*
begin (to)	cominciare	*ko-meen-char-eh*
beginning	il principio	*preen-chee-pyo*
behind	dietro	*dye-tro*
believe (to)	credere	*kre-dair-eh*
bell	il campanello	*kam-pa-nel-lo*
belong (to)	appartenere	*ap-par-te-nair-eh*
below	sotto	*sot-to*
belt	la cintura	*cheen-too-ra*
bench	la panchina	*pan-kee-na*
bend	la curva	*koor-va*
berth	il letto	*let-to*
best	il migliore	*meel-yor-eh*
bet	la scommessa	*skom-mes-sa*

better	meglio/migliore	*mel-yo/meel-yor-eh*
between	fra	*fra*
bicycle	la bicicletta	*bee-chee-klet-ta*
big	grande	*gran-deh*
bill	il conto	*kon-to*
binoculars	il binocolo	*bee-no-ko-lo*
bird	l'uccello *m*	*oo-chel-lo*
birthday	il compleanno	*kom-ple-an-no*
bite (to)	mordere	*mor-dair-eh*
bitter	amaro	*a-ma-ro*
blanket	la coperta	*ko-pair-ta*
bleach (to)	ossigenare	*os-see-jen-ar-eh*
bleed (to)	sanguinare	*san-gwee-nar-eh*
blind	cieco	*chye-ko*
blister	la vescica	*ve-shee-ka*
blood	il sangue	*san-gweh*
blouse	la blusa	*bloo-za*
blow *hit*	il colpo	*kol-po*
blow (to)	soffiare	*sof-fyar-eh*
(on) board	a bordo	*a bor-do*
boarding house	la pensione	*pen-syo-neh*
boat	il battello	*bat-tel-lo*
body	il corpo	*kor-po*

bone	l'osso *m*	*os-so*
bonfire	il falò	*fa-lo*
book	il libro	*leeb-ro*
book (to)	riservare	*ree-zair-var-eh*
boot *for foot*	lo stivale	*stee-va-leh*
border	la frontiera/il confine	*front-yair-a/kon-fee-neh*
bored	annoiato	*an-no-ya-to*
boring	noioso	*no-yo-zo*
borrow (to)	prendere in prestito	*pren-dair-eh een pres-tee-to*
both	entrambi	*en-tram-bee*
bother (to) *annoy*	disturbare	*dees-toor-bar-eh*
bottle	la bottiglia	*bot-teel-ya*
bottle opener	il cavatappi	*ka-va-tap-pee*
bottom	il fondo	*fon-do*
bow tie	la cravatta a farfalla	*kra-vat-ta a far-fal-la*
bowl	la scodella	*sko-del-la*
box *container*	la scatola	*ska-to-la*
theatre	il palco	*pal-ko*
box office	il botteghino	*bot-te-gee-no*
boy	il ragazzo	*ra-gat-so*
bracelet	il braccialetto	*bra-cha-let-to*
braces	le bretelle	*bre-tel-leh*

brain	il cervello	*chair-vel-lo*
brains	le cervella	*chair-vel-la*
branch *tree*	il ramo	*ra-mo*
office	la filiale/ la succursale	*feel-ya-leh/sook-koor-sa-leh*
brassière	il reggiseno	*red-jee-se-no*
break (to)	rompere	***rom**-pair-eh*
breakfast	la (prima) colazione	*pree-ma ko-lat-syo-neh*
breathe (to)	respirare	*res-peer-ar-eh*
brick	il mattone	*mat-to-neh*
bridge	il ponte	*pon-teh*
bright *light*	lucente	*loo-chen-teh*
bring (to)	portare	*por-tar-reh*
British	britannico	*bree-**tan**-nee-ko*
broken	rotto	*rot-to*
brooch	la spilla	*speel-la*
brother	il fratello	*fra-tel-lo*
bruise (to)	ammaccarsi	*am-mak-kar-see*
brush	la spazzola	***spat**-so-la*
brush (to)	spazzolare	*spat-so-lar-eh*
bucket	la secchia	*sek-kya*
buckle	la fibbia	*feeb-bya*
build (to)	costruire	*kos-tru-eer-eh*
building	l'edificio *m*	*e-dee-fee-cho*

bunch *flowers, keys*	il mazzo	*mad-zo*
buoy	la boa	*bo-a*
burn (to)	bruciare	*broo-char-eh*
burst (to)	scoppiare	*skop-pyar-eh*
bus	l'autobus *m*	*ow-to-boos*
bus lane	corsia dei pullman	*kor-see-a day pool-man*
bus stop	la fermata d'autobus	*fair-ma-ta dow-to-boos*
business	gli affari	*af-far-ee*
busy	occupato	*ok-koo-pa-to*
but	ma	*ma*
butterfly	la farfalla	*far-fal-la*
button	il bottone	*bot-to-neh*
buy (to)	comprare	*kom-prar-eh*

C

cab	il taxi	*taxi*
cabin	la cabina	*ka-bee-na*
calculator	il calcolatore	*kal-ko-la-tor-eh*
calendar	il calendario	*ka-len-dar-yo*
call *telephone*	la chiamata	*kya-ma-ta*
call (to) *summon*	chiamare	*kya-mar-eh*
visit	visitare	*vee-zee-tar-eh*
calm	calmo	*kal-mo*

camp (to)	**accamparsi**	*ak-kam-par-see*
camp site	**un camping**	*camping*
can (to be able)	**potere**	*po-tair-eh*
can *tin*	**il barattolo**	*ba-rat-to-lo*
can opener	**l'apriscatole** *m*	*ap-ree-ska-to-leh*
Canada	**Canada** *m*	*ka-na-da*
Canadian	**canadese**	*ka-na-de-zeh*
cancel (to)	**cancellare**	*kan-chel-lar-eh*
candle	**la candela**	*kan-de-la*
canoe	**la canoa**	*ka-no-a*
cap	**il berretto**	*ber-ret-to*
capital city	**la capitale**	*ka-pee-ta-leh*
car	**la macchina**	*mak-kee-na*
car park	**il parcheggio**	*par-ked-jo*
carafe	**la caraffa**	*ka-raf-fa*
caravan	**la roulotte**	*roo-lot*
care	**la cura**	*koo-ra*
careful	**attento**	*at-ten-to*
careless	**disordinato**	*dee-zor-dee-na-to*
caretaker	**il/la custode**	*koos-to-deh*
carpet	**il tappeto**	*tap-pe-to*
carry (to)	**portare**	*por-tar-eh*
cash	**i contanti**	*kon-tan-tee*
cash (to)	**incassare**	*een-kas-sar-eh*

cashier	**il cassiere**	*kas-syair-eh*
casino	**il casinò**	*ka-zee-**no***
castle	**il castello**	*kas-tel-lo*
cat	**il gatto**	*gat-to*
catalogue	**il catalogo**	*ka-**ta**-lo-go*
catch (to)	**prendere**	***pren**-dair-eh*
cathedral	**la cattedrale/ il duomo**	*kat-te-dra-leh/ dwo-mo*
Catholic	**cattolico**	*kat-**to**-lee-ko*
cave	**la grotta**	*grot-ta*
cement	**il cemento**	*che-men-to*
central	**centrale**	*chen-tra-leh*
centre	**il centro**	*chen-tro*
century	**il secolo**	***se**-ko-lo*
ceremony	**la cerimonia**	*che-ree-mo-nya*
certain(ly)	**certo**	*chair-to*
chain *jewellery*	**la catena**	*ka-te-na*
chair	**la sedia**	*sed-ya*
chambermaid	**la cameriera**	*ka-mair-yair-a*
chance	**il caso**	*ka-zo*
(small) change	**gli spiccioli**	***spee**-cho-lee*
change (to)	**cambiare**	*kam-byar-eh*
chapel	**la cappella**	*kap-pel-la*
charge *money*	**il costo**	*kos-to*

charge (to) *money*	**far pagare**	*far pa-gar-eh*
cheap	**a buon mercato**	*a bwon mair-ka-to*
check (to)	**controllare**	*kon-trol-lar-eh*
chef	**il capocuoco**	*ka-po-kwo-ko*
cheque	**l'assegno** *m*	*as-sen-yo*
chess	**il gioco degli scacchi**	*jo-ko del-yee skak-kee*
chess set	**gli scacchi**	*skak-kee*
child	**il bambino**	*bam-bee-no*
chill (to)	**mettere in fresco**	***met****-tair-eh een fres-ko*
china	**la porcellana**	*por-chel-la-na*
choice	**la scelta**	*shel-ta*
choose (to)	**scegliere**	***shel****-yair-eh*
church	**la chiesa**	*kye-za*
cigar	**il sigaro**	***see****-ga-ro*
cigarette	**la sigaretta**	*see-ga-ret-ta*
cinema	**il cinema**	***chee****-ne-ma*
circle *theatre*	**la galleria**	*gal-lair-ee-a*
circus	**il circo**	*cheer-ko*
city	**la città**	*cheet-**ta***
class	**la classe**	*klas-seh*
clean	**pulito**	*poo-lee-to*
clean (to)	**pulire**	*poo-leer-eh*
cleansing cream	**la crema detergente**	*kre-ma de-tair-jen-teh*
clear	**chiaro**	*kya-ro*

cliff	**la scogliera**	*skol-yair-a*
climb (to)	**arrampicarsi**	*ar-ram-pee-kar-see*
cloakroom	**il guardaroba**	*gwar-da-ro-ba*
clock	**l'orologio** *m*	*or-o-lo-jo*
close (to)	**chiudere**	***kyoo***-*dair-eh*
closed	**chiuso**	*kyoo-zo*
cloth	**la stoffa**	*stof-fa*
clothes	**i vestiti**	*ves-tee-tee*
cloud	**la nube**	*noo-beh*
coach	**il pullman**	*pool-man*
coast	**la costa**	*kos-ta*
coat	**il soprabito**	*sop-**ra**-bee-to*
coathanger	**l'attaccapanni** *m*	*at-tak-ka-pan-nee*
coin	**la moneta**	*mo-ne-ta*
cold	**freddo**	*fred-do*
cold (to have a)	**essere raffreddato**	***es***-*se-reh raf-fred-da-to*
collar	**il colletto**	*kol-let-to*
collect (to)	**raccogliere**	*rak-**kol**-yair-eh*
colour	**il colore**	*ko-lor-eh*
comb	**il pettine**	***pet***-*tee-neh*
come (to)	**venire**	*ve-neer-eh*
come in	**entrate**	*en-tra-teh*
comfortable	**comodo**	***ko***-*mo-do*

company	**la compagnia**	*kom-pan-yee-a*
compartment *train*	**lo scompartimento**	*skom-par-tee-men-to*
compass	**la bussola**	***boos**-so-la*
compensation	**il risarcimento**	*ree-zar-chee-men-to*
complain (to)	**lagnarsi**	*lan-yar-see*
complaint	**la lagnanza**	*lan-yant-sa*
complete	**completo**	*kom-ple-to*
computer	**il computer**	*computer*
concert	**il concerto**	*kon-chair-to*
concert hall	**la sala dei concerti**	*sa-la day kon-chair-tee*
concrete	**il calcestruzzo**	*kal-che-stroot-so*
condition	**la condizione**	*kon-dect-syo-nch*
condom	**il preservativo**	*pre-zair-va-tee-vo*
conductor *bus*	**l'autista**	*ow-tis-ta*
congratulations	**congratulazioni**	*kon-gra-too-lat-syo-nee*
connect (to)	**connettere**	*kon-**net**-tair-eh*
connection *train, etc.*	**la coincidenza**	*ko-een-chee-dent-sa*
consul	**il console**	***kon**-so-leh*
consulate	**il consolato**	*kon-so-la-to*
contact lenses	**le lenti a contatto**	*len-tee a kon-tat-to*
contain (to)	**contenere**	*kon-te-nair-eh*
contraceptive	**is contraccetivo**	*kon-tra-che-tee-vo*
contrast	**il contrasto**	*kon-tras-to*

convenient	**conveniente**	*kon-ven-yen-teh*
convent	**il convento**	*kon-ven-to*
conversation	**la conversazione**	*kon-vair-sat-syo-neh*
cook	**il cuoco**	*kwo-ko*
cook (to)	**cucinare**	*koo-chee-nar-eh*
cool	**fresco**	*fres-ko*
copper	**il rame**	*ra-meh*
copy	**la copia**	*ko-pya*
copy (to)	**copiare**	*ko-pyar-eh*
cork	**il tappo**	*tap-po*
corkscrew	**il cavatappi**	*ka-va-tap-pee*
corner	**l'angolo** *m*	*an-go-lo*
correct	**corretto**	*kor-ret-to*
corridor	**il corridoio**	*kor-ree-do-yo*
cosmetics	**i cosmetici**	*kos-me-tee-chee*
cost	**il costo**	*kos-to*
cost (to)	**costare**	*kos-tar-eh*
costume jewellery	**la bigiotteria**	*bee-jot-tair-ee-a*
cottage	**la casetta di campagna**	*ka-zet-ta dee kam-pan-ya*
cotton	**il cotone**	*ko-to-neh*
cotton wool	**l'ovatta** *f*	*o-vat-ta*
couchette	**la cuccetta**	*koo-chet-ta*
count (to)	**contare**	*kon-tar-eh*

country *nation*	il paese	pa-e-zeh
not town	la campagna	kam-pan-ya
course *dish*	la portata	por-ta-ta
cousin	il cugino	koo-jee-no
cover charge	il coperto	ko-pair-to
crash *collision*	l'urto *m*	oor-to
credit card	la carta di credito	kar-ta dee **kre**-dee-to
cross	la croce	kro-cheh
cross (to)	attraversare	at-tra-vair-sar-eh
cross country skiing	lo sci di fondo	shee dee fon-do
crossroads	il crocevia	kro-che-vee-a
crystal	il cristallo	krees-tal lo
cul de sac	il vicolo cieco	**vee**-ko-lo chye-ko
cufflinks	i gemelli	je-mel-lee
cup	la tazza	tat-sa
cupboard	l'armadio *m*	ar-ma-dyo
cure (to)	guarire	gwa-reer-eh
curious	curioso	koo-ree-o-zo
curl	il riccio	ree-cho
current	la corrente	kor-ren-teh
curtain	la tenda	ten-da
cushion	il cuscino	koo-shee-no
customs	la dogana	do-ga-na

customs officer	l'ufficiale di dogana *m*	*oof-fee-cha-leh dee do-ga-na*
cut	il taglio	*tal-yo*
cut (to)	tagliare	*tal-yar-eh*
cycling	il ciclismo	*chee-kleez-mo*
cyclist	il/la ciclista	*chee-klees-ta*

D

daily	quotidiano	*kwo-tee-dya-no*
damaged	danneggiato	*dan-ned-ja-to*
damp	umido	*oo-mee-do*
dance	il ballo	*bal-lo*
dance (to)	ballare	*bal-lar-eh*
danger	pericolo	*pair-ee-ko-lo*
dangerous	pericoloso	*pair-ee-ko-lo-zo*
dark	scuro	*skoo-ro*
date *appointment*	l'appuntamento *m*	*ap-poon-ta-men-to*
calendar	la data	*da-ta*
daughter	la figlia	*feel-ya*
day	il giorno	*jor-no*
dead	morto	*mor-to*
dead end street	la strada senza uscita	*stra-da send-za oo-shee-ta*
deaf	sordo	*sor-do*
dealer	il commerciante	*kom-mair-chan-teh*

dear	caro	*ka-ro*
decanter	la caraffa	*ka-raf-fa*
decide (to)	decidere	*de-chee-dair-eh*
deckchair	la sedia a sdraio	*sed-ya a zdra-yo*
declare (to)	dichiarare	*dee-kyar-ar-eh*
deep	profondo	*pro-fon-do*
delay	il ritardo	*ree-tar-do*
deliver (to)	consegnare	*kon-sen-yar-eh*
delivery	la consegna	*kon-sen-ya*
demi-pension	la mezza pensione	*med-za pen-syo-neh*
dentist	il dentista	*den-tees-ta*
dentures	la dentiera	*dent-yair-a*
deodorant	il deodorante	*de-o-dor-an-teh*
depart (to)	partire	*par-teer-eh*
department	il dipartimento	*dee-par-tee-men-to*
department stores	i grandi magazzini	*gran-dee ma-gad-zee-nee*
departure	la partenza	*par-tent-sa*
dessert	i dolci	*dol-chee*
detour	la deviazione	*de-vyat-syo-neh*
dial (to)	comporre il numero	*kom-por-reh eel noo-mair-o*
dialling code	il prefisso	*pre-fees-so*
diamond	il diamante	*dee-a-man-teh*
dice	i dadi	*da-dee*
dictionary	i dizionario	*deet-syo-nar-yo*

diet	la dieta	dye-ta
diet (to)	stare a dieta	star-eh a dye-ta
different	differente	deef-fair-en-teh
difficult	difficile	deef-fee-chee-leh
dine (to)	pranzare	pran-zar-eh
dining room	la sala da pranzo	sa-la da pran-zo
dinner	il pranzo	prand-zo
dinner jacket	il smoking	smoking
direct	diretto	dee-ret-to
direction	la direzione	dee-ret-syo-neh
dirty	sporco	spor-ko
disappointed	deluso	de-loo-zo
discount	lo sconto	skon-to
dish	il piatto	pyat-to
disinfectant	il disinfettante	dees-een-fet-tan-teh
distance	la distanza	dees-tant-sa
disturb (to)	disturbare	dees-toor-bar-eh
ditch	il fosso	fos-so
dive (to)	tuffarsi	toof-far-see
diving board	il trampolino di lancio	tram-po-lee-no dee lan-cho
divorced	divorziato	dee-vort-sya-to
do (to)	fare	far-eh
dock (to)	attraccare	at-trak-kar-eh

doctor	il medico	*me-dee-ko*
dog	il cane	*ka-neh*
doll	la bambola	***bam**-bo-la*
door	la porta	*por-ta*
double	doppio	*dop-pyo*
double bed	il letto matrimoniale	*let-to mat-ree-mo-nya-leh*
double room	la camera matrimoniale	*ka-mair-a mat-ree-mo-nya-leh*
down (stairs)	giù	*joo*
dozen	la dozzina	*dot-see-na*
draughty	pieno di correnti d'aria	*pye-no dee kor-ren-tee dar-ya*
draw (to)	disegnare	*dee-zen-yar-eh*
drawer	il cassetto	*kas-set-to*
drawing	il disegno	*dee-zen-yo*
dream	il sogno	*son-yo*
dress	l'abito *m*	*a-bee-to*
dressing gown	la vestaglia	*ves-tal-ya*
dressmaker	il sarto	*sar-to*
drink (to)	bere	*be-reh*
drinking water	acqua potabile	*ak-wa po-**ta**-bee-leh*
drive (to)	guidare	*gwee-dar-eh*
driver	il conduttore	*kon-doot-tor-eh*
driving licence	il patente	*pa-ten-teh*
drop (to)	cadere	*ka-dair-eh*

drunk	**ubriaco**	*oo-bree-a-ko*
dry	**secco, asciutto**	*sek-ko, a-shoot-to*
during	**durante**	*doo-ran-teh*
duvet	**il duvet**	*duvet*
dye	**la tinta**	*teen-ta*

E

each	**ciascuno**	*chas-koo-no*
early	**di buon'ora**	*dee bwon or-a*
earrings	**gli orecchini**	*or-ek-kee-nee*
east	**est** *m*	*est*
Easter	**pasqua** *f*	*pas-kwa*
easy	**facile**	*fa-chee-leh*
eat (to)	**mangiare**	*man-jar-eh*
edge	**la sponda**	*spon-da*
eiderdown	**il piumino**	*pyoo-mee-no*
elastic	**l'elastico** *m*	*e-las-tee-ko*
electric socket	**la presa elettrica**	*pre-za el-et-tree-ka*
electricity	**l'elettricità**	*el-et-tree-chee-ta*
elevator	**l'ascensore** *m*	*a-shen-sor-eh*
embarrassed	**imbarazzato**	*eem-ba-rad-za-to*
embassy	**l'ambasciata** *f*	*am-ba-sha-ta*
emergency exit	**l'uscita di sicurezza** *f*	*oo-shee-ta dee see-koo-ret-sa*

empty	**vuoto**	*vwo-to*
end	**la fine**	*fee-neh*
end of no-parking zone	**la fine del divieto di parcheggio**	*fee-neh del dee-vye-to dee par-ked-jo*
engaged *people*	**fidanzato**	*fee-dant-sa-to*
busy	**occupato**	*ok-koo-pa-to*
engine	**il motore**	*mo-tor-eh*
England	**Inghilterra** *f*	*een-geel-ter-ra*
English	**inglese**	*een-gle-zeh*
enjoy (to)	**godere**	*go-dair-eh*
enjoy oneself (to)	**divertirsi**	*dee-vair-teer-see*
enough	**abbastanza**	*ab-bas-tant-sa*
enquiries	**gli informazioni**	*een-for-mat-syo-nee*
enter (to)	**entrare**	*en-trar-eh*
entrance	**l'ingresso** *m*	*een-gres-so*
entrance fee	**l'entrata** *f*	*en-tra-ta*
envelope	**la busta**	*boos-ta*
equipment	**l'attrezzatura** *f*	*at-tret-sa-too-ra*
escalator	**la scala mobile**	*ska-la **mo**-bee-leh*
escape (to)	**scappare**	*skap-par-eh*
estate agent	**l'agente immobiliare** *m*	*a-jen-teh eem-mo-beel-yar-eh*
E.U.	**U.E. (Unione Europea)**	*oo-eh (oo-nyo-neh e-oo-ro-pe-a)*
Europe	**l'Europa** *f*	*e-oo-ro-pa*

even *not odd*	**pari**	*pa-ree*
evening	**la sera**	*se-ra*
event	**l'evento** *m*	*e-ven-to*
every	**ogni**	*on-yee*
everybody	**ognuno**	*on-yoo-no*
everything	**tutto**	*toot-to*
everywhere	**dovunque**	*do-voon-kweh*
example	**l'esempio** *m*	*e-zem-pyo*
excellent	**eccellente**	*e-chel-len-teh*
except	**eccetto**	*e-chet-to*
excess	**l'eccesso** *m*	*e-ches-so*
exchange bureau	**il cambio**	*kam-byo*
exchange rate	**il cambio**	*kam-byo*
excursion	**la gita**	*jee-ta*
excuse (to)	**scusare**	*skoo-zar-eh*
exhibition	**la mostra**	*mos-tra*
exit	**l'uscita** *f*	*oo-shee-ta*
expect (to)	**aspettare**	*as-pet-tar-eh*
expensive	**costoso**	*kos-to-zo*
express *letter*	**espresso**	*es-pres-so*
express train	**il rapido**	*ra-pee-do*
extra	**extra/in più**	*extra/een pyoo*
eye shadow	**l'ombretto** *m*	*om-bret-to*

F

fabric	il tessuto	tes-soo-to
face	la faccia	fa-cha
face cloth	pezzuola per lavarsi	pet-swo-la pair la-var-see
face cream	la crema per il viso	kre-ma pair eel vee-zo
fact	il fatto	fat-to
factory	la fabbrica	fab-bree-ka
fade (to)	scolorire	sko-lor-eer-eh
faint (to)	svenire	zve-neer-eh
fair colour	chiaro	kya-ro
fête	la fiera	fyair-a
fall (to)	cadere	ka-dair-eh
family	la famiglia	fa-meel-ya
far	lontano	lon-ta-no
fare	il prezzo (del biglietto)	pret-so (del beel-yet-to)
farm	la fattoria	fat-tor-ee-a
farmer	l'agricoltore m	ag-ree-kol-tor-eh
farmhouse	la fattoria	fat-tor-ee-a
farther	più lontano	pyoo lon-ta-no
fashion	la moda	mo-da
fast	veloce	ve-lo-cheh
fat	grasso	gras-so
father	il padre	pa-dreh

fault	**lo sbaglio**	*zbal-yo*
fear	**la paura**	*pa-oo-ra*
feed (to)	**alimentare**	*a-lee-men-tar-eh*
feeding bottle	**il biberon**	*bee-be-ron*
feel (to)	**sentire**	*sen-teer-eh*
felt-tip pen	**il pennarello**	*pen-na-rel-lo*
female *adj*	**femminile**	*fem-mee-nee-leh*
ferry	**il traghetto**	*tra-get-to*
fetch (to)	**andare a prendere**	*an-dar-eh a pren-dair-eh*
fever	**la febbre**	*feb-breh*
a few	**alcuni**	*al-koo-nee*
fiancé(e)	**il fidanzato/la fidanzata**	*fee-dant-sa-to/ fee-dant-sa-ta*
field	**il campo**	*kam-po*
field glasses	**il binocolo**	*bee-no-ko-lo*
fight (to)	**combattere**	*kom-bat-tair-eh*
fill/ fill in (to)	**riempire**	*ree-em-peer-eh*
film	**il film/la pellicola**	*film/pel-lee-ko-la*
find (to)	**trovare**	*tro-var-eh*
fine *money*	**la multa**	*mool-ta*
finish (to)	**finire**	*fee-neer-eh*
finished	**finito**	*fee-nee-to*
fire	**il fuoco**	*fwo-ko*
fire escape	**l'uscita di sicurezza**	*oo-shee-ta dee see-koo-ret-sa*

fire extinguisher	l'estintore *m*	*es-teen-tor-eh*
fireworks	i fuochi d'artificio	*fwo-kee dar-tee-fee-cho*
first	primo	*pree-mo*
first aid	il pronto soccorso	*pron-to sok-kor-so*
first class	la prima classe	*pree-ma klas-seh*
fish	il pesce	*pe-sheh*
fish (to)	pescare	*pes-kar-eh*
fisherman	il pescatore	*pes-ka-tor-eh*
fit (to)	star bene	*star be-neh*
flag	la bandiera	*ban-dyair-a*
flat *adj*	piatto	*pyat-to*
noun	l'appartamento *m*	*ap-par-ta-men-to*
flavour	il sapore	*sa-por-eh*
flea market	il mercato delle pulci	*mair-ka-to del-leh pool-chee*
flight	il volo	*vo-lo*
flood	l'inondazione *f*	*een-on-dat-syo-neh*
floor *ground*	il pavimento	*pa-vee-men-to*
storey	il piano	*pya-no*
floorshow	il cabaret	*ka-ba-reh*
flower	il fiore	*fyor-eh*
fly	la mosca	*mos-ka*
fly (to)	volare	*vo-lar-eh*
fog	la nebbia	*neb-bya*

fold (to)	**piegare**	*pye-gar-eh*
follow (to)	**seguire**	*seg-weer-eh*
food	**il cibo**	*chee-bo*
foot	**il piede**	*pye-deh*
football	**il calcio**	*cal-cho*
footpath	**il sentiero**	*sen-tyair-o*
for	**per**	*pair*
forbid (to)	**vietare**	*vye-tar-eh*
foreign	**straniero**	*stran-yair-o*
forest	**la foresta**	*for-es-ta*
forget (to)	**dimenticare**	*dee-men-tee-kar-eh*
fork	**la forchetta**	*for-ket-ta*
forward	**avanti**	*a-van-tee*
forward (to)	**inoltrare**	*een-ol-trar-eh*
fountain	**la fontana**	*fon-ta-na*
fragile	**fragile**	*fra-jee-leh*
free	**libero**	*lee-bair-o*
freight	**il nolo**	*no-lo*
fresh	**fresco**	*fres-ko*
fresh water	**l'acqua dolce** *f*	*ak-wa dol-cheh*
friend	**l'amico** *m*/**l'amica** *f*	*a-mee-ko/a-mee-ka*
friendly	**amichevole**	*a-mee-ke-vo-leh*
from	**da**	*da*

front	**il fronte**	*fron-teh*
frontier	**la frontiera**	*fron-tyair-a*
frost	**la brina**	*bree-na*
frozen	**congelato**	*kon-je-la-to*
fruit	**il frutto**	*froot-to*
full	**pieno**	*pye-no*
full board	**la pensione completa**	*pen-syo-neh kom-ple-ta*
fun	**il divertimento**	*dee-vair-tee-men-to*
funny	**divertente**	*dee-vair-ten-teh*
fur	**la pelliccia**	*pel-lee-cha*
furniture	**il mobilio**	*mo-beel-yo*

G

gallery	**la galleria**	*gal-lair-ee-a*
gamble (to)	**giocare d'azzardo**	*jo-kar-eh dat-sar-do*
game	**il gioco**	*jo-ko*
garage	**il garage**	*ga-**raj***
garbage	**i rifiuti**	*reef-yoo-tee*
garden	**il giardino**	*jar-dee-no*
gas	**il gas**	*gaz*
gate	**il cancello**	*kan-chel-lo*
gentlemen	**signori, uomini**	*seen-yor-ee, **wo**-mee-nee*
genuine	**autentico**	*ow-**ten**-tee-ko*

get (to)	**ottenere**	*ot-te-nair-eh*
get off (to)	**scendere**	*shen-dair-eh*
get on (to)	**salire**	*sa-leer-eh*
get up (to)	**alzarsi**	*alt-sar-see*
gift	**il regalo**	*re-ga-lo*
gift wrap (to)	**fare una confezione regalo**	*far-eh oon-a kon-fet-syo-neh re-ga-lo*
girl	**la ragazza**	*ra-gat-sa*
give (to)	**dare**	*dar-eh*
glad	**contento**	*kon-ten-to*
glass	**il bicchiere**	*beek-kyair-eh*
glasses	**gli occhiali**	*ok-kya-lee*
gloomy	**oscuro**	*os-koo-ro*
glove	**il guanto**	*gwan-to*
go (to)	**andare**	*an-dar-eh*
god	**dio** *m*	*dee-o*
gold	**l'oro** *m*	*or-o*
gold-plate	**il vasellame d'oro**	*va-sel-la-meh do-ro*
golf course	**il campo di golf**	*kam-po dee golf*
good	**buono**	*bwo-no*
government	**il governo**	*go-vair-no*
granddaughter	**la nipote**	*nee-po-teh*
grandfather	**il nonno**	*non-no*
grandmother	**la nonna**	*non-na*

grandson	il nipote	nee-po-teh
grass	l'erba *f*	air-ba
grateful	grato	gra-to
great	grande	gran-deh
Great Britain	la Gran Bretagna	gran bre-ta-nya
ground	il terreno/la terra	ter-re-no/ter-ra
grow (to)	crescere	kre-shair-eh
guarantee	la garanzia	gar-ant-see-a
guard	la guardia	gwar-dya
guest	l'ospite *m/f*	os-pee-teh
guest house	la pensione	pen-syo-neh
guide	la guida	gwee-da
guide book	la guida	gwee-da
guided tour	il giro organizzato	jee-ro or-ga-neet-sa-to

H

hair	i capelli	ka-pel-lee
hair brush	la spazzola da capelli	spat-so-la da ka-pel-lee
hair dryer	l'asciugacapelli *m/* il fon	a-shoo-ga-ka-pel-lee/fon
hair spray	la lacca per capelli	lak-ka pair ka-pel-lee
hairpin	la forcina	for-chee-na
half	mezzo	med-zo
half board	la mezza pensione	med-za pen-syo-neh

half fare	metà prezzo *m*	*me-ta pre-tso*
hammer	il martello	*mar-tel-lo*
hand	la mano	*ma-no*
handbag	la borsetta	*bor-set-ta*
handkerchief	il fazzoletto	*fat-so-let-to*
handmade	fatto a mano	*fat-to a ma-no*
hang (to)	attaccare/ appendere	*at-tak-kar-eh/ap-pen-dair-eh*
hanger	l'attaccapanni *m*	*at-tak-ka-pan-nee*
happen (to)	accadere	*ak-ka-dair-eh*
happy	felice	*fe-lee-cheh*
happy birthday	buon compleanno	*bwon kom-ple-an-no*
harbour	il porto	*por-to*
hard	duro	*doo-ro*
harmful	dannoso	*dan-no-zo*
harmless	innocuo	*een-nok-wo*
hat	il cappello	*kap-pel-lo*
have (to)	avere	*a-vair-eh*
he	egli/lui	*el-yee, loo-ee*
head	la testa	*tes-ta*
headphones	la cuffia	*koof-fya*
health	la salute	*sa-loo-teh*
hear (to)	sentire	*sen-teer-eh*
heart	il cuore	*kwor-eh*

heat	il calore	ka-lor-eh
heating	il riscaldamento	rees-kal-da-men-to
heavy	pesante	pe-zan-teh
hedge	la siepe	sye-peh
heel *shoe*	il tacco	tak-ko
helicopter	l'elicottero *m*	e-lee-**kot**-tair-o
help	l'aiuto *m*	a-yoo-to
help (to)	aiutare	a-yoo-tar-eh
hem	l'orlo *m*	or-lo
her *adj*	suo	soo-o
her *pron*	lei	lay
here	qui	kwee
high	alto	al-to
hike (to)	fare un'escursione a piedi	fa-reh oon-es-koor-syo-neh a pye-dee
hill	la collina	kol-lee-na
him	lui	loo-ee
hire (to)	noleggiare	no-led-jar-eh
his	suo	soo-o
history	la storia	stor-ya
hitchhike (to)	fare l'autostop	fa-reh low-to-**stop**
hobby	il passatempo	pas-sa-tem-po
hold (to)	tenere	te-nair-eh
hole	il buco	boo-ko

holiday	la vacanza	va-kant-sa
hollow	vuoto/concavo	vwo-to/kon-ka-vo
(at) home	a casa	a ka-za
honeymoon	la luna di miele	loo-na dee mye-leh
hope	la speranza	spe-ran-za
hope (to)	sperare	spe-rar-eh
horse	il cavallo	ka-val-lo
horse races	le corse di cavalli	kor-seh dee ka-val-lee
horse riding	l'equitazione	ek-wee-tat-syo-neh
hose	il tubo flessibile	too-bo fles-**see**-bee-leh
hospital	l'ospedale m	os-pe-da-leh
host/hostess	l'ospite m/f	**os**-pee-teh
hostel	l'ostello m	os-tel-lo
hot	caldo	kal-do
hot water bottle	la borsa d'acqua calda	bor-sa dak-wa kal-da
hotel	l'albergo m	al-bair-go
hotel keeper	l'albergatore m	al-bair-ga-tor-eh
hour	l'ora f	or-a
house	la casa	ka-za
how?	come?	ko-meh
how much/many?	quanto/quanti?	kwan-to/kwan-tee
hungry (to be)	aver fame	a-**vair** fa-meh
hunt (to)	cacciare	ka-char-eh

hurry (to)	**affrettarsi**	*af-fret-tar-see*
hurt (to)	**far male**	*far ma-leh*
husband	**il marito**	*ma-ree-to*
hydrofoil	**l'aliscafo** *m*	*a-lee-ska-fo*

I

I	**io**	*ee-o*
ice	**il ghiaccio**	*gya-cho*
ice cream	**il gelato**	*je-la-to*
ice lolly	**il ghiacciolo**	*gya-cho-lo*
identify (to)	**identificare**	*ee-den-tee-fee-kar-eh*
if	**se**	*seh*
imagine (to)	**immaginare**	*eem-ma-jee-nar-eh*
immediately	**subito**	*soo-bee-to*
immersion heater	**il riscaldatore a immersione**	*rees-kal-da-tor-eh a eem-mair-syo-neh*
important	**importante**	*eem-por-tan-teh*
in	**in, a**	*een, a*
include (to)	**includere**	*een-kloo-dair-eh*
included	**compreso**	*kom-pre-zo*
inconvenient	**scomodo**	*sko-mo-do*
incorrect	**scorretto**	*skor-ret-to*
independent	**independente**	*een-de-pen-den-teh*

indoors	**in casa**	*een ka-za*
industry	**l'industria** *f*	*een-doos-trya*
inexpensive	**poco costoso**	*po-ko kos-to-zo*
inflammable	**infiammabile**	*een-fyam-**ma**-bee-leh*
inflatable	**pneumatico**	*pne-oo-**ma**-tee-ko*
inflation	**l'inflazione** *f*	*een-flat-syo-neh*
information	**l'informazione** *f*	*een-for-mat-syo-neh*
ink	**l'inchiostro** *m*	*een-kyos-tro*
inn	**l'osteria** *f*	*os-tair-ee-a*
insect	**l'insetto** *m*	*een-set-to*
insect bite	**la puntura d'insetto**	*poon-too-ra deen-set-to*
insect repellent	**la lozione anti-insetti**	*lot-syo-neh an-tee-een-set-tee*
inside	**dentro**	*den-tro*
instead	**invece**	*een-ve-cheh*
instructor	**l'istruttore** *m*	*ees-troot-tor-eh*
insurance	**l'assicurazione** *f*	*as-see-koo-rat-syo-neh*
insure (to)	**assicurarsi**	*as-see-koo-rar-see*
interest	**l'interesse** *m*	*een-tair-es-seh*
interested	**interessato**	*een-tair-es-**sa**-to*
interesting	**interessante**	*een-tair-es-san-teh*
Internet	**Internet**	*internet*
interpreter	**l'interprete** *m*	*een-**tair**-pre-teh*

into	in, dentro	*een, den-tro*
introduce (to)	**presentare**	*pre-zen-tar-eh*
invitation	**l'invito** *m*	*een-vee-to*
invite (to)	**invitare**	*een-vee-tar-eh*
Ireland	**Irlanda** *f*	*eer-lan-da*
Irish	**irlandese**	*eer-lan-de-zeh*
iron (to)	**stirare**	*steer-ar-eh*
island	**l'isola** *f*	*ee-zo-la*
it	**lo**	*lo*
Italian	**italiano**	*ee-tal-ya-no*
Italy	**Italia** *f*	*ee-tal-ya*

J

jacket	**la giacchetta**	*jak-ket-ta*
jar	**la brocca**	*brok-ka*
jelly fish	**la medusa**	*me-doo-za*
Jew	**l'ebreo** *m*	*e-bre-o*
jewellery	**la gioielleria**	*joy-el-lair-ee-a*
Jewish	**ebraico**	*e-bray-ko*
job	**il lavoro**	*la-vo-ro*
journey	**il viaggio**	*vyad-jo*
jump (to)	**saltare**	*sal-ta-reh*
jumper	**il maglione**	*mal-yo-neh*

K

keep (to)	**tenere**	*te-nair-eh*
keep in the right-hand lane	**tenere la destra/ stare nella corsia di destra**	*te-nair-eh la des-tra/ sta-reh nel-la kor-see-a dee des-tra*
key	**la chiave**	*kya-veh*
kick (to)	**dare calci a**	*da-reh kal-chee a*
kind *adj*	**gentile**	*jen-tee-leh*
king	**il re**	*reh*
kiss	**il bacio**	*ba-cho*
kiss (to)	**baciare**	*ba-cha-reh*
kitchen	**la cucina**	*koo-chee-na*
knee	**il ginocchio**	*jee-nok-kyo*
knife	**il coltello**	*kol-tel-lo*
knock (to)	**bussare**	*boos-sar-eh*
know (to) *fact*	**sapere**	*sa-pair-eh*
person	**conoscere**	*ko-**no**-shair-eh*

L

label	**l'etichetta** *f*	*e-tee-ket-ta*
lace	**il merletto**	*mair-let-to*
ladies	**signore/donne**	*seen-yor-eh/don-neh*
lake	**il lago**	*la-go*
lamp	**la lampada**	*lam-pa-da*

land	la terra	*ter-ra*
landing *plane*	l'atterraggio *m*	*at-ter-rad-jo*
stairs	il pianerottolo	*pya-nair-**ot**-to-lo*
landlady/lord	la padrona/il padrone di casa	*pa-dro-na/pa-dro-neh dee ka-za*
landmark	il punto di riferimento	*poon-to dee ree-fe-ree-men-to*
landscape	il paesaggio	*pa-e-zad-jo*
lane	il vicolo	*vee-ko-lo*
language	la lingua	*leen-gwa*
large	grande	*gran-deh*
last	ultimo	*ool-tee-mo*
late	tardi	*tar-dee*
laugh (to)	ridere	*ree-dair-eh*
launderette	la lavanderia automatica	*la-van-dair-ee-a ow-to-ma-tee-ka*
lavatory	il bagno/la toilette	*ba-nyo/twa-let*
lavatory paper	la carta igienica	*kar-ta ee-jen-ee-ka*
law	la legge	*led-jeh*
lawn	il prato inglese	*pra-to een-gle-zeh*
lawyer	l'avvocato *m*	*av-vo-ka-to*
lead (to)	condurre	*kon-door-reh*
leaf	la foglia	*fol-ya*
leak (to)	perdere	*pair-dair-eh*
learn (to)	imparare	*eem-pa-rar-eh*

least	minimo	*mee-nee-mo*
at least	almeno	*al-me-no*
leather	la pelle	*pel-leh*
leave (to) *abandon*	lasciare	*la-shar-eh*
go away	partire	*par-teer-eh*
left *opp. right*	sinistro	*see-nees-tro*
left luggage	il deposito bagagli	*de-po-zee-to ba-gal-yee*
leg	la gamba	*gam-ba*
lend (to)	prestare	*pres-**tar**-eh*
length	la lunghezza	*loon-get-sa*
less	meno	*me-no*
lesson	la lezione	*let-syo-neh*
let (to) *allow*	permettere	*pair-**met**-tair-eh*
rent	affittare	*af-feet-tar-eh*
letter	la lettera	*let-tair-a*
level crossing	il passaggio a livello	*pas-sad-jo a lee-vel-lo*
library	la biblioteca	*beeb-lee-o-te-ka*
licence	la patente	*pa-ten-teh*
life	la vita	*vee-ta*
lifebelt	la cintura di salvataggio	*cheen-too-ra dee sal-va-tad-jo*
lifeboat	il battello di salvataggio	*bat-tel-lo dee sal-va-tad-jo*
lifeguard	il bagnino	*ban-yee-no*

lift	l'ascensore *m*	*a-shen-sor-eh*
light	la luce	*loo-cheh*
colour	chiaro	*kya-ro*
weight	leggero	*led-je-ro*
light bulb	la lampadina	*lam-pa-dee-na*
lighthouse	il faro	*fa-ro*
lightning	il lampo	*lam-po*
like (to) *it pleases me*	mi piace	*mee pya-cheh*
wish	volere	*vo-lair-eh*
like *prep*	come	*ko-meh*
like that	così	*ko-**zee***
line	la linea	***lee**-ne-a*
linen	la tela	*te-la*
lingerie	la biancheria per signore	*byan-kair-ee-a pair seen-yor-eh*
lipsalve	la pomata per labbra	*po-ma-ta pair lab-bra*
lipstick	il rossetto	*ros-set-to*
liquid *adj*	liquido	***lee**-kwee-do*
noun	il liquido	***lee**-kwee-do*
listen (to)	ascoltare	*as-kol-tar-eh*
little *amount*	poco	*po-ko*
size	piccolo	***peek**-ko-lo*
live (to)	vivere	***vee**-vair-eh*

local	locale	*lo-ka-leh*
lock	la serratura	*ser-ra-too-ra*
lock (to)	chiudere a chiave	***kyoo**-dair-eh a kya-veh*
long	lungo	*loon-go*
look at (to)	guardare	*gwar-dar-eh*
look for (to)	cercare	*chair-kar-eh*
look like (to)	sembrare	*sem-brar-eh*
loose chippings	materiale instabile sulla strada	*ma-te-rya-leh een-**sta**-bee-leh sul-la stra-da*
lorry	il camion	*ka-myon*
lose (to)	perdere	***pair**-dair-eh*
lost property office	gli oggetti smarriti	*od-jet-tee zmar-ree-tee*
(a) lot	molto	*mol-to*
loud	forte	*for-teh*
love (to)	amare	*a-mar-eh*
lovely	bello	*bel-lo*
low	basso	*bas-so*
lucky	fortunato	*for-too-na-to*
luggage	i bagagli	*ba-gal-yee*
lunch	il pranzo	*prand-zo*

M

magazine	**la rivista**	*ree-vees-ta*
maid	**la cameriera**	*ka-mair-yair-a*
mail	**la posta**	*pos-ta*
main street	**la strada principale**	*stra-da preen-chee-pa-leh*
make (to)	**fare**	*far-eh*
make love (to)	**fare l'amore**	*far-eh la-mo-reh*
make-up	**il trucco**	*trook-ko*
male *adj*	**maschile**	*mas-kee-leh*
man	**l'uomo** *m*	*wo-mo*
man-made	**artificiale**	*ar-tee-fee-cha-leh*
manage (to)	**dirigere**	*dee-**ree**-jair-eh*
manager	**il direttore**	*dee-ret-tor-eh*
manicure	**la manicure**	*ma-nee-koo-reh*
many	**molti**	*mol-tee*
map *country*	**la carta geografica**	*kar-ta je-o-**gra**-fee-ka*
town, small area	**la mappa**	*map-pa*
market	**il mercato**	*mair-ka-to*
market place	**la piazza del mercato**	*pyat-sa del mair-ka-to*
married	**sposato**	*spo-za-to*
marsh	**il palude**	*pa-loo-deh*
Mass	**la messa**	*mes-sa*
massage	**il massaggio**	*mas-sad-jo*

match *light*	il fiammifero	*fyam-mee-fair-o*
sport	la partita	*par-tee-ta*
material *fabric*	la stoffa	*stof-fa*
mattress	il materasso	*ma-tair-as-so*
maximum speed	il limite massimo di velocità	*lee-mee-teh **mas**-see-mo dee ve-lo-chee-**ta***
me	mi, me	*mee, meh*
meal	il pasto	*pas-to*
mean (to)	voler dire	*vo-lair deer-eh*
measurements	le misure	*mee-zoo-reh*
meet (to)	incontrare	*een-kon-trar-eh*
memory stick	pennina (USB)	*la pen-nee-na (oo-es-seh-bee)*
mend (to)	riparare	*ree-pa-rar-eh*
menstruation	le mestruazioni	*mes-troo-at-syo-nee*
mess	la confusione	*kon-foo-zyo-neh*
message	il messaggio	*mes-sad-jo*
messenger	il messaggero	*mes-sad-je-ro*
metal	il metallo	*me-tal-lo*
midday	mezzogiorno	*med-zo-jor-no*
middle	centro, mezzo	*chen-tro, med-zo*
middle-aged	di una certa età	*dee oon-a chair-ta e-**ta***
middle class *adj*	borghese	*bor-ge-zeh*
noun	il ceto medio	*che-to med-yo*

midnight	**mezzanotte**	*med-za-not-teh*
mild	**mite**	*mee-teh*
mill	**il mulino**	*moo-lee-no*
mine *pron*	**il mio/la mia** *sing*, **i miei/le mie** *pl*	*mee-o/mee-a/mee-ay/ mee-eh*
minute	**il minuto**	*mee-noo-to*
mirror	**lo specchio**	*spek-kyo*
Miss	**signorina**	*seen-yor-ee-na*
miss (to) *train, etc.*	**perdere**	*pair-dair-eh*
mistake	**lo sbaglio**	*zbal-yo*
mix (to)	**mescolare**	*mes-ko-lar-eh*
mixed	**mescolato/misto**	*mes-ko-la-to/mees-to*
mobile phone	**il telefonino/ cellulare**	*te-le-fo-nee-no/ chel-loo-la-reh*
modern	**moderno**	*mo-dair-no*
moisturizer	**la crema idratante**	*kre-ma eed-ra-tan-teh*
moment	**il momento**	*mo-men-to*
monastery	**il monastero**	*mo-nas-te-ro*
money	**il denaro/i soldi**	*de-na-ro/sol-dee*
monk	**il monaco**	*mo-na-ko*
month	**il mese**	*me-zeh*
monument	**il monumento**	*mo-noo-men-to*
moon	**la luna**	*loon-a*
moorland	**la brughiera**	*broog-yair-a*

moped	il motorino/il ciao	mo-tor-ee-no/cha-o
more	(di) più	(dee) pyoo
morning	la mattina	mat-tee-na
mortgage	l'ipoteca f	ee-po-te-ka
mosque	la moschea	mos-ke-a
mosquito	la zanzara	zan-za-ra
most	il più/la più	pyoo
mother	la madre	ma-dreh
motor bike	la moto	mo-to
motor boat	la motobarca	mo-to-bar-ka
motor cycle	la motocicletta	mo-to-chee-klet-ta
motor racing	la corsa automobilistica	kor-sa ow-to-mo-bee-lees-tee-ka
motorway	l'autostrada	ow-to-stra-da
motorway toll	il casello/pedaggio autostradale	ka-zel-lo/pe-dad-jo ow-to-stra-da-leh
mountain	la montagna	mon-tan-ya
mouse	il topo	to-po
mouth	la bocca	bok-ka
mouthwash	il colluttorio	kol-loot-tor-yo
move (to)	muovere	mwo-vair-eh
Mr	signor	seen-yor
Mrs	signora	seen-yor-a
much	molto	mol-to

museum	il museo	*moo-ze-o*
music	la musica	*moo-zee-ka*
muslim	musulmano	*moo-sool-ma-no*
muslin	la mussola	*moos-so-la*
must *to have to*	dovere	*do-vair-eh*
my	mio	*mee-o*
myself	io stesso	*ee-o stes-so*

N

nail *carpentry*	il chiodo	*kyo-do*
finger	l'unghia *f*	*oon-gya*
nailbrush	lo spazzolino da unghie	*spat-so-lee-no da oon-gyeh*
nailfile	la limetta da unghie	*lee-met-ta da oon-gyeh*
nail polish	lo smalto per unghie	*smal-to pair oon-gyeh*
name	il nome	*no-meh*
napkin	il tovagliolo	*to-val-yo-lo*
nappy	il pannolino	*pan-no-lee-no*
narrow	stretto	*stret-to*
narrow road	la strada stretta	*stra-da stret-ta*
natural	naturale	*na-too-ra-leh*
near	vicino	*vee-chee-no*
nearly	quasi	*kwa-zee*

necessary	**necessario**	*ne-ches-sar-yo*
necklace	**la collana**	*kol-la-na*
need (to)	**aver bisogno di**	*a-vair bee-zon-yo dee*
needle	**l'ago** *m*	*a-go*
nephew	**il nipote**	*nee-po-teh*
never	**mai**	*my*
new	**nuovo**	*nwo-vo*
New Zealand	**la Nuova Zelanda**	*nwo-va dze-lan-da*
New Zealander	**neozelandese**	*ne-o-dze-lan-de-zeh*
news	**le notizie** *f*	*no-teet-syeh*
newspaper	**il giornale**	*jor-na-leh*
next	**prossimo**	*pros-see-mo*
nice	**carino**	*ka-ree-no*
niece	**la nipote**	*nee-po-teh*
nightclub	**il locale notturno**	*lo-ka-leh not-toor-no*
nightdress	**la camicia da notte**	*ka-mee-cha da not-teh*
no through road	**strada bloccata**	*stra-da blok-ka-ta*
nobody	**nessuno**	*nes-soo-no*
noisy	**rumoroso**	*roo-mo-ro-zo*
non-alcoholic	**analcolico**	*a-nal-ko-lee-ko*
none	**nessuno**	*nes-soo-no*
no one	**nessuno**	*nes-soo-no*
normal	**normale**	*nor-ma-leh*
north	**nord** *m*	*nord*

nosebleed	l'emorragia nasale *f*	*e-mor-ra-jee-a na-za-leh*
not	non	*non*
note	il biglietto	*beel-yet-lo*
notebook	il taccuino	*tak-kwee-no*
nothing	niente	*nyen-teh*
notice	l'avviso *m*	*av-vee-zo*
notice (to)	osservare	*os-sair-var-eh*
novel	il romanzo	*ro-man-zo*
now	ora/adesso	*or-a/a-des-so*
number	il numero	***noo**-mair-o*
nylon	il nailon	*nylon*

O

obtain (to)	ottenere	*ot-te-nair-eh*
occasion	l'occasione *f*	*ok-ka-zyo-neh*
occupation	l'occupazione *f*	*ok-koo-pat-syo-neh*
occupied	occupato	*ok-koo-pa-to*
ocean	l'oceano *m*	*o-**che**-a-no*
odd *not even*	dispari	***dees**-pa-ree*
strange	strano	*stra-no*
of	di	*dee*
of course	naturalmente	*na-too-ral-men-teh*
offer	l'offerta *f*	*of-fair-ta*
office	l'ufficio *m*	*oof-fee-cho*

official *adj*	**ufficiale**	*oof-fee-cha-leh*
noun	**l'ufficiale** *m*	*oof-fee-cha-leh*
often	**spesso**	*spes-so*
ointment	**l'unguento** *m*	*oon-gwen-to*
OK	**okay/va bene**	*OK/va be-neh*
old	**vecchio**	*vek-kyo*
on	**su, sopra**	*soo, sop-ra*
on foot	**a piedi**	*a pye-dee*
on time	**in orario**	*een or-ar-yo*
once	**una volta**	*oon-a vol-ta*
one way	**senso unico**	*sen-so **oo**-nee-ko*
online	**online/in linea**	*online/een **lee**-ne-a*
only	**soltanto**	*sol-tan-to*
open (to)	**aprire**	*ap-reer-eh*
open *adj*	**aperto**	*a-pair-to*
open-air	**all'aperto**	*al-la-pair-to*
opening	**l'apertura** *f*	*a-pair-too-ra*
opera	**l'opera** *f*	*o-pair-a*
opportunity	**l'occasione** *f*	*ok-ka-zyo-neh*
opposite	**opposto**	*op-pos-to*
optician	**l'ottico** *m*	*ot-tee-ko*
or	**o**	*o*
orchard	**l'orto** *m*	*or-to*

orchestra	l'orchestra *f*	*or-kes-tra*
order (to)	**ordinare**	*or-dee-nar-eh*
ordinary	**solito**	*so-lee-to*
other	**altro**	*al-tro*
ought	**dovere**	*do-vair-eh*
our, ours	**nostro**	*nos-tro*
out(side)	**fuori**	*fwo-ree*
out of order	**guasto**	*gwas-to*
out of stock	**esaurito**	*e-zow-ree-to*
over	**sopra**	*sop-ra*
overtaking prohibited	**vietato il sorpasso/ sorpassare**	*vye-ta-to eel sor-pas-so/ sor-pas-sa-reh*
over there	**là**	*la*
overcoat	**il soprabito**	*sop-ra-bee-to*
overnight	**per la notte**	*pair la not-teh*
owe (to)	**dovere**	*do-vair-eh*
owner	**il proprietario**	*prop-rye-tar-yo*

P

pack (to)	**impaccare**	*eem-pak-kar-eh*
packet	**il pacchetto**	*pak-ket-to*
paddle (to)	**sguazzare**	*sgwat-sar-eh*
paddling pool	**la piscina per bambini**	*pee-shee-na pair bam-bee-nee*

page	**la pagina**	*pa-jee-na*
paid	**pagato**	*pa-ga-to*
pain	**il dolore**	*do-lor-eh*
painkiller	**l'antidolorifico** *m*	*an-tee-do-lor-**ee**-fee-ko*
paint (to)	**dipingere**	*dee-**peen**-jair-eh*
painting	**la pittura/il quadro**	*peet-too-ra/kwad-ro*
pair	**il paio**	*pa-yo*
palace	**il palazzo**	*pa-lat-so*
pale	**pallido**	***pal**-lee-do*
panties	**le mutande**	*moo-tan-deh*
paper	**la carta**	*kar-ta*
parcel	**il pacco**	*pak-ko*
park	**il parco**	*par-ko*
park (to)	**parcheggiare**	*par-ked-jar-eh*
parking for disabled	**il parcheggio per disabili**	*par-ked-jo pair dee-**sa**-bee-lee*
parking meter	**il parchimetro**	*par-**kee**-met-ro*
parking ticket	**la multa per divieto di sosta**	*mool-ta pair dee-vye-to dee sos-ta*
parliament	**il parlamento**	*par-la-men-to*
part	**la parte**	*par-teh*
party *fête*	**la festa**	*fes-ta*
political	**il partito**	*par-tee-to*
pass (to)	**passare**	*pas-sar-eh*

passenger	il passeggero	pas-sed-je-ro
passport	il passaporto	pas-sa-por-to
past *adj*	passato	pas-sa-to
noun	il passato	pas-sa-to
path	il sentiero	sen-tyair-o
patient	il paziente	pat-syen-teh
pavement	il marciapiede	mar-cha-pye-deh
pay (to)	pagare	pa-gar-eh
payment	il pagamento	pa-ga-men-to
peace	la pace	pa-cheh
peak	la cima	chee-ma
pearl	la perla	pair-la
pebble	il ciottolo	**chot**-to-lo
pedal	il pedale	pe-da-leh
pedestrian	il pedone	pe-do-neh
pedestrian crossing	l'attraversamento pedonale *m*	at-tra-vair-sa-men-to pe-do-nal-eh
pedestrian precinct	la zona pedonale	dzo-na pe-do-nal-eh
(fountain) pen	la penna (stilografica)	pen-na (stee-lo-***gra***-fee-ka)
pencil	la matita	ma-tee-ta
penknife	il temperino	tem-pe-ree-no
pensioner	il pensionato	pen syo na to
people	la gente	jen-teh

perfect	**esatto/perfetto**	*e-zat-to/pair-fet-to*
performance	**lo spettacolo**	*spet-ta-ko-lo*
perfume	**il profumo**	*pro-foo-mo*
perhaps	**forse**	*for-seh*
perishable	**deperibile**	*de-pair-ee-bee-leh*
permit	**il permesso**	*pair-mes-so*
permit (to)	**permettere**	*pair-met-tair-eh*
person	**la persona**	*pair-so-na*
per person	**a persona**	*a pair-so-na*
personal	**personale**	*pair-so-nal-eh*
petticoat	**la sottana**	*sot-ta-na*
photograph	**la fotografia**	*fo-to-gra-fee-a*
photographer	**il fotografo**	*fo-to-gra-fo*
piano	**il pianoforte**	*pya-no-for-teh*
pick (to) *choose*	**scegliere**	*shel-yair-eh*
gather, pick up	**cogliere**	*kol-yair-eh*
picnic	**il picnic**	*peek-neek*
piece	**il pezzo**	*pet-zo*
pier	**il molo**	*mo-lo*
pillow	**il guanciale**	*gwan-cha-leh*
(safety) pin	**la spilla (di sicurezza)**	*speel-la (dee see-koo-ret-sa)*
pipe	**la pipa**	*pee-pa*

place	il posto	pos-to
plain	semplice	sem-plee-cheh
plan	il piano	pya-no
plant	la pianta	pyan-ta
plastic	plastica	plas-tee-ka
plate	il piatto	pyat-to
play *theatre*	la commedia	kom-me-dya
play (to)	giocare	jo-kar-eh
player	il giocatore	jo-ka-tor-eh
please	per favore	pair fa-vor-eh
pleased	contento	kon-ten-to
plenty of	molto, molti	mol-to, mol-tee
pliers	le pinze	peent-seh
plug *bath*	il tappo	tap-po
electric	la spina elettrica	spee-na el-et-tree-ka
pocket	la tasca	tas-ka
point	il punto	poon-to
poisonous	velenoso	ve-le-no-zo
police station	il commissariato di polizia	kom-mees-sar-ya-to dee pol-eet-see-a
policeman	il poliziotto	pol-eet-syot-to
political	politico	po-lee-tee-ko
politician	il politico	po-lee-tee-ko

politics	la politica	po-*lee*-tee-ka
pollution	l'inquinamento *m*	een-kwee-na-men-to
pond	lo stagno	stan-yo
poor	povero	*po*-vair-o
pope	il papa	pa-pa
popular	popolare	po-po-lar-eh
porcelain	la porcellana	por-chel-la-na
port	il porto	por-to
possible	possibile	pos-*see*-bee-leh
post (to)	imbucare	eem-boo-kar-eh
post box	la buca delle lettere	boo-ka del-leh *let*-tair-eh
post office	l'ufficio postale *m*	oof-fee-cho pos-ta-leh
postcard	la cartolina postale	kar-to-lee-na pos-ta-leh
postman	il postino	pos-tee-no
postpone	rimandare	ree-man-dar-eh
pound	la sterlina	stair-lee-na
(face) powder	la cipria	*cheep*-ree-a
prefer (to)	preferire	pre-fe-reer-eh
pregnant	incinta	een-cheen-ta
prepare (to)	preparare	pre-pa-rar-eh
present *gift*	il regalo	re-ga-lo
president	il presidente	pre-zee-den-teh

press (to)	**premere**	*pre-mair-eh*
pretty	**carino**	*ka-ree-no*
price	**il prezzo**	*pret-so*
priest	**il prete**	*pre-teh*
prime minister	**il primo ministro**	*pree-mo mee-nees-tro*
print	**la stampa**	*stam-pa*
print (to)	**stampare**	*stam-par-eh*
private	**privato**	*pree-va-to*
problem	**il problema**	*prob-le-ma*
profession	**la professione**	*pro-fes-syo-neh*
programme	**il programma**	*pro-gram-ma*
promise	**la promessa**	*pro-mes-sa*
promise (to)	**promettere**	*pro-**met**-tair-eh*
protestant	**protestante**	*pro-tes-tan-teh*
provide (to)	**fornire**	*for-neer-eh*
public	**pubblico**	*poob-blee-ko*
public holiday	**la festa nazionale**	*fes-ta nat-syo-na-leh*
pull (to)	**tirare**	*tee-rar-eh*
pure	**puro**	*poo-ro*
purse	**il borsellino**	*bor-sel-lee-no*
push (to)	**spingere**	*speen-jair-eh*
put (to)	**mettere**	*met-tair-eh*
pyjamas	**il pigiama**	*pee-ja-ma*

Q

quality	**la qualità**	*kwa-lee-ta*
quantity	**la quantità**	*kwan-tee-ta*
quarter	**il quarto**	*kwar-to*
queen	**la regina**	*re-jee-na*
question	**la domanda**	*do-man-da*
quick	**presto**	*pres-to*
quiet	**tranquillo**	*tran-kweel-lo*

R

race	**la corsa**	*kor-sa*
racecourse	**l'ippodromo** *m*	*eep-po-dro-mo*
radiator	**il radiatore**	*rad-ya-tor-eh*
radio	**la radio**	*rad-yo*
railway	**la ferrovia**	*fer-ro-vee-a*
rain	**la pioggia**	*pyod-ja*
rainbow	**l'arcobaleno**	*ar-ko-ba-le-no*
raincoat	**l'impermeabile** *m*	*eem-pair-me-a-bee-leh*
(it is) raining	**piove**	*pyo-veh*
rare	**raro**	*ra-ro*
rash	**l'esantema** *m*	*e-zan-te-ma*
rate	**la tariffa**	*ta-reef-fa*
rather	**piuttosto**	*pyoot-tos-to*

raw	**crudo**	*kroo-do*
razor	**il rasoio**	*ra-zo-yo*
razor blade	**la lametta per barba**	*lam-et-ta pair bar-ba*
reach (to)	**raggiungere**	*rad-**joon**-jair-eh*
read (to)	**leggere**	***led**-jair-eh*
ready	**pronto**	*pron-to*
real	**vero**	*ve-ro*
really	**veramente**	*ve-ra-men-teh*
reason	**la ragione**	*ra-jo-neh*
receipt	**la ricevuta**	*ree-che-voo-ta*
receive (to)	**ricevere**	*ree-**che**-vair-eh*
recent	**recente**	*re-chen-teh*
recipe	**la ricetta**	*ree-chet-ta*
recognize (to)	**riconoscere**	*ree-ko-**no**-shair-eh*
recommend	**raccomandare**	*rak-ko-man-dar-eh*
refill	**riempire**	*ryem-peer-eh*
refrigerator	**il frigorifero**	*free-go-**ree**-fe-ro*
refund	**il rimborso**	*reem-bor-so*
registered letter	**la lettera raccomandata**	***let**-tair-a rak-ko-man-da-ta*
relatives	**i parenti**	*pa-ren-tee*
religion	**la religione**	*re-lee-jo-neh*
remember (to)	**ricordare**	*ree-kor-dar-eh*
rent (to)	**affittare**	*af-feet-tar-eh*
repair (to)	**riparare**	*ree-pa-rar-eh*

repeat (to)	**ripetere**	*ree-**pe**-tair-eh*
reply (to)	**rispondere**	*rees-**pon**-dair-eh*
reservation	**la prenotazione**	*pre-no-tat-syo-neh*
reserve (to)	**prenotare/riservare**	*pre-no-tar-eh/ ree-zair-var-eh*
reserved	**prenotato**	*pre-no-ta-to*
restaurant	**il ristorante**	*rees-tor-an-teh*
restaurant car	**il vagone ristorante**	*va-go-neh rees-tor-an-teh*
restricted parking	**parcheggio limitato**	*par-ked-jo lee-mee-ta-to*
return (to)	**ritornare**	*ree-tor-nar-eh*
reward	**la ricompensa**	*ree-kom-pen-sa*
ribbon	**il nastro**	*nas-tro*
rich	**ricco**	*reek-ko*
right *opp. left*	**destro**	*des-tro*
opp. wrong	**corretto**	*kor-ret-to*
right (to be)	**aver ragione**	*a-**vair** ra-jo-neh*
ring *finger*	**l'anello** *m*	*a-nel-lo*
ripe	**maturo**	*ma-too-ro*
rise (to)	**sorgere**	***sor**-jair-eh*
river	**il fiume**	*fyoo-meh*
road	**la strada**	*stra-da*
road map	**la carta stradale**	*kar-ta stra-da-leh*
road sign	**il cartello stradale**	*kar-tel-lo stra-da-leh*
road works	**lavori in corso**	*la-vor-ee een kor-so*

rock	**lo scoglio**	*skol-yo*
roll *bread*	**il panino**	*pa-nee-no*
roll (to)	**rotolare**	*ro-to-lar-eh*
roof	**il tetto**	*tet-to*
room	**la stanza**	*stant-sa*
rope	**la fune**	*foo-neh*
round	**rotondo**	*ro-ton-do*
rowing boat	**la barca a remi**	*bar-ka a re-mee*
rubber	**la gomma**	*gom-ma*
rubbish	**le immondizie/i rifiuti**	*eem-mon-deet-syeh/ ree-fyoo-tee*
rucksack	**il sacco da montagna**	*sak-ko da mon-tan-ya*
ruins	**le rovine**	*ro-vee-neh*
run (to)	**correre**	*kor-rair-eh*
rush hour	**l'ora di punta** *f*	*or-a dee poon-ta*

S

sad	**triste**	*trees-teh*
saddle	**la sella**	*sel-la*
safe *adj*	**sicuro**	*see-koo-ro*
noun	**la cassaforte**	*kas-sa-for-teh*
sail (to)	**andare in barca vela**	*an-dar-eh een bar-ka ve-la*
sailing boat	**la barca vela**	*bar-ka ve-la*

sailor	**il marinaio**	*ma-ree-na-yo*
saint	**il santo/la santa**	*san-to/san-ta*
sale *clearance*	**la svendita**	*sven-dee-ta*
(for) sale	**in vendita**	*een **ven**-dee-ta*
salesman	**il commesso (di negozio)**	*kom-mes-so (dee ne-got-syo)*
saleswoman	**la commessa (di negozio)**	*kom-mes-sa (dee ne-got-syo)*
salt	**il sale**	*sa-leh*
salt water	**l'acqua salata** *f*	*ak-wa sa-la-ta*
same	**stesso**	*stes-so*
sand	**la sabbia**	*sab-bya*
sandals	**i sandali**	*san-da-lee*
sanitary towel	**l'assorbente igienico** *m*	*as-sor-ben-teh ee-**jen**-ee-ko*
satisfactory	**soddisfacente**	*sod-dees-fa-chen-teh*
saucer	**il piattino**	*pyat-tee-no*
save (to) *money*	**risparmiare**	*rees-par-myar-eh*
rescue	**salvare**	*sal-var-eh*
say (to)	**dire**	*deer-eh*
scald (to)	**scottare**	*skot-tar-eh*
scarf	**la sciarpa**	*shar-pa*
scenery	**il paesaggio**	*pa-e-zad-jo*
scent	**il profumo**	*pro-foo-mo*

school	la scuola	skwo-la
scissors	le forbici	for-bee-chee
Scotland	Scozia f	skot-sya
Scottish	scozzese	skot-se-zeh
scratch (to)	graffiare	graf-fyar-eh
screw	la vite	vee-teh
sculpture	la scultura	skool-too-ra
sea	il mare	mar-eh
sea food	i frutti di mare	froot-tee dee mar-eh
seashore	la spiaggia	spyad-ja
seasickness	il mal di mare	mal dee mar-eh
season	la stagione	sta-jo-neh
seat	il posto	pos-to
seat belt	la cintura di sicurezza	cheen-too-ra dee see-koo-ret-sa
second	secondo	se-kon-do
second hand	di seconda mano	dee se-kon-da ma-no
see (to)	vedere	ve-dair-eh
seem (to)	parere	pa-rair-eh
self-catering	casa da affitto	ca-za da af-feet-to
self-contained	indipendente	een-dee-pen-den-teh
sell (to)	vendere	ven-dair-eh
send (to)	mandare	man-dar-eh

separate *adj*	a parte	*a par-teh*
serious	serio	*sair-yo*
serve (to)	servire	*sair-veer-eh*
service	il servizio	*sair-veet-syo*
service *church*	il servizio religioso	*sair-veet-syo re-lee-jo-zo*
service charge	il servizio	*sair-veet-syo*
several	parecchi	*pa-rek-kee*
sew (to)	cucire	*koo-cheer-eh*
shade *colour*	la tinta	*teen-ta*
shade/shadow	l'ombra *f*	*om-bra*
shallow	basso	*bas-so*
shampoo	lo shampoo	*sham-poo*
shape	la forma	*for-ma*
share (to)	dividere	*dee-**vee**-dair-eh*
sharp	tagliente	*tal-yen-teh*
shave (to)	farsi la barba	*far-see la bar-ba*
shaving brush	il pennello	*pen-nel-lo*
shaving cream	la crema da barba	*kre-ma da bar-ba*
she	essa, lei	*es-sa, lay*
sheet	il lenzuolo	*lend-zwo-lo*
shelf	lo scaffale	*skaf-fa-leh*
shell	la conchiglia	*kon-keel-ya*
shelter	il riparo	*ree-pa-ro*

shine (to)	**splendere**	*splen-dair-eh*
shingle	**i ciottoli**	*chot-to-lee*
ship	**la nave**	*na-veh*
shipping line	**la compagnia di navigazione**	*kom-pan-yee-a dee na-vee-gat-syo-neh*
shirt	**la camicia**	*ka-mee-cha*
shock	**il colpo**	*kol-po*
shoe	**la scarpa**	*skar-pa*
shoelaces	**le stringhe da scarpe**	*streen-geh da skar-peh*
shoe polish	**la tinta da scarpe**	*teen-ta da skar-peh*
shop	**la bottega**	*bot-te-ga*
shopping centre	**il centro dei negozi**	*chen-tro day ne-got-see*
shore	**la spiaggia**	*spyad-ja*
short	**corto**	*kor-to*
shorts	**i calzoncini**	*kalt-son-chee-nee*
shoulder	**la spalla**	*spal-la*
show	**lo spettacolo**	*spet-**ta**-ko-lo*
show (to)	**mostrare**	*mos-trar-eh*
shower	**la doccia**	*do-cha*
shut (to)	**chiudere**	*kyoo-dair-eh*
shut *adj*	**chiuso**	*kyoo-zo*
side	**il lato**	*la-to*
sights	**le vedute**	*ve-doo-teh*

sightseeing	**il giro turistico**	*jee-ro toor-ees-tee-ko*
sign	**il segno**	*sen-yo*
sign (to)	**firmare**	*feer-mar-eh*
silver	**l'argento** *m*	*ar-jen-to*
simple	**semplice**	*sem-plee-cheh*
since	**da**	*da*
sing (to)	**cantare**	*kan-tar-eh*
single *just one*	**singolo**	*seen-go-lo*
unmarried	**scapolo** *of man*	*ska-po-lo*
	nubile *of woman*	*noo-bee-leh*
single room	**la camera ad un letto**	*ka-mair-a ad oon let-to*
sister	**la sorella**	*so-rel-la*
sit (to)	**sedere**	*se-dair-eh*
sit down (to)	**accomodarsi**	*ak-ko-mo-dar-see*
size	**la misura**	*mee-zoo-ra*
skate (to)	**pattinare**	*pat-tee-nar-eh*
ski (to)	**sciare**	*shee-ar-eh*
skid (to)	**slittare**	*sleet-tar-eh*
skirt	**la gonna**	*gon-na*
sky	**il cielo**	*che-lo*
sleep (to)	**dormire**	*dor-meer-eh*
sleeper	**il vagone letto**	*va-go-neh let-to*
sleeping bag	**il sacco a pelo**	*sak-ko a pe-lo*

sleeve	la manica	*ma*-nee-ka
slice	la fetta	*fet-ta*
slip *garment*	la sottoveste	*sot-to-ves-teh*
slippers	le pantofole/le ciabatte	*pan-to-fo-leh/ cha-bat-teh*
slowly	lentamente	*len-ta-men-teh*
slow traffic	rallentamento traffico	*ral-len-ta-men-to **traf**-fee-ko*
small	piccolo	***peek**-ko-lo*
smart	elegante	*e-le-gan-teh*
smell	l'odore *m*	*o-dor-eh*
smile	sorridere	*sor-**ree**-dair-eh*
smoke (to)	fumare	*foo-mar-eh*
no smoking	vietato fumare	*vye-ta-to foo-mar-eh*
snack	lo spuntino	*spoon-tee-no*
snorkel	il respiratore a tubo	*res-pee-ra-tor-eh a too-bo*
snow	la neve	*ne-veh*
(it is) snowing	nevica	***ne**-vee-ka*
so	così	*ko-**zee***
soap	il sapone	*sa-po-neh*
soap powder	il sapone in polvere	*sa-po-neh een **pol**-vair-eh*
sober	sobrio	*sob-ryo*
socket *electrical*	la presa (elettrica)	*pre-za e-**let**-tree-ka*
socks	i calzini	*kalt-see-nee*

soft	molle	*mol-leh*
sold	venduto	*ven-doo-to*
sold out	esaurito	*e-zow-ree-to*
sole *shoe*	la suola	*swo-la*
solid	solido	*so-lee-do*
some	qualche	*kwal-keh*
somebody	qualcuno	*kwal-koo-no*
something	qualcosa	*kwal-ko-za*
sometimes	qualche volta	*kwal-keh vol-ta*
somewhere	qualche parte	*kwal-keh par-teh*
son	il figlio	*feel-yo*
song	la canzone	*kant-so-neh*
soon	presto	*pres-to*
sour	acido	*a-chee-do*
south	sud	*sood*
souvenir	il souvenir/il ricordo	*souvenir/ree-kor-do*
space	lo spazio	*spat-syo*
spanner	la chiave	*kya-veh*
speak (to)	parlare	*par-lar-eh*
speciality	la specialità	*spe-cha-lee-**ta***
spectacles	gli occhiali	*ok-kya-lee*
speed	la velocità	*ve-lo-chee-**ta***
speed limit	il limite di velocità	***lee**-mee-teh dee ve-lo-chee-**ta***

spend (to)	**spendere**	*spen-dair-eh*
spice	**la spezia**	*spet-sya*
spoon	**il cucchiaio**	*kook-kya-yo*
sport	**lo sport**	*sport*
sprain (to)	**slogare**	*zlo-gar-eh*
spring *water*	**la sorgente**	*sor-jen-teh*
season	**la primavera**	*pree-ma-vair-a*
square *adj*	**quadrato**	*kwad-ra-to*
noun	**la piazza**	*pyat-sa*
stage	**il palcoscenico**	*pal-ko-she-nee-ko*
stain	**la macchia**	*mak-kya*
stained	**macchiato**	*mak-kya-to*
stairs	**le scale**	*ska-leh*
stalls	**le poltrone**	*pol-tro-neh*
stamp	**il francobollo**	*fran-ko-bol-lo*
stand (to)	**stare in piedi**	*star-eh een pye-dee*
start (to)	**cominciare**	*ko-meen-char-eh*
statue	**la statua**	*stat-wa*
stay (to)	**stare**	*star-eh*
step *foot*	**il passo**	*pas-so*
stick	**il bastone**	*bas-to-neh*
stiff	**rigido**	*ree-jee-do*
still *time*	**ancora**	*an-ko-ra*
not moving	**immobile**	*eem-mo-bee-leh*

sting	**la puntura**	*poon-too-ra*
stolen	**rubato**	*roo-ba-to*
stone	**la pietra**	*pye-tra*
stool	**lo sgabello**	*zga-bel-lo*
stop (to)	**fermare**	*fair-mar-eh*
store	**il magazzino**	*ma-gad-zee-no*
storm	**la tempesta**	*tem-pes-ta*
straight	**diritto**	*dee-reet-to*
straight on	**a diritto**	*a dee-reet-to*
strap	**la cinghia**	*cheen-gya*
stream	**il ruscello**	*roo-shel-lo*
street	**la strada**	*stra-da*
street map	**lo stradario**	*stra-dar-yo*
string	**lo spago**	*spa-go*
strong	**forte**	*for-teh*
student	**lo studente**	*stoo-den-teh*
style	**lo stile**	*stee-leh*
suburb	**la periferia**	*pair-ee-fair-ee-a*
subway	**il sottopassaggio**	*sot-to-pas-sad-jo*
suddenly	**improvvisamente**	*eem-prov-vee-za-men-teh*
suede	**il camoscio**	*ka-mo-sho*
suit	**l'abito** *m*	*a-bee-to*
suitcase	**la valigia**	*va-lee-ja*

summer	l'estate *f*	*es-ta-teh*
sun	il sole	*so-leh*
sunbathing	il bagno di sole	*ban-yo dee so-leh*
sunburn	la scottatura di sole	*skot-ta-too-ra dee so-leh*
sunglasses	gli occhiali da sole	*ok-kya-lee da so-leh*
sunhat	il cappello da sole	*kap-pel-lo da so-leh*
sunny	soleggiato	*so-led-ja-to*
sunshade	il parasole	*pa-ra-so-leh*
suntan cream	la pomata solare	*po-ma-ta so-lar-eh*
supermarket	il supermercato	*soo-pair-mair-ka-to*
supper	la cena	*che-na*
sure	sicuro	*see-koo-ro*
surfboard	il sandolino	*san-do-lee-no*
surgery	l'ambulatorio *m*	*am-boo-la-tor-yo*
surprise	la sorpresa	*sor-pre-za*
surprise (to)	sorprendere	*sor-**pren**-dair-eh*
surroundings	i dintorni	*deen-tor-nee*
sweater	il maglione	*mal-yo-neh*
sweet	dolce	*dol-cheh*
sweets	le caramelle	*ka-ra-mel-leh*
swell (to)	gonfiare	*gon-fyar-eh*
swim (to)	nuotare	*nwo-tar-eh*
swimming pool	la piscina	*pee-shee-na*

swings	l'altalena *f*	*al-ta-le-na*
Swiss	svizzero	*sveet-se-ro*
switch *light*	l'interruttore *m*	*een-tair-root-tor-eh*
Switzerland	Svizzera	*sveet-se-ra*
synagogue	la sinagoga	*see-na-go-ga*

T

table	la tavola/il tavolo	*ta-vo-la/ta-vo-lo*
tablecloth	la tovaglia	*to-val-ya*
tablet	la pastiglia	*pas-teel-ya*
tailor	il sarto	*sar-to*
take (to)	prendere	*pren-dair-eh*
talk (to)	parlare	*par-lar-eh*
tall	alto	*al-to*
tampon	il tampone	*tam-po-neh*
tank	il serbatoio	*sair-ba-to-yo*
tap	il rubinetto	*roo-bee-net-to*
tapestry	l'arazzo *m*	*a-rat-so*
taste	il gusto	*goos-to*
taste (to)	gustare	*goos-tar-eh*
tax	la tassa	*tas-sa*
taxi	il taxi	*taxi*
teach (to)	insegnare	*een-sen-yar-eh*

tear *eye*	la lacrima	*lak-ree-ma*
tear (to)	**strappare**	*strap-par-eh*
telephone	**il telefono**	*te-le-fo-no*
telephone (to)	**telefonare**	*te-le-fo-nar-eh*
telephone call	**la telefonata**	*te-le-fo-na-ta*
telephone directory	**l'elenco telefonico** *m*	*e-len-ko te-le-fo-nee-ko*
telephone number	**il numero di telefono**	*noo-mair-o dee te-le-fo-no*
telephone operator	**il centralino**	*chen-tra-lee-no*
television	**la televisione**	*te-le-vee-zyo-neh*
tell (to)	**raccontare**	*rak-kon-tar-eh*
temperature	**la temperatura**	*tem-pe-ra-too-ra*
temporary	**provvisorio**	*prov-vee-zor-yo*
tennis	**il tennis**	*tennis*
tent	**la tenda**	*ten-da*
tent peg	**il cavicchio per tenda**	*ka-veek-kyo pair ten-da*
tent pole	**il palo per tenda**	*pa-lo pair ten-da*
terrace	**la terrazza**	*ter-rat-sa*
text message	**il messaggino**	*mes-sad-jee-no*
than	**che, di**	*keh, dee*
that	**quello**	*kwel-lo*
the	**il/lo/la/i/gli/le**	*eel/lo/la/ee/lyee/leh*
theatre	**il teatro**	*te-at-ro*
their, theirs	**loro**	*lo-ro*

them	li, loro	*lee, lo-ro*
then	poi, allora	*poy, al-lor-a*
there	lì, là	*lee, la*
there is	c'è	*cheh*
there are	ci sono	*chee so-no*
thermometer	il termometro	*tair-**mo**-met-ro*
these	questi	*kwes-tee*
they	essi/loro	*es-see/lo-ro*
thick	grosso	*gros-so*
thief	il ladro	*lad-ro*
thin	sottile	*sot-tee-leh*
thing	la cosa	*ko-za*
think (to)	pensare	*pen-sar-eh*
thirsty (to be)	aver sete	*a-**vair** se-teh*
this	questo	*kwes-to*
those	quelli	*kwel-lee*
thread	il filo	*fee-lo*
throat	la gola	*go-la*
through	attraverso	*at-tra-vair-so*
throw (to)	gettare	*jet-tar-eh*
thunder	il tuono	*two-no*
thunderstorm	la tempesta	*tem-pes-ta*
ticket	il biglietto	*beel-yet-to*

ticket office	**la biglietteria**	*beel-yet-tair-ee-a*
tide	**la marea**	*ma-re-a*
tie	**la cravatta**	*kra-vat-ta*
tight	**stretto**	*stret-to*
tights	**la calzamaglia**	*kalt-sa-mal-ya*
time	**il tempo**	*tem-po*
timetable	**l'orario** *m*	*o-rar-yo*
tin	**il barattolo**	*ba-rat-to-lo*
tin opener	**l'apriscatole** *m*	*ap-ree-skat-to-leh*
tip *money*	**la mancia**	*man-cha*
tip (to) *money*	**dare una mancia**	*dar-eh oon-a man-cha*
tired	**stanco**	*stan ko*
to	**a/in**	*a/een*
tobacco (brown)	**il tabacco (scuro)**	*ta-bak-ko (skoo-ro)*
together	**insieme**	*een-sye-meh*
toilet	**il gabinetto**	*ga-bee-net-to*
toilet paper	**la carta igienica**	*kar-ta ee-jen-ee-ka*
toll	**il pedaggio**	*pe-dad-jo*
tomorrow	**domani**	*do-ma-nee*
tongue	**la lingua**	*leen-gwa*
too *also*	**anche**	*an-keh*
excessive	**troppo**	*trop-po*
too much/many	**troppo/troppi**	*trop-po/trop-pee*

toothbrush	**lo spazzolino da denti**	*spat-so-lee-no da den-tee*
toothpaste	**il dentifricio**	*den-tee-free-cho*
toothpick	**lo stuzzicadenti**	*stoot-see-ka-den-tee*
top	**la cima**	*chee-ma*
torch *electric*	**la lampadina tascabile**	*lam-pa-dee-na tas-ka-bee-leh*
torn	**strappato**	*strap-pa-to*
touch (to)	**toccare**	*tok-kar-eh*
tough	**duro**	*doo-ro*
tourist	**il turista**	*too-rees-ta*
tourist office	**l'agenzia turistica**	*a-jent-see-a too-**rees**-tee-ka*
towards	**verso**	*vair-so*
towel	**l'asciugamano** *m*	*a-shoo-ga-ma-no*
tower	**la torre**	*tor-reh*
town	**la città**	*cheet-**ta***
town hall	**il municipio**	*moo-nee-cheep-yo*
toy	**il giocattolo**	*jo-**kat**-to-lo*
traffic	**il traffico**	***traf**-fee-ko*
traffic jam	**l'ingorgo di traffico** *m*	*een-gor-go dee **traf**-fee-ko*
traffic lights	**il semaforo**	*se-**ma**-for-o*
train	**il treno**	*tre-no*

trainers	le scarpe da ginnastica/ da tennis	skar-peh da jeen-na-stee-ka/da tennis
transfer	trasferire	tras-fe-reer-eh
translate (to)	tradurre	tra-door-reh
travel (to)	viaggiare	vyad-jar-eh
travel agent	l'agenzia di viaggi f	agent-see-a dee vyad-jee
treat (to)	trattare	trat-tar-eh
medical	curare	koo-rar-eh
treatment	la cura	koo-ra
tree	l'albero m	al-bair-o
trip	il viaggio	vyad-jo
trouble	il guaio	gwa-yo
trousers	i pantaloni	pan-ta-lo-nee
true	vero	vair-o
trunk luggage	il baule	ba-oo-leh
trunks	i calzoncini	kalt-son-chee-nee
truth	la verità	ve-ree-ta
try, try on (to)	provare	pro-var-eh
tunnel	la galleria	gal-lair-ee-a
turn (to)	voltare	vol-tar-eh
turning	la svolta	zvol-ta
tweezers	le pinzette	peent-set-teh
twisted	slogato	zlo-ga-to

U

ugly	**brutto**	*broot-to*
umbrella	**l'ombrello** *m*	*om-brel-lo*
uncle	**lo zio**	*tsee-o*
uncomfortable	**scomodo**	***sko**-mo-do*
unconscious	**svenuto**	*zve-noo-to*
under	**sotto**	*sot-to*
underground	**la metropolitana**	*met-ro-po-lee-ta-na*
underneath	**sotto**	*sot-to*
underpants	**le mutande**	*moo-tan-deh*
understand	**capire**	*ka-peer-eh*
underwear	**la biancheria intima**	*byan-kair-ee-a **een**-tee-ma*
United Kingdom	**il Regno Unito**	*ren-yo oo-nee-to*
university	**l'università** *f*	*oo-nee-vair-see-**ta***
unpack (to)	**disfare le valigie**	*dees-far-eh leh va-lee-jeh*
until	**fino a**	*fee-no a*
unusual	**insolito**	*een-**so**-lee-to*
up	**sopra**	*sop-ra*
upstairs	**di sopra**	*dee sop-ra*
urgent	**urgente**	*oor-jen-teh*
us	**noi/ci**	*noy/chee*
use (to)	**usare**	*oo-zar-eh*

useful	utile	*oo-tee-leh*
useless	inutile	*een-oo-tee-leh*
usual	solito	*so-lee-to*

V

vacant	libero	*lee-bair-o*
vacation	la vacanze	*va-kant-seh*
valid	valido	*va-lee-do*
valley	la valle	*val-leh*
valuable	di valore	*dee va-lor-eh*
value	il valore	*va-lor-eh*
vase	il vaso	*va-zo*
VAT	IVA	*ee-va*
vegetables	la verdura	*vair-doo-ra*
vegetarian	vegetariano	*ve-je-tar-ya-no*
vein	la vena	*ve-na*
ventilation	la ventilazione	*ven-tee-lat-syo-neh*
very	molto	*mol-to*
very little	pochissimo	*po-kees-see-mo*
very much	moltissimo	*mol-tees-see-mo*
vest	la maglietta	*mal-yet-ta*
viaduct	il viadotto	*vee-a-dot-to*
view	la vista	*vees-ta*

village	**il villaggio**	*veel-lad-jo*
vineyard	**il vigneto**	*veen-ye-to*
violin	**il violino**	*vyo-lee-no*
visa	**il visto**	*vees-to*
visit	**la visita**	***vee**-zee-ta*
visit (to)	**visitare**	*vee-zee-tar-eh*
voice	**la voce**	*vo-cheh*
voltage	**il voltaggio**	*vol-tad-jo*
voucher	**il buono**	*bwo-no*
voyage	**il viaggio**	*vyad-jo*

W

wait (to)	**aspettare**	*as-pet-tar-eh*
waiter	**il cameriere**	*ka-mair-yair-eh*
waiting room	**la sala d'aspetto**	*sa-la das-pet-to*
waitress	**la cameriera**	*ka-mair-yair-a*
wake (to) *someone*	**svegliare**	*zvel-yar-eh*
wake up (to)	**svegliarsi**	*zvel-yar-see*
Wales	**Galles** *m*	*gal-lez*
walk (to)	**passeggiare**	*pas-sed-jar-eh*
wallet	**il portafoglio**	*por-ta-fol-yo*
want (to)	**volere**	*vo-lair-eh*
wardrobe	**il guardaroba**	*gwar-da-ro-ba*

warm	**caldo**	*kal-do*
wash (to)	**lavare**	*la-var-eh*
waste	**il rifiuto**	*ree-fyoo-to*
waste (to)	**sprecare**	*spre-kar-eh*
watch	**l'orologio** *m*	*o-ro-lo-jo*
water	**l'acqua** *f*	*ak-wa*
waterfall	**la cascata**	*kas-ka-ta*
waterproof	**impermeabile**	*eem-pair-me-a-bee-leh*
water ski-ing	**lo sci nautico**	*shee naw-tee-ko*
wave	**l'onda** *f*	*on-da*
way	**la via**	*vee-a*
we	**noi**	*noy*
wear (to)	**indossare**	*een-dos-sar-eh*
weather	**il tempo**	*tem-po*
weather forecast	**le previsioni del tempo**	*pre-vee-syo-nee del tem-po*
website	**il sito internet**	*see-to internet*
wedding ring	**la fede**	*fe-deh*
week	**la settimana**	*set-tee-ma-na*
weekend	**il fine settimana**	*fee-neh set-tee-ma-na*
weigh (to)	**pesare**	*pe-zar-eh*
weight	**il peso**	*pe-zo*
well *adv*	**bene**	*be-neh*

well *water*	**il pozzo**	*pot-so*
Welsh	**gallese**	*gal-le-zeh*
west	**ovest**	*o-vest*
wet	**bagnato**	*ban-ya-to*
what?	**che cosa?**	*keh ko-za*
wheel	**la ruota**	*rwo-ta*
wheelchair	**la sedia a rotelle**	*se-dya a ro-tel-leh*
when?	**quando?**	*kwan-do*
where?	**dove?**	*do-veh*
which?	**quale?**	*kwa-leh*
while	**mentre**	*men-treh*
who?	**chi?**	*kee*
whole	**intero**	*een-te-ro*
whose?	**di chi?**	*dee kee*
why?	**perché?**	*pair-keh*
wide	**largo**	*lar-go*
widow	**la vedova**	***ve**-do-va*
widower	**il vedovo**	***ve**-do-vo*
wife	**la moglie**	*mol-yeh*
wild	**selvaggio**	*sel-vad-jo*
win (to)	**vincere**	***veen**-chair-eh*
wind	**il vento**	*ven-to*
window	**la finestra**	*fee-nes-tra*

wine merchant	**la rivendita di vino**	*ree-**ven**-dee-ta dee vee-no*
wing	**l'ala** *f*	*a-la*
winter	**l'inverno** *m*	*een-vair-no*
winter sports	**gli sport invernali**	*sport een-vair-na-lee*
wish (to)	**desiderare**	*de-zee-dair-ar-eh*
with	**con**	*kon*
without	**senza**	*send-za*
woman	**la donna**	*don-na*
wonderful	**meraviglioso**	*me-ra-veel-yo-zo*
wood *forest*	**il bosco**	*bos-ko*
timber	**il legno**	*len-yo*
word	**la parola**	*pa-ro-la*
work	**il lavoro**	*la-vo-ro*
work (to)	**lavorare**	*la-vo-rar-eh*
worried	**preoccupato**	*pre-ok-koo-pa-to*
worse	**peggiore**	*ped-jor-eh*
worth (to be)	**valore**	*va-lor-eh*
wrap	**avvolgere**	*av-**vol**-jair-eh*
write (to)	**scrivere**	***scree**-vair-eh*
writing paper	**la carta da scrivere**	*kar-ta da **scree**-vair-eh*
wrong	**sbagliato**	*zbal-ya-to*
wrong (to be)	**aver torto**	*a-**vair** tor-to*

Y

yacht	lo yacht	yacht
year	l'anno m	an-no
yesterday	ieri	yair-ee
you	tu/voi/lei	too/voy/lay
young	giovane	jo-van-eh
your	tuo/vostro/suo	too-o/vos-tro/soo-o
youth hostel	l'ostello della gioventù m	os-tel-lo del-la jo-ven-**too**

Z

zip	la chiusura lampo	kyoo-zoo-ra lam-po
zoo	lo zoo	zoo

INDEX